A VIEW FROM THE MARGINS

A VIEW FROM THE MARGINS

PRATAP SINGH

GYAN

A View From the Margins

ISBN: 978-81-212-1095-9

Rs. 250

Published in 2011 in India by
Gyan Publishing House
23, Main Ansari Road, Darya Ganj
New Delhi-110002
Phones : 23282060, 23261060
Fax : 011-23285914
E-mail: books@gyanbooks.com
Website: www.gyanbooks.com

Laser Type Setting by: Rudra Computer Graphics, Delhi
Printed at : Chawla Offset Printers, Delhi

Dedicated

To all those who stood up to voice against any kind of oppression and discrimination

Disclaimer

This is a work of fiction. All characters appearing in this work are fictitious, except few liberties with regard to the names of three heavenly departed sadhus. Any other resemblances and similarities to real persons, living or dead are purely coincidental and the author hereby disclaim for them.

Contents

Preface

A moment of reflection can change things in life. Something similar happened to me. The conception of this fictional work flowed from an incident that took place in Canada a few years ago, and to which I was a direct witness. That incident, involving enlightened people of Indian-origin, worked as a wiper to remove the haze of the naivety of my thinking that what I had experienced as a Dalit was confined to a particular set of people living in a different cultural milieu. But in this foreign land, considered to be an epitome of racial tolerance, my encounter was with a class of people of Indian-origin who, given their longstanding existence in that tolerant society, were supposed to be above the trashy, petty considerations of caste discrimination. However, what was observed on their part was far beyond my imagination. Their noxious and siege mentality towards the weakest sections of India, called Dalits, impelled me to record all what had hitherto remained deeply buried in my heart. Following the episode, all those past unpleasant experiences with which I had lived throughout life, and had never thought them of much significance, began bothering my mind alarmingly. In a fleeting moment, all those memories of the past, filled with hatred, violence, injustice, oppression and torture came alive. Thus took the birth of this book.

However, the idea of writing the book could not have fructified had I not received the desired cooperation from my family. My first gratitude goes to my wife Premlata and two sons - Antariksh and Ashwani - who, when they needed me most, gave me ample time to sit back to put together and correlate all thoughts scribbled in my two old diaries. Without their sacrifice, the book could never be completed. Considerably inspiring was the encouragement I received from A. K. Tandon, a colleague in Consulate General of India in Jalalabad, who after going through the scribbled story kept goading me to have it typed out. I then began working on it. To have the scattered portions of the story typed out was no less than a challenge for me. In doing this, I was assisted by Kishore Asthana, N. K. Sharma and D. D. Singh to whom I owe big thanks.

February 13, 2011 **Pratap Singh**

1

Overseas Indians' Deep-rooted Prejudices

It was a bright day of July. Gentle cool breeze was blowing offering a wonderfully pleasant weather, soothing both body and mind. The clear blue sky over high-rise buildings, scattered here and there in the city of Ottawa, the Capital of Canada, appeared like a vast umbrella. People of Indian origin settled in here, had gathered to celebrate community picnic in the prestigious Vincet Massy Park, a favourite local destination for outdoor activities.

Since I dealt with community affairs in Ottawa-based Indian Mission, the President of India-Canada Association invited me as a special guest to participate in the event. I drove to the site along with my family consisting wife, two sons and myself.

As I was looking around to spot the Indian community people, suddenly the fragrance of Indian dishes like *Pakora*, *Puri*, and *Samosa,* hit my nose, making me to instantly figure out that Indians must be where the smell of the dishes was coming from. I at once, followed by my family, headed towards the direction to discover that I had no misunderstanding of typical Indian dishes under preparation to be served to the Indian community picknickers.

Surrounded by tall cedar trees, the park presented a beautiful landscape displaying a mosaic appearance. There gathered people of various nationalities like Lebanese, Chinese, Mexicans and Pakistanis occupying different corners in the park.

Women from Indian community, forming a group, had grabbed benches in one corner of the park, whereas men had comfortably taken their seats near them on the ground, covered with nicely trimmed grass looking like a green carpet rolled out, especially for welcoming the picnickers. Several aged women in the group wore colored baggy shorts and tops, making them appear a little funny with their protruding tummies and bulging buttocks. The women soon plunged into their familiar conversation, which revolved largely around their most favourite subjects such as cooking, knitting, weaving, shopping and so on.

On the other hand, the gents made them busy in discussions pertaining to Indian history, culture, politics and economy, with each one of them trying to prove his scholasticism on India. Given that after settling in Canada, many of them, had not visited even once their country of birth, their knowledge and understanding about the latest developments there could hardly be credible. Nevertheless they were more concerned about developments in India than discussing issues regarding their adopted country.

Highly elated and proud of India's recent progress in various areas, they were offering their specialized opinions on what was further required to transform India into a superpower of the 21st century. Citing examples of India's strides in information technology, they were more than certain that the day was not very far when India, in every respect, would be the powerhouse of the world. They would then proudly fly the flag of Indian supremacy the world over. I was truly gladdened to observe such a kind and caring attitude on their part towards India.

Their discussion via economy, politics, technology and culture travelled to various Indian states. They finally concentrated their attention on Uttar Pradesh and Bihar. Highlighting socio-economic backwardness of these provinces, almost all of them sounded pessimistic, bashing the leadership of the two states.

As the ongoing debate was heating up, a mature Person of India Origin (PIO) holding a very senior position in the Central Government of Canada chipped in. Expressing his dismay on the backwardness and ever- declining conditions of Bihar and Uttar Pradesh he said, 'Do you know why U.P. and Bihar have lagged behind the rest of the country?' he continued.

'For the last several years the two states are being ruled by *Chude* and *Chamar* politicians who have no vision. People in these states are fools that they allow such unscrupulous elements to come to power. The low castes Chief Ministers currently ruling there are solely responsible for the fast deteriorating socio-economic and political conditions. After all, they have low caliber and thus not intellectually competant to govern. How do the upper castes put up with them?'

Interestingly, this elderly man had lived in Canada for over 40 years. Yet, he was more concerned about developments in India than Canada. He continued with his patronizing lecture. 'We feel proud of India's recent progress; however, it doesn't auger well for the upper castes with low castes occupying crucial positions. How could the people at the lowest rung of society be allowed to rule over the people who, for centuries, had been at the helm of affairs?'

To hear such demeaning words from Dr. Shutter, otherwise a highly educated, experienced and seemingly liberal person, I got a little disillusioned. Until now, I held different opinion of overseas Indians. I believed that they must have embraced all those liberal, secular and democratic values that are fundamental features of a multicultural society like Canada.

Alas! I was deeply mistaken. To my astonishment, I found them more obscurant as far as the belief and practice of casteism was concerened. Dr. Shutter, whose views on the low castes mentioned above, perhaps reflected the overall mindset of a certain class of Indians, including members of religions such as Hindus, Muslims, Sikhs and Christians towards low castes called Dalits.

I was peeved at their seized mentality towards the underpriviliged of India, but bearing in mind my official position, I restrained myself from expressing any sentiments.

It was ironical to observe them having in their mind the same deep- rooted hatred and prejudice against the Indian outcast, particularly when they were themselves enjoying full freedom, and equality of status and opportunity while living in Canada. In order to safeguard their interests and assert for their rights they had even formed community associations; and they would not hesitate in accusing the local authorities of racial discrimination if they felt that they had not received proper treatment. However, in case of India, Overseas Indians did not appreciate the fact that Dalits, through their assertion and participation in the political process, were also making a meaningful contribution towards strengthening the democratic institutions in the country.

It was also incomprehensible as to how it was going to adversally affect the life of people like Dr. Shutter if Dalits were to occupy respectable position in Indian society after having them educated.

As Dr. Shutter was making ascerbic remarks against Dalits and their politicians, he kept receiving a manifest applause from most of his fellow Indian immigrants. They said in unison, 'With these so-called Dalits coming into government services on the basis of reservation, our youth are being prevented from occupying important positions in administrative services. The reason for fast spreading corruption in the country's administration and the frequent political instability, seen in several states of India can be ascribed to the emergence of caste-based political parties floated by a few Dalit and backward class leaders.'

They added, 'These Dalits are poisonous insects like mosquitoes that multiply and spread diseases by sucking our blood. Every one of us, including you, would prefer killing a mosquito to letting it bite and suck our blood. Dalits in India are exactly doing that and they therefore need to be stopped.'

Throughout my life, I had experienced a bitter taste of exploitation, discrimination, prejudice and oppression at the hands of people with Dr. Shutter's mentality. Unable to suppress my sentiments, I decided to reason out, 'Dr. Shutter, please let me know how *Chude* and *Chamar* are responsible for the poverty, backwardness and corruption rampant in India? I would also like to know how you, a Sikh, whose religion has no place for casteism and untouchability demonstrate so much abhorrence towards Dalits?'

'Mr. Preet, you must know that till yesterday all these people used to undertake menial jobs; and today they claim to be equal to us. How can we put up with this situation? How can we allow shoes worn in feet, to sit on our head? After all you can't change blood.'

'Dr. Shutter, you left India long ago; and today you are living in one of the most developed and liberal societies of the world. Why has your rigid casteist mentality not yet changed, particularly when you no longer remain concerned towards India after having obtained Canadian citizenship?' I demanded, trying to provoke him further to give vent to his frustration.

'Yes, it is true that I immigrated to Canada over fourty years ago; but I am still an Indian by blood that I brought along with my social initiations, values and cultural heritage. My upbringing took place in a high caste Sikh family, and I can hardly forget and abandon my cultural roots,' said Dr. Shutter further reinforcing his point of view.

On earlier occasions also, I had the opportunity to interact with Indians residing in countries of West Asia. They too in no way were different from their counterparts in the developed countries. Towards Dalits, they had the same mentality of hatred, disdain and prejudice.

Nevertheless, Dr. Shutter's conservative approach towards Dalits and backwards impelled me to probe further into the mindset of other overseas Indians to know their views on casteism.

Bearing this in mind, I increased my interaction manifold with Indian immigrant community in Canada. Without giving an air of my own caste origins, I would enthusiastically participate in all relgious ceremonies organized by many of them at the local temple. I observed that even during the course of puja ceremonies there were repeated caste references, although on such occasions they were totally out of context. Obviously, they were there to reinforce the concept of casteism. It was noteworthy that on these occasions participants were always found more interested in discussing caste related issues back in India. In social gatherings as well, the issue of Dalit-backward politics was always a hot topic for discussion among the guests.

On a few occasions, in light and inocous way I asked them, 'Why do you indulge in Dalit-bashing when you have many more relevant things to discuss?' In reply, they would say, 'We discuss all this because it disturbs us a lot to see lower castes taking centrestage in society.' I would then ask, 'How would you feel if alike Dalits you are subjected to some kind of discrimination in Canada?'

They would retort, 'We have established ourselves on the basis of our high education and better abilities. In intellectuality, intelligence and hard work, there is no match to us, Indians. So, if there is any discrimination against us, we will call it sheer racism.' Some real fun I would get out of these comments!

Reactionary mentality of Indian community, settled in America, came to fore a few years ago when a popular Canadian magazine carried an article highlighting the miserable human conditions that Dalits were compelled to live in. The intellectual class of the immigrant communities was enraged against the editor of the magazine, accusing him of deliberately maligning their image. Putting forth their arguments and defending their position they through written mails and talk shows reasoned out, 'Discrimination, in some form or the other, exists almost in all societies of the world. However, Dalits are not treated as badly as blacks in the developed North America.'

Having met with people of such siege mentality and that too, in a liberal society, I said to myself, 'Oh God! Situation back home in India has really improved a lot. With a few exceptions and aberrations, no one in India looks at Dalits with so much disdainfullness.'

One day, I received an invitation from Dr. Shutter for dinner at his residence. Given his malice towards the down-troddens, I had developed some sort of negativity toward him and was therefore reluctant to accept his invitation. I was sure that there I would have to put up with the same rubbish talks. However, aware of my position in the Embassy, I shed off my perplexity and finally decided to join him for dinner. After all, my main purpose now was to know the caste credentials of more and more immigrant Indians.

Party began at 6.30 pm. The drawing room really looked like a wedding hall. Although it was very spacious, given large number of guest it was hardly adequate to accommodate them all.

Having downed 3-4 pegs of whisky, the guests began to discuss common issues relating primarily to their families and businesses. Then, the intellectually oriented invitees soon moved to discuss important global issues. American aggression of Iraq and war against terrorism was the hottest issue that figured prominently in their discussion. Having bashed America for its evil designs to control the world, they shifted their focus on developments in India.

Presently, a female guest namely Purva Agarwal hailing from Rajasthan, butted in saying, 'yes, things are changing for better in India; however, some unpleasant developments are also taking place in society. You know, in Rajasthan, even Dalits have started asserting in a way with which we can hardly put up. Having acquired some wealth and power, they have stopped respecting us. Governments at our cost are pampering them. In this way, they are depleting the national resources. Not only does the State provide them reservations in services, but also grants their children scholarships apart from arranging lunch for them at school. This is quite irrational on the part of respective governments. This amounts to spreading inequality in society. If this is allowed to continue, it will eventually lead to disintegration of the country.'

'Yes, I absolutely agree with you, Mrs. Agarwal. Government should immediately stop encouraging mediocrity. Not all are equal in society. We cannot keep doctors and engineers at par with workers. Similarly, Dalits cannot be equal to Upper Castes. In my view, there is need to change the basic structure of the Indian Constitution, which provides equal rights to all without taking into account origins of people's culture and educational background.' said Dr. Shutter, the host, supporting and reinforcing Mrs. Agarwal's views on Dalits.

Continuing his tirade, Shutter said, 'You see, the Dalit and Muslim population in India is increasing very rapidly. The day is not very far when, if not checked, they will outnumber the aggregate of Upper Castes and capture power only through ballot. That will be the darkest day in the history of India!'

Having heard such radical views from a highly educated lot of professionals of Indian origin, I was truly aghast. Suddenly, incidents of bitter experiences that I had to suffer in the caste-ridden village society began flashing on my mind. My memories flew back to my childhood when my grandfather had related me a long story of his continous persecution by the Upper Caste.

2

Dhyani Singh – The Grandfather

Grandfather was a brave and bold man. Never afraid of being insulted, humiliated, or even killed, he called a spade a spade. He had zero tolerance with any kind of injustice and would always oppose it with his full might. As a result, he had become a thorn in the flesh of higher castes. He was more loathsome to the landed propertied class who, at any cost, wanted his status as a landholder to finish. By virtue of his land holding, he had not only consolidated his own economic condition, but also had gradually begun to assert for equal rights for other Dalits and Backward communities, thereby antagonizing all the high castes in the village. Becoming a landholder himself, he had set an example before his community people. Following him, many more people from his tribe had become landholders. With that happening, they had stopped working as unpaid bonded labours for Rajput landlords. Durganand Singh, the chieftain of Rajput Thakurs foresaw in the economic consolidation of Dalits a great danger to his tribesmen's hegemony over villagers. For this, he held grandfather squarely responsible.

Sensing a potential danger from grandfather, Durganand Singh and his men decided to decimate him so that in future he could not try to augment his position further by acquiring more land. Fomenting problems after problems, they tried to implicate him in several false cases of robbery, brigandage, arson and even of rape. For years, he was systematically harassed. Unable to make him buckle under their pressure they resorted to other tricks. Launching a malicious campaign against him, they began to concoct all sorts of weird stories as if he was thriving and amassing wealth at the cost of other Dalits. To fill his tribemen's mind with envy, the Thakurs instigated them that Dhyani was no longer as one of them. To prove their point they would tell them that while they were still living in abject poverty, Dhyani at the same time had made fortunes. Thakur Durganand's tricks worked in his favour. He easily succeeded in creating fissures in Dalit ranks, which as a single largest segment in the village were a force to reckon with. By virtue of being their leader, grandfather had gained prominence in the area.

3

Machinations Against Grandfather

Zamindar Durganand Singh was elected as Director of the local Farmers' Co-operative Society. Prior to him, grandfather held this post and he had proved himself efficient and competent as the elected representative of the farmers. Though an illiterate, he had admirable political and administrative acumen. Zamindar Thakur Durganand Singh was never happy with grandfather holding such an important position.

Now being at the helm of affairs himself, Durganand Singh was determined to reduce grandfather to an insignificant position, making it impossible for him to regain his status and raise his head high before Thakurs. With this evil design, Durganand Singh hatched a conspiracy against grandfather to get him implicated in a forgery case.

Taking advantage of his influence over other members of the cooperative society, Durganand Singh, in misuse of his official position, forged documents to raise heavy loans in the name of grandfather and his elder son (uncle). With the investment of this money, he established a sugar industry at his agricultural farm. With his venture thriving, within a short span of period he made great fortunes. On the other hand, unaware of this, grandfather at the same time was sinking in the ocean of debt.

To his great shock, one day, grandfather received a notice, with a warning that his entire property would be attached if he failed to pay the loan on due date. Feeling like stricken by a thunderbolt, for the following several days, he remained confused, disturbed and highly agitated, stretching at the same time his mind to recall if he ever had taken such loan or stood a guarantee for someone. Convinced that he never took any loan himself nor did he ever stand a guarantee for someone, he realized that there was some deep-rooted conspiracy against him.

In order to get down to the bottom of the matter, grandfather approached his connections in the town, who through their reliable sources, found out that it was Durganand Singh who had taken loan by producing forged documents on behalf of him.

Aware of the consequences of litigation and unable to decide on the next move to get over the situation, grandfather approached Durganand Singh with a proposal for an out of court settlement. Showing the notice to Chieftain Thakur he said, 'Chaudhari Sahab, you must be aware of this notice served on me for repayment of the loan, which I have never taken. I have found out that you took loan on our behalf by producing fake documents.'

The Thakur maintained his studied silence. To find no reply forthcoming, grandfather added, 'Look I am not in favour of moving the court and wish to resolve this issue directly with you even if I have to suffer some financial losses. However, I somehow want to bury this matter forever. Please do not try to drag me into litigation and agree to my proposal. If you do that I am even willing to give you a lump sum amount to settle the loan.'

Displaying his adamant and intransigent attitude, the Thakur replied, 'I have no idea about this loan. I do not understand why you are complaining to me. The loan is in your name; you have been served noticed for that; so why don't you settle it?'

'Chowdhury Sahib, please don't feign your innocence. You know everything in the matter. I can see you unnecessarily are trying to drag me into court proceedings that I want to avoid. I would certainly not like to sell my agriculture land for fighting a court case. I therefore wish that with a part of the loan shared by me, even though I am not liable, the matter be resolved between us. Please show some flexibility to settle the matter,' urged grandfather.

Realizing that grandfather was truckling to his ill designs, the Thakur said sarcastically, 'Arey Dhyani, given your several bigahs of agriculture land and with your sons employed in the local sugar mill, you should have no problem in repaying the loan. Since the loan is in your name, you had better pay it, particularly, when you received a notice. As for me, I am not concerned with it.'

Grandfather made several sincere efforts for the resolution of this thorny issue. He even solicited the intervention of the prominent local people in the matter, but the Thakur refused to relent.

Having tried all possible methods to bury hatchet with the Thakur, grandfather realized that he had no other option, but to move the court for justice. He then filed a case against the Thakur. A thorough inquiry into the matter found the Thakur guilty of forgery of documents. Soon court proceedings started against him. Before every next hearing in the court, he warned grandfather of dire consequences if he persisted in pursuing the case. Ignoring all such threats, grandfather pursued the case vigorously. The lower court sentenced Thakur ten years of imprisonment. Upon this, he filed an appeal with the high court, which upheld lower court's decision. Thakur then approached the Supreme Court with last appeal. His main aim now was economic debilitation of grandfather to the extent that in future he had no chance to recover.

In the Supreme Court, the case remained pending for several years. During this period, grandfather's plight had become obvious. So many miseries visited him simultaneously. First, he had to sell several bighas of agriculture land to follow up the case in the Supreme Court. Unable to mobilize adequate resources he had to dispose even of all jewelry available with the family. During the period, Thakur's henchmen didn't allow him to irrigate his crops. Even when he somehow managed to grow them with the help of rain god, Thakur's cattle grazed upon them or if the crops ever ripened, they were set ablaze in the fields.

For years, grandfather continued to suffer like this. With the income coming from father and two uncles, he somehow survived. Meanwhile due to non-availability of money he abandoned pursuing the case in the Supreme Court and lost all his hope to get justice. Then to his great astonishment one day, he got the news that Thakur Durganand Singh received a sentence of ten years imprisonment alongwith a financial penalty. On receiving this news, overtaken by emotions, he cried a lot. That day he was a truly proud man. Despite facing all odds, he stood up against his mighty enemies and succeeded in having their evil designs exposed.

With incarceration of Thakur, his reputation no doubt had beaten down. He however was happy to see that a Dalit, who aspired to become equal to Thakur landlords was reduced to a pauper.

After serving his full period of sentence, Zamindar Durganand Singh was released from jail. He resumed his sugar business as usual. He had no feeling of guilt or any semblance of remorse for being in jail. His tribesmen and other villagers still held him in high esteem.

On the other hand, life for grandfather had no longer remained the same, as it used to be earlier when he owned a large land holding. For following several years, family suffered from all scarcities. However, after a few years, things began to look bright and people gradually started interacting with him, sharing concerns of the village community. In order to normalize his relationship, even Thakur Durganand Singh had now begun cozying up to grandfather to garner latter's support to win the next village president's elections. On a few occasions, in light moments I found grandfather complaining to the Thakur that the latter was responsible for his ruination.

4

Betrayal of Gandhiji by Self-Proclaimed Gandhians

Grandfather, even though an illiterate himself, understood the value of education in life. Ambitious as he was, he made all persistent efforts to carve a place for himself in society by consolidating his economic condition. Being a Dalit, he however was fully aware of his limitations to assert in a caste-ridden society. Entangled in some problem or the other through out his life, he was unable to educate his three sons i.e. father and two uncles. He would always complain ruefully about his inability to provide education to his sons.

He, therefore, was more conscious about the education of his Gen-next. Being the eldest grandchild, he pinned his all hopes on me. He knew before hand that the upper castes would put obstacles in his way if he tried to enroll his grand children in the school. With all this in mind, he still resolved to put his grandchildren in the school.

He wished to see me a highly educated man holding an important position in the government. Learning from his past bitter experiences, he was now convinced that to attain an honourable status in society was possible only through good education. Telling me stories from the lives of great leaders like Mahatma Gandhi, Dr. B.R. Ambedkar, Pandit Jawaharlal Nehru and Netaji Subhash Chandra Bose, he would always inpire me to be something big in life. I had grown old enough to understand things around. When senior government officials visited our village, grandfather, pointing to them, would say, 'They are big people. You should make yourself something like them.' Impeccably dressed, and sophisticated in mannerism, they would speak a different kind of language distinguishing them from common people.

These visiting high-ranking officials fascinated me so much that I too began harbouring an ambition to become like one of them. However, given the bad economic condition of family, I at times felt that perhaps my ambition would remain purely a daydream especially when being a Dalit even the caste barrier could come in my way to move up in life. Notwithstanding such negative thoughts, I was determined to move ahead to educate myself.

Situation that emerged in the country immediately after independence appeared to be somewhat conducive for the weaker sections of society. There was now a slight positive change in the attitude of upper caste Hindus, Muslims, Sikhs and other religions towards Dalits. This positive change in their attitude, to large extent, could be because of provisions in the Indian Constitution for the protection of their rights. The change, however, was limited to only urban areas where people, perhaps because of their modern education, had begun to change. In villages, the higher castes' outlook towards underdogs of India had not changed at all, as they were not yet prepared to shed off their deep-rooted biases against them.

During election time, many white-clad congressmen would visit Dalit bastis (settlements) seeking latter's votes. To welcome these visiting leaders Dalits would spread out string cots for them to sit, but they never sat on them. Instead, they would remain standing, keeping Dalits at the same time engaged in sweet talks and telling them about all what their party had been doing for their welfare. Interestingly, when Dalits offered them tea, water or any eatables, they would make some pretext or the other to avoid drinking and eating at the former's household. Nevertheless, Dalits would feel highly elated with these congressmen visitng them.

5

Facing Opposition for Admission in the Primary School

It was the first day of July. I was then about six years old. That day in the morning mother gave me a soap bath, dressed me nicely and sent me over to grandfather at the chaupal, where he was engaged in talks with visitors. He himself had fixed this day for my admission in the primary school, but he seemed to have forgotten about it. Approaching him, I reminded, 'Grandfather, you told me to be ready this time to go with you to the school for admission. Could you take me there, now?'

'Oh! My child, I really forgot about it. Do not worry, I will take you there right away,' he said.

He then immediately stood up and holding my hand in his he led me to the school, only a few yards away from our house. On reaching there, we found that all the four teachers sat on their chairs in the front yard. Bowing his head a little down towards the teachers, grandfather wished them. Following him, with my hands folded up I too said, 'Namaste Masterji.' Pointing to me and looking towards grandfather, the headmaster asked, 'Arrey Dhyani, who is this boy?'

'He is my eldest grandson, Masterji. I have brought him here for admission', replied grandfather.

'Admission! Dhyani, you know that your condition nowadays is not good. You are still in debt. I have also come to know that you are finding it difficult to arrange two square meals for your family. Despite this, you want to admit your child in school. You rather send him to work for Chaudhary Durganand Singh than putting him here. Instead of squandering your money unnecessarily on his education, you need to first stabilize your family by mobilizing more resources. By the way, you must now have realized that your confrontation with the Thakurs proved too costly for you. Your quarrelsome attitude has just ruined you, reducing to a pauper. I would advise you to tender your apologies to Rajputs to please them in order to avoid facing the same situation in future.'

'Masterji, I had no intention of confronting Thakurs or any other caste. You know what Chaudhari Durganand did to me. Despite my best efforts to settle the matter out of court, he dragged me into litigation. And what happened subsequently, he is solely responsible for that. It wasn't my fault. So, what should I tender my apologies for?' replied grandfather.

'Dhyani, you always annoyed Thakurs with your unpalatable actions. There is a long list of your irksome actions. First, you put the suffix 'Singh' behind your name. Secondly, you acquired several acres of agricultural land aspiring to claim an equal status with Thakurs. Thirdly, projecting yourself as a leader and spokesperson of your entire community, you challenged the upper caste ascendancy in the village. Not content with all this, you created a sort of revolt in society by instigating your castemen to abandon menial jobs. And now you are here to admit your grandchild in the school – an act which will further enrage the upper castes,' commented the headmaster.

'Masterji, I do not understand why you are talking about all this,' asked grandfather.

'Well, Dhyani, I am trying to explain to you the proverb that an elephant is suitable for royals only, and not for a man like you, living in a hut,' added the headmaster.

'Masterji, I do not understand the meaning of your proverb. And by the way, how is it applicable in this case where I am simply asking you to grant my grandson admission.' demanded grandfather.

'Let me tell you in plain words, Dhyani. Education is not meant for people like you. It behoves only the cultured and civilized people. In the past also, some backward caste people tried to educate their children by putting them in this school, and you must know that majority of them were unable to continue their studies. I doubt if your grandchild would be able to pursue his studies,' explained the headmaster.

'If backward caste children didn't continue their studies it doesn't mean that my grandson too would not be able to do so. I don't understand why you are telling me this,' argued out grandfather.

'I knew beforehand, Dhyani; you would argue like this. But let me tell you that before I consider your request for admission, I need to seek the consent of Chaudhary Durganand Singh and other prominent men from higher castes as without bringing it to their notice, I suo motu cannot admit your grandson.' told the headmaster frowning his forehead.

'How do others have any say in this matter? As far as I know it is you who has to decide on it,' demanded grandfather, slightly raising his voice.

'Dhyani, you always irk people by your quarrelsome attitude. I am trying to explain to you some practical problem but you seem to pick a fight with me. Do you understand how upper castes would react to your grandson's admission without their knowledge? So, wait for a couple of days and then come to me,' advised the headmaster to postpone the issue.

'Masterji, tell me clearly if you are going to admit my grandchild today, or not. I am not bothered about upper castes, as they have no right to decide on the matter concerning me. Yes, if you have any problem in granting admission, let me know about it. I will get you orders from district education department for the admission of my grandson. In case, I fail to do so I will give away this child to some missionary school where he would get free of cost good English education, subsequently becoming a Christian himself. Anyhow, I wish him to be educated. That is my resolve,' said grandfather fumbling with an element of threatening.

Being fully aware of grandfather's obsessive nature to pursue matters in courts and government offices, and anticipating the problem he might land himself in, the headmaster immediately toned down and said 'Dhyani, I think you got angry. You need not take trouble in approaching the district authorities for admission. I will enroll your child today itself. Okay?'

'Masterji, I thank you from my heart for this favour,' responded grandfather smilingly.

Admitted in the school, I happily returned home with grandfather.

6

Persecution at the Primary School

That day mother woke up me a bit early in the morning. Having given me a nice cool bath and dressing me with the newly stitched attires, she applied fragrant oil to my hair and put a black mark on my forehead to ward off evil eyes. She then fed me a spoonful of yoghurt mixed with jaggery, considered auspicious before a new beginning. With a small sachet swung over my shoulders, I walked to the chaupal from where grandfather escorted me to my first day at school.

Standing in a corner, I looked around to find a place to sit. There were four rows of students. The first two rows had coir mattresses rolled out, whereas in the other two, students sat on the gunny mats brought from home.

To find me standing there, one of the teachers, pointing towards a place at the end of the fourth row, asked me sternly, 'Aye, what are you looking for? Go and sit there, behind.' As I had not brought my own gunny mat, I walked to the far end of the last row and finding a place there, I took my seat beside a student. Seeing me grabbing a seat near the boy, the teacher said furiously 'You fool! I didn't ask you to sit there. Sit on the ground. And don't forget to bring your own mat from tomorrow onwards.' Shaken and petrified, I walked a few steps away past that boy to take a seat on the ground.

Assigning my first lesson, the teacher instructed me to pick up a broom from the store and sweep the entire courtyard. I at once started sweeping. It took me over an hour to clean the entire courtyard. After finishing the work, I felt thirsty and looked around for water. On a wooden platform, erected in a corner, were sitting two pitchers of water. There was another pitcher placed down on the ground, a few yards away from the wooden platform. Unsuspecting, I filled a jug with water from one of the pitchers on the wooden platform. I was just about to drink water when one of the teachers noticed me. Rising swiftly from his chair, he rushed towards me shouting. Approaching me, he violently snatched the jug from my hands and threw it on the ground. He then said to me screamingly, 'Bloody fool! Don't you know that the pitcher from which you took water is exclusively for the upper caste students? For you low castes, there is that separate pitcher on the ground. With your touch, you have polluted the pot. Why are you looking at me now? Collect that pitcher from there and smash it.'

Absolutely shaken and fearful, with trembling feet I walked up to the platform to remove the pitcher. Lifting it from there, I brought it to the brick lane outside the school premises and tumbled it. This way, I learnt my first lesson that I was a lowly being. The teacher then handed out a schedule for my additional duties that included dusting regularly the chairs, tables and coir mattresses after taking them out from the storeroom. After closure of school, when other students ran merrily towards home, I would roll up coir mattresses and put them back into the storeroom along with the chairs and tables.

On learning about my admission in school, Thakur Durganand immediately sent for the Headmaster who at once, accompanied by his colleagues, dashed towards his chaupal where the latter had now been joined by his clan men also.

Having seated the teachers comfortably on string stools existing across him, the Thakur said,

'Teachers, I am surprised to learn that Dhyani chamar's grandson has joined school. Before admitting him, you didn't even bother to inform us let alone seeking our consent. How did it happen?'

'I did this all in the interest of Hindu community.' replied the headmaster.

'Funny! How is it in the interest of the whole community with a Dalit boy getting himself educated and aspiring to become something in life?' demanded Thakurs.

'You know, I tried my best to dissuade Dhyani from seeking admission for his grandson. When I refused to relent in, he threatened to put the boy in a missionary school. Do you think that a Dalit boy receiving education in a missionary school was in our interest? Missionaries are more than willing to lap them up. You understand this. Allowing Dhyani to enroll his grandchild with a Christian school could open a can of worms. Thereafter, you could have hardly prevented other Dalits from putting their wards there. Who knows that after getting education in a missionary school these Dalit boys and girls would not have converted to Christianity?' explained the headmaster.

On hearing this, Thakur Durganand said,

'Hmm, this Dhyani chamaar is really a dangerous man; he is certainly up to some mischief. Admission for his grandson may be just his pretext to create troubles for us. In denial of admission, he would be looking for an opportunity to forge unity among his caste men.'

For a few minutes, Thakurs conferred among themselves and then announced,

'Masterji, we think your decision is right. Being aware of your capability, we believe you will keep this child of that swine Dhyani in his proper place. Ensure that that bastard boy, under your watchful eyes, is not able to learn anything antithetical to the interests of upper castes. We are sure you will do everything possible for not allowing him to be rebellious. Taking into account all that transpired between you and Dhyani, we agree with your view point.'

For several months, I continued to do only cleaning, dusting, watering plants and digging new flowerbeds. I could learn only a few words by following other students, who would sound loud when mugging up their lessons. I had begun to pronounce and even write those words on takhti (wooden board). Once, teacher gave us homework to write numerals from 1 to 100 on takhti. Alike several other students, I wrote them correctly. After checking my takhti, the teacher remarked,

'How come you were able to write these numbers so accurately, with barely being in the class for few months? Is there someone who teaches you at home?'

'Masterji, I learnt to write them here itself. I have no one at home to teach me', I informed the teacher.

'Hmm, it seems you have learnt all this in your mother's womb', said the teacher sarcastically.

In those days teacher gave severe punishment to indisciplined students. However, in awarding punishment, they always discriminated in favour of upper caste students. Once, a classmate made a false complaint against me. The teacher at once instructed me to stand up at my place. Having made me stand, he angrily walked up to me and slapped me on both cheeks.

'You, a low caste, have the audacity to misbehave with an upper caste boy! How can you do this?' demanded the teacher twisting my right ear piercingly.

'I did not do anything, Masterji.' replied I.

The teacher got more furious and instructed me to squat on my knees, holding my ears with both hands crossed in between the legs. Not satisfied with this, the teacher asked some classmates to put ten bricks on my back with warning that if any brick fell off, the punishment would be extended for another hour. For half an hour, when I did not show any sign of giving in, the teacher commented sarcastically,

'Look at this haraamzada (illegitimate), he does not seem to feel any pain. People rightly say that God has blessed these untouchables with additional bones in their bodies.'

'Well, they are made for such things', remarked the other teacher.

Every alternate day, one punishment or the other was coming my way at school on false complaints from other students, who were certainly dragging glee out of my chagrin. Scared of going to school, I began to sneak out of there by bunking the classes.

Infact, I was tired of dusting, cleaning, digging, and watering flowers in the school. Therefore, after bunking the classes, I would stealthly disappear into the nearby fields to hide myself there to come out only when the school closed. One-day teachers saw me going out of the class. Calling out from behind, he said

'Ay, listen, where are you going?'

To hear him calling me I sprinted towards the fields and did not show up until the school shut. Next day, four-five tough students from the school came to our house. Holding by hands and legs and suspending me in the air, they took me forcibly to the school. Throughout the way, I kept crying, shouting and abusing them trying to break free of their clutches. Seeing the students holding me up, the teacher cried out,

'Arrey, leave him. I will teach him a good lesson. If he doesn't attend the school voluntarily, you will go and bring him over here in this way. I can see he is trying to avoid attending to the work assigned to him.'

Staring at me with a bad look, he then said sternly, 'Now, what are you looking at? Come here. Do you see that flowerbed? Go there, at once. Pick up the spade lying there, and dig the land repeatedly to make it soft until it is ready for plantation. Scared of receiving further thrashing, reluctantly, I walked coyly towards the area, holding spade in my hand. The school had four teachers – two Thakurs, one Brahmin and one Bania. They paid scant attention towards teaching. Rather, they would discuss social and political events focusing largely on Dalits.

Meanwhile, several other Dalit students had joined the school. As the upper caste students did not mingle and make friends with us, we formed our own group. Teachers had earmarked a corner for us to sit in school. Our upper caste brothers would always ridicule us by making dirty remarks, addressing us, not by our personal names but by caste. To our great shock, even teachers would join them and jeer at us citing all kinds of weird examples to prove our born-lowliness. Feeling totally out of place, study hardly interested us. Despite teachers total apathy towards us we continued to pick up things ourselves. I was now in class V and as per my date of birth registered arbitrarily by the headmaster, I was fourteen years old. Rather than focusing on my study, I would pay more attention to teachers' ongoing discussion primarily based on Dalit related issues.

On an occasion, I found teachers indulged in Dalit-bashing, with headmaster commenting, 'Yes, buddies. The wind is blowing in wrong direction. These untouchables of yesteryears, having abandoned their traditional occupations like scavenging, sweeping and cleaning, have begun educating themselves to take up government jobs. They are now no longer available to work at our farms. If this continues, our own sons will have to work as labourers.'

Endorsing him, another teacher spoke up, 'I agree with you, sir. The way things are going nowadays in favour of lower castes, it is bound to disturb the balance of society. The very idea that yesterday's untouchables would sit beside us as our equals sends shivers down my spine.'

With no idea of teachers' reaction, I asked them 'Sir, why do you think that Dalits should always work for you and not get education?'

On hearing this, the teacher instructed me to stand up at my place and repeat the question. Summoning up courage, I repeated it. I had not yet completed that I received a heavy blow on my face from the teacher saying, '*Tu Harami, char akshar kya seekh gaya, ab toone hamaare bhi saamne jabaan kholni shuru kar dee.* (You bastard, as you have learnt a few letters, you have even begun to question us?)' The teacher then, clutching my shoulders, shook me violently, throwing me down to the ground. It was my first attempt in the class to ask a question.

Schoolteachers commanded great respect among upper castes as they played important role in setting political agenda for all villages under school's jurisdication. People very often invited them over lunches at their residences. Once, Thakur Durganand Singh arrived at the school to invite them personally over lunch. Seeing him approaching, the headmaster at once arose from his chair and pulling a chair close to him, he said, 'come please, Chaudhary Sahib. Please take your seat.'

Sitting on the chair and pulling a long breath Chaudhary Durganand said, 'Masterji, Gandhiji won us independence. This was undoubtedly his great contribution. But don't you think he also created more disturbances in society by granting liberty and equality to all riff-raff.'

'Thakur Sahab, I understand your concern. Gandhiji really did us in by agreeing to that '*harami*' Ambedkar's unreasonable demands for equal rights for his people.' the headmaster replied.

On hearing this, I approached the headmaster asking 'Sir, why were you hurling abuses on Dr. Ambedkar who was greatly respected by even Mahatma Gandhi himself.'

Evading a direct reply to my question, he said, 'Arrey, you are still too young to understand these things. Go and concentrate on your studies.'

On earlier occasions, the headmaster would definitely thrash me for asking such questions, but he was now unusually soft with me. This could possibly be because of his involvement in an incident to which I was the sole witness.

7

Headmaster Caught Red-Handed

It was a cold windy day of December. Sugarcane harvest season was on. Most of the men were away to the local sugar mill to work, whereas women were busy in the fields to arrange fodder for cattle. The village looked quite desolate.

At interval, all students and teachers, barring the headmaster, had gone home for lunch. After lunch, on my way back to school, I stopped by our cattle yard – only a few yards away – where my mother was busy in constructing a pyramid of cow-dung cakes. As no one had returned yet to school afer interval, I decided to bear a hand in mother's work. Still busy in assisting her, I noticed the headmaster suddenly leaving and heading towards his sugarcane fields in the west. Normally, he never left the school like this particularly when no other teacher was there.

After a while, I took leave of mother and went straight to the school. Standing in the courtyard, I looked towards the direction the headmaster had just left. I could see only his back. I observed that he was almost rushing. Within a few moments, he disappeared into the thick sugarcane fields. For some silly reasons, I grew curious to know where he was heading so hurriedly. I at once climbed up the stairs to get to the roof of school. From there, I noticed him waving at someone. Then I saw a girl moving towards him. I got further curious to know as to what was going on between them. Climbing down quickly, I virtually ran along the divider towards the fields.

After walking a little distance, I found the girl, headmaster's niece - his elder cousin's daughter – standing on a divider between the two sugarcane fields. Avoiding her attention, I hid myself behind a dense cluster of sugarcanes. Absolutely still, I stood there waiting for what was going to happen next. Meanwhile, headmaster emerged from the other side and waived at the girl, who soon followed him. With headmaster's right hand wrapped around the girl's back, he led her inside the sugarcane field. Over-cautious that I might be seen and the sound of my footsteps be heard, I tiptoed behind them along the divider leading to the field they had just entered.

Within a few moments, I spotted them in a thick corner. I stopped short of walking near them. I stood just two-three yards away from them and could see their every movement. With headmaster's both hands on her shoulders, the girl was now pulling down her *salwar*. After putting off quickly her clothes, she went down on her knees, with headmaster still standing in front of her. Then the headmaster sat down and pushed her gently backward. The girl lay now on her back with her legs raised up. Sitting in between her legs, the headmaster quickly held up her legs up and bringing his erected dick close to her, he made a quick push forward. With their eyes closed and heads rested at each other's shoulders, they held each other tightly in arms making fast movement back and forth, gasping hoarsely. I had no idea of what was happening between them. For a few moments, I continued to watch them. However, I soon realized my mistake when they separated from each other. To find me there, they quickly grasped for their clothes. Putting on her *salwar* and tying it, the girl in a fraction of second disappeared from the scene, whereas the headmaster, putting on his *pyjama*, moved speedily towards me shouting angrily, *'Tu, mader chodh, bhosdiwale, yahan kya kar raha hai? Thahar ja, teri abhi khabar leta hoon.'* (What are you doing here, mother fucker! Hold on, I will accost you right now.) Saying this, he rushed towards me with blood shots. I at once stepped back and ran away from the scene. The headmaster tried to catch hold of me but he could not as he was already out of breath. I arrived at the school much before him.

By that time, most of the students had returned to the school after interval. The other teachers had not yet come back. Pursuing me, the headmaster had now reached the school. He was still breathing fast. Pulling up a chair, he sat on it. I could see him throwing angry glance towards me. After a while, he signaled me to come to him. Though I was trembling with fear, obeying him I grudgingly walked up to him. Without looking at me, headmaster asked quite affectionately, 'Did you tell anyone about what you saw there? Listen, I will not spank you if you tell me the truth'

'Masterji, I didn't tell anyone yet and will never. Please forgive me for my mistake.' I pleaded with folded hands.

The headmaster now appeared to be quite relaxed. Rising from his chair and putting his hands on my shoulders, he said, *'Achcha, Achcha, daro mat. Main tumhen peetunga nahin. Aaj se tum agli pankti mein baithna. Main doosre teachron se bhi keh doonga ki wei tumhen dante ya peete nahin. Kintu ek baat yaad rakhna ki kisi ke saamne bhi iss bare mein kabhi munh nahi kholna hai.'* (Ok, OK, don't be scared. I will not spank you. From henceforth, you sit in the front row, and I will inform other teachers not to scold or thrash you. However, remember one thing! You will never ever open your mouth before anyone about it.)

8

Mother's Woes

One good trait that I liked most in my father was his physical prowess and fearlessness. This had won him copious laurels from people. He was a good wrestler and weight lifter. What made him outstanding in the village was his ability to overwhelm and pin down even physically bigger-sized opponents in the wrestling game.

On the other hand, he was bad-tempered and abusive, never shy to pick fight with anyone. His ill-treatment of mother and illicit relationship with another woman would always trouble me a lot. Because of his habits, there would be frequent quarrels, clashes and verbal brawl in the family. Unable to bear quietly, mother tried to raise her voice, but it always resulted in her thrashing, revilement, starving etc. These were, indeed, very bad days. At the slightest pretext, father would come down with severe beating. On occasions, she was seriously injured and screamed through the night, but neither of my two aunts showed sympathy with her. Her sufferings at the hands of father were immeasurable.

Filled with exemplary courage, strong will power and compassion, mother was absolutely committed to her children. Even when she was down with her grievous injuries, she would manage to get up early in the morning to cook for us siblings before we set out for school.

We were a large joint family, consisting of grandfather, uncles and aunts, ten cousins and we five siblings, including a sister. On the whole, except the first few years, the family atmosphere was far from peaceful and harmonious. On trifle matters, there would be fierce fighting between father and two uncles with grandfather adding fuel to the fire by siding with the two uncles even though they were wrong. Initially, mother, out of deference, never opened her mouth in front of grandfather. However, when her patience gave in, she began to resent over his biased attitude against father. Two aunts had further aggravated the situation by joining hands in opposition to mother. They would always concoct stories to poison grandfather's ears, provoking him to harass mother.

As I narrated elsewhere, by nature, grandfather was hotheaded and arbitrary. He had zero tolerance for any family member opposing him. He disliked mother due to this reason. On the other hand, my two aunts held grudge against mother as she had four sons, while they had none.

Mother would cook all three meals - breakfast, lunch and dinner - for the entire family of twenty-two members. After finishing the pantry work, she would hand over the kitchen to my elder aunt (Taayi) who, accompanied by the younger aunt (Chachi), served the food. When the men folks, led by grandfather, would line up along the wall to have food, it was the elder aunt, who always was there for service. Grandfather would always complain sarcastically that the *maharani* never showed up in the kitchen. Interestingly, my aunt never disclosed that mother had been preparing the food. Instead, her general reply would be that she was taking rest inside, as she was not well, thereby further crystallizing grandfather's impression that mother was a shirker and her illness was only a pretext to avoid attending to kitchen chores. This continued for days, months and years. Taayi was also helping in projecting mother in a poor light. Grandfather on his part hardly bothered to verify the facts. Nevertheless, mother continued to work with devotion. Grandfather remained oblivious of mother stoking fire in the earthen oven, three times a day for the entire family.

Mother's persecution at the hands of grandfather, two uncles and aunts had intensified. Despite this, father remained insensitive towards her. Mother was living with all this for the sake of her children. While, my uncles and aunts would rest at home during harsh winters and scorching summers, mother would accompany father to work in the fields. She would do all that to help father who hardly took note of her sacrifices.

When we brothers grew up, grandfather would pressurize us to go and work in the fields. He never did that in case of our cousins. We never objected to him, however, mother was not happy with this arrangement. The two uncles who worked in factory, used to keep their earnings with them. Their money never reached father, whereas the entire family used the farm produce. Surprisingly, father never objected too. Instead, grandfather's remarks on mother would carry him away.

Mother had now begun to see clearly the tricks of two aunts who out of their jealousy never wanted her to raise her children well. Fed up with frequent fights and scuffles, mother finally demanded for partition of agricultural land. At this grandfather was furious. He said to mother unequivocally,

'Splitting of land would be possible only after my death. At no cost, I am going to give you any share from farmland. If you are not happy in the joint family, you are free to go your way.'

Grandfather's hard stance over this issue resulted in frequent rumblings in the family. Meanwhile, mother persisted in her demand, forcing finally grandfather to split farmland. Not to be defeated, he too came up with a well-contrived plan for split of farmland.

As narrated above, intrinsically, grandfather was inclined towards uncles and their children. Therefore, he split the land into four parts-one each for him, two uncles, and father. He would then pass on his share to two uncles, who, with addition of his share, never faced food scarcity throughout the year. Logically, with a larger number of members, our family unit needed his share the most but he denied. As a result, we always felt severe shortage of food grains to meet our needs.

When mother realised that her two sisters-in-law were responsible for presenting a negative image of hers in the eyes of father-in-law, she tried to explain to him, but was snubbed saying, 'How dare you; you better know I do not allow ladies to open their mouth. And you have the temerity to come over to discuss things with me!' After that, she could not summon up further courage to clear the air.

Once grandfather called in his three sons and said, 'In a joint family, every member should not be expected to make equal contribution. While some work more, others do not. This is necessary in the interest of family unity and solidarity. Joint families run by the rule 'From everybody according to his ability, to everybody according to his need'. You all need to remain united. However, the one with more male children needs to contribute more to meet the household expenses.'

Grandfather further elaborated, 'I notice nowadays my children getting out of control. One of my daughters-in-law is hell-bent upon disturbing family's peace and unity, and tarnishing my image in the community. She often avoids domestic chores like cooking under the pretext of ill ness.'

Of course, he was alluding to mother. At this, for the first time, father's dim sense of understanding suddenly brightened. As he was about to get up and say something, grandfather, pointing his finger at him, stopped him tersely, 'If I speak about your spouses, none of you should argue in their defence. I am hurt as one of my daughters-in-law always argues with me. And my own son is responsible for this state of affairs.' Hearing this, father got quiet and could not speak up.

Strangely, grandfather always adopted democratic means – mediation, arbitration, dialogues and negotiations – to help settle others disputes. But when it came to his own household, he had absolute control over affairs and never brooked the idea of democracy in it.

Once, elder aunt, without any obvious reason, rushed to the chaupal before lunch hours. Seated comfortably on his charpoy, grandfather that time was puffing at his smoking pipe. Approaching him, she started crying loudly. When grandfather asked her the reason, she complained, 'It has become difficult for us to breathe easily in the house; we have the responsibility for all the household work, but she (mother) doesn't allow us to do that; today, she laid hands upon us and threw the kneaded dough to dogs; she is not allowing us to enter the kitchen'.

It was a good pretext for grandfather to give vent to his hatred and anger towards mother. Fretted and fumed, he immediately dashed to the house, joined by younger uncle. Reaching there, he began hurling filthiest abuses upon mother, who was bewildered and somewhat terrorized to see him in the fit of rage. Unable to understand what was wrong with him, she began walking away. Grandfather then lifted a staff from the ground and began beating her. Not satisfied with this, younger uncle also joined the chorus and he too hit her several times with a bamboo. I jumped in to save her, as I could no longer stand her being assaulted so brutally.

In protest, I did not take my dinner that evening. It was shocking to find father not taking any notice of the incident let all alone showing any care for her. He spent his time mostly in fields. Whenever mother tried to speak to him about her problems, he silenced her with reproach, 'I will do nothing that spoils my father's image in the community.'

Harsh, painful and humiliating conditions in the family were taking their heavy toll on mother's mental and physical health. Her appetite was no longer normal as she now took very little food, maybe just to keep herself alive. As a result, she had turned into a skeleton. She was hardly capable to stand on her own.

One day, in the late afternoon, when she was lying in a charpoy in the foreyard of the house, she heard the sound of grandfather's footsteps approaching the haveli. Women, both within and outside the family, could easily learn about his arrival by the unique mannerism of his foot tapping. As soon as she realized about his presence, she hurriedly tried to step out of the charpoy. Suddenly, she felt darkness around and fell down on the ground hitting her right arm against a rusted iron object lying there. She somehow stood up and dragged herself inside.

Seeing that her hand bleeded profusely, she took out a cotton swab and soaking it in the kerosene oil, she cleaned the injured part. Thereafter, she forgot about the injury. After a few days, she felt excruciating pain in the injured arm from nail to shoulder. She also noticed the unusual swelling perhaps caused by infection.

Within a few days, yellowish mucus began oozing out of her arm. Day and night, she would lament, but father paid no attention. Instead, he would believe grandfather who told him that there was nothing serious and she was making her small injury an excuse to visit her parents to avoid working in the fields during the forthcoming harvest season.

One evening, on returning home, when father saw mother lying on charpoy, he got furious. Without checking the fact, he began hurling filthy abuses on her, 'Wicked lady! You are a nuisance, hell bent upon disturbing peace of the family. Under the pretext of a small injury, you are all the time lying idle. You have turned the house into a gloomy place by wailing day and night.'

To see father saying this, I grew highly angry, but I restrained myself from displaying my rage. Mother's condition continued to deteriorate. Within the next few days, she was completely bed-ridden. Unbearable pain was now killing her. I would stand beside her bed for hours, with my eyes glued to her pale face. At times, it was so pathetic that I too broke down and then we together would share the grief. With her arms clutched into each other, she would plead loudly, 'This is killing me. I can't take it any more. Please take me to the doctor to have this bloody hand amputated. I want to live for my children. I know if I die, no one is going to look after them.'

With the passage of another week, the brownish slimy secretion from her injury began flowing out automatically. One morning, when father found her saree stained with yellow-reddish spots all over, he realized for the first time the gravity of the problem. Walking to her cot, he bent down and picked up the injured arm to have a close look at it. No sooner did he touch the hand than she wriggled out cryingly to ease it from him. Upon her cry, father immediately dropped her hand with a jerk and said angrily, '*Saali, ab kyon is tarah chilla rahi hai. Us din se to tune bataya naheen ki itni takleef ho gayi hai.*' (Bloody woman, why are you crying now? You never told me about the real extent of your pain).

He continued angrily, 'You have come to ruin us. Now that harvesting season is near, I guess you have deliberately caused this injury to avoid working in the fields. You are of no use to us. I don't need you. I have no money for your treatment. Your parents have given nothing worthwhile to be considered for spending on you.'

For a few moments, mother looked at father in disbelief. Then covering her face with a corner of her saree she turned away. She sobbed unrelentingly. Father, without saying anything further, left the house fretting.

One of our community women hailed from the village close to mother's native place. She addressed mother as her elder sister and we called her Mausi. She was going to visit her parents. Before departure, she came to see mother enquiring if she wanted to convey any message to her family.

To see mother's condition, Mausi was shocked. Showing her sympathy with her, she said, 'I did not know your condition was this serious. I am sorry that I couldn't visit you earlier. I am deeply shocked to find no one around to look after you. Men and women – all - in this family are cruel and inhumane. Tell me what exactly you want me to convey to Taayi (Aunt)'

'Please request her to come and see me just once. God knows if I would be alive to go and see my mother, brothers and their families. This is the only favour I ask you. I want to see my younger brother. If he is not available in the village, please advise mother to inform him right away', pleaded mother with welled-up eyes.

At this, Mausi felt deeply moved. Recovering herself, she tried to console mother, 'You need not worry. I will tell taayi all what I have seen with my own eyes. I am going to tell her everything - your persecution and involvement of the whole family in the conspiracy to kill you.'

9

Father's Escapades

It was a dusty evening. I had just returned after a long day in the fields. Suddenly, I heard someone wailing in the haveli. I paced up towards there. I saw mother and granny weeping with their heads on each other's shoulders. Mother was intermittently relating her woes to granny, who in turn, was describing her own sorrows she had experienced as a widow. Mother was granny's favourite among three daughters. While mother and granny were sharing their sorrows, my uncles were making fun of them. They assumed that mother would go away with granny and that there was very little prospect of her return, as, according to their calculations, she would not survive in the present condition.

That night nobody in the family, including father, spoke affectionately with granny. From their attitude, she could easily judge that all the family members were against her daughter and wanted to get rid of her. Granny, in a feeble voice, tried to reason out with father but before she could finish, father walked out, leaving her hurt, humiliated and disappointed.

Next morning, without having breakfast, granny herself prepared mother by wrapping her in saree to take her along.

When they were about to leave, grandfather entered haveli. To see mother in a new saree, standing beside her mother, he remarked, 'Chaudhraniji! (His mode of addressing granny) I knew it. *Bahu's* only motive was to go back to you, and she was looking for a pretext to leave the house. I am wondering about the quality of family values she has inherited. Since her arrival here, she has been spoiling peace of my family by sowing the seeds of discord among brothers; and she avoids working in the household on one pretext or the other.'

Granny wanted to respond but she held back, out of respect towards grandfather in line with Indian ethos and sensitivity of her relationship with him. On his part, grandfather continued with his barrage of bitter words, 'Yes, one more thing, Chaudhraniji. We all are tired of her crying day and night. I don't think she has any serious illness. If you think she has any, you are free to take her with you. I don't have resources to freak out on useless matters like her made-up sickness. If you decide to take her along, please ensure that she returns only when she has recovered.'

Hearing this, Granny felt silent. Summoning some degree of courage, she pleaded, 'Chaudhry Saheb! Being her mother, I know my daughter better than you all do. I am in the knowledge of her illness, the reasons for her sufferings and the treatment meted out to her by each member of the family. My daughter is on deathbed and you claim that she is using her illness as a pretext to go with me. I cannot leave her behind to die like an orphan as long as I am alive. Despite being a widow, I am fully capable to take care of my children.'

Mother went back with granny, leaving me behind in the custody of my two aunts. I was young but did understand things. My younger brother, who still needed to be breastfed by mother, went along with her.

After mother's departure, father tried to see that I did not miss mother. However, within a week, I began feeling her absence. I would whimper and insist upon visiting her but my cries had hardly any effect upon him. I would be emotional when my aunts served meal to my cousins and I would sulk in a remote corner of the house. My elder aunt would angrily rebuke me whenever I insisted on dining along with my cousins. 'You are not going to die in a few minutes. Wait until they have finished eating. I don't have another thali (serving plate) to serve you meal along with them.'

On some pretext or the other, she would make me wait for food. After my cousins had finished, she would put some leftover on my plate, asking me to sit aside and eat. Though I was child, I could understand fairly well the reason behind this poor treatment. Her deep-seated jealousy towards mother flowed from the fact that she still did not have a son. On the other hand, mother never thought ill of aunts on any count.

Surprisingly, one-day father enquired, 'Why do you look so weak?' I did not reply. He seemed to have noticed my declining health. On finding me quiet, he repeated, 'Do you miss your mother? Why do you bother about her? I am here to take care of you'. I remained quiet again. Then, suddenly tears began rolling down my cheeks. 'You are a boy. Be bold and courageous. Don't take these small things to heart. We will go there in a few days to bring your younger brother back to give you company', said he trying to console me.

With every passing day, I was weakening. I had no appetite left. Throughout the night, I would lay awake on my charpoy, thinking about my mother. Father would always go to chaupal to sleep while I had to sleep with my cousins in the haveli.

Nearly five months had gone by; there was no news of mother. Sadly, father too never bothered to enquire. Granny, after taking mother from our place, sent her to her elder sister's (mausi) house for treatment. One fine morning, mausi's brother-in-law visited us to break the good news about mother's fast recovery. When he told this, grandfather, instead of thanking him, was sarcastic, 'Oh! Afterall, she survived! Not good news! She will continue nagging us'.

In the evening, when father returned from fields, grandfather informed him about mother's recovery. He said, 'Now that she has recovered, you better go and bring her back. Crop is ready for harvest. Additional help will be handy.'

I accompanied father to mausi's place. As I had visited mausi earlier also, I knew the location of their house. No sooner did we reach the village, than I left father behind and sprinted towards the house. From the muddy entrance porch, I could notice that mother was sitting on the charpoy with her back towards the door. I walked up to her and shut her eyes with my palms standing behind her. Uttering who it was, she groped my hands in an effort to recognize me. I was standing very close to her and she could feel my breath. Recognizing me instantly, she pulled me around and hugged me lovingly with tears in her eyes. Stroking my head and planting kisses on my cheeks, she inquired, 'Who brought you here? Is your father with you?' In reply to her last question, I just nodded in affirmative. 'How are your aunts?' she continued. 'You have thinned a lot. I hope you had proper meals?' Mother was still shooting off innocuous enquiries when father entered the scene. Without even looking at her, he just passed the charpoy mother perched on, and went straight to the guest room in a corner.

After spending about a week's time with mausi, all of us left for home.

Even after her return from there, mother continued her medication. In a couple of months, she completely cured. After recovery, she resumed her household chores. However, my two aunts and uncles did not seem to relish the idea of mother's return and the subsequent cordiality between father and mother. For the present, there held truce between father and mother.

Things appeared to be going happily normal. Then mother somehow came to know about father's extra-marital relations with a woman. Around this time, an incident, involving father and the woman, living a few yards from our house, took place. This created turbulence in the family.

It was summer. During this time, people in the villages would sleep in the open-air outside their houses. One day when mother and father were both sleeping out in the foreyard, father got up silently. He first lit up a beedi (sort of small cigar), and had his pulls at it for a few minutes. Stepping out of his charpoy, he walked to mother. He bent over her to see whether she was asleep. Once assured, he left the house. Father had no inkling that mother was awake. She was, in fact, pretending to be asleep and observing his movements quietly. No sooner did he leave, than mother got up and followed him into the direction of his departure keeping a little distance between herself and on-the-move father. Once there, father hurriedly walked into the gate of the courtyard where the woman was sleeping in the open with a little baby beside her. Mother also walked up to the gate and stopped by. Then slouching against the wall, she peeped into the courtyard. Perhaps, the woman was already awake, as mother could hear her whisperings. The woman, soon, removed the baby from her charpoy and put it into a baby-cot nearby. With enough room now on the charpoy to accommodate him, father quickly leapt into it and spread him all over her. Both were now breathing hoarsely, holding each other tightly in their arms. Mother, could not stand watching the scene and turned immediately back to the house.

She laid back into the charpoy and started sobbing uncontrollably. When father got back, her cries grew louder. In shrill voice, she confronted him, 'You had gone to that randi (prostitute). You have been neglecting me for her. Why do you visit her stealthily? Why don't you keep her openly? I had heard about your relations with her, but never believed it, always taking you to be a committed husband. Now I am going to tell everyone. They should know how reputed and honourable your family is, something your father is boastful and proud of. People in the community must also know about the true character of your family.'

First, father was listening quietly. He then flared up and stepped down the charpoy. He walked angrily to mother's charpoy and yelling at her, he hurled the filthiest abuses.

He said, 'Badmaash Aurat (Wicked woman)! You have the audacity to open your mouth against me in the public to disgrace our family. Haramzaadi (bastard), you spy on me. You shameless woman followed me there. You don't have any hesitation or fear while going out of the house at this late hour.'

He then violently dragged mother out of charpoy. Holding her by hair, he felled her on the ground. Crying with pain, mother was writhing to release herself from his clutches but to no avail. Hearing commotion, I woke up and came out into the yard from inside the house to witness father kicking her all over. Thrashed mercilessly, she could not breathe or express herself. She was trying to say something, but her voice was too feeble to hear. She was almost half-dead. She lay there, still. Then she moved her hand, but was still unable to speak. For another few moments, she kept lying on the ground, as she was not yet able to stand up. Looking towards me, she pointed to the pitcher of water. Her throat was dry to make it difficult for her to speak. I immediately filled a glass and taking some water into my palm; I splashed her face with it and then dropped another palm of water into her mouth. A little later, mother regained her consciousness and sat up. With my little strength, I helped her stand on her legs and administered her to her charpoy.

Father was now absolutely quiet. Perhaps, he realised that I had overheard everything, transpiring between them.

I was expecting something nasty to happen the next day. Surprisingly, mother did not rake up the issue at all. Perhaps, out of shame, fear and concern for the sake of her children, she preferred to keep quiet. Father, however, did not change his ways. Emboldened by mother's silence, he continued unabashedly his sexual escapades. There was no semblance of mitigation in mother's miseries. Her sufferings, insults and humiliation at the hands of her husband, two sisters-in-law, brothers-in-law and father-in-law continued as earlier.

10

First Taste of Untouchability

Alike elsewhere, even in rural India women then ruled the domestic world of their families, whereas male members handled only the external affairs. Women, copared to men, were more orthodox. To ensure strict observance of religious and social practices in the family, they had a final say as far as dealing with intra-caste matters is concerned.

I was then a grade three student in the village primary school. One of my classmates was from backward community. We would very often play together in the school as well as the fields around. Perhaps, the boy, like me, also did not have much idea about high or low social status.

It was the month of October - harvesting season for paddy and preparation time for the next wheat crop. The ploughed-up fields, bright gold in color, looked extremely beautiful to attract young boys for playing country-games like high jump, long jump, kabaddi and wrestling offering them ready-made arena. Both of us were returning home after the school. Suddenly, we heard someone calling us. Turning around, we found some senior boys waving at us to stop. Within moments, we were face to face.

The grown-up boys decided to play kabaddi. Given our age and physique, we were no match to play a rustic game like that with almost young boys, but on their insistence, we followed them up to the fields. Within half an hour, more and more boys our age joined us. While young boys began playing kabaddi by forming two teams, we tiny beings indulged in petty sports like race, push ups, gulli-danda etc. Having played for nearly two hours, we put on our clothes to return home.

On way back home, I stopped by my classmate's house - located a few yards before our house. On seeing him back, his mother showered him with a barrage of questions, 'Where have you been all day long? You have not eaten anything since morning. Look here, what have you made of yourself? I am very angry with you. You remain away without permission for so long. I will neither talk to you nor give you any food today.'

The boy was sort of a spoilt child. He too retorted, 'All right. I too will not talk to you, and I am again going to play.'

'All right, go away', said his mother.

Then suddenly rising from the charpoy, she cupped affectionately his face in her palms. Taking water from the pitcher, placed nearby on the stand, she splashed his mouth, and then dabbed his face with the border of her saree. Having seated him on sting cot lying in front of their thatched house, she went in saying, 'Now, be seated, and wait!'

I kept standing beside him. Soon, his mother, with a thali (tray) on her hand lined with two chapattis and daal (lentil), emerged from the house. With food before him, the boy started whimpering and pushed the thali away. 'Arrey beta, eat, eat; you have eaten nothing since morning. You must be very hungry', said the mother. 'No, no! You always give me the same food. I don't like lentil everyday,' grumbled the boy.

Without any sense of discrimination - right or wrong, pure or impure, high or low - I picked up a chapatti from his thali and holding it out to him, I said, 'Arrey yaar, eat it. Your mother is offering you food with so much love and affection'.

I still held the chapatti. Seeing this, the boy's mother swiftly rushed towards me. Snatching the chapati from my hands, she said angrily, 'Oh! What have you done? You should not have touched it. You have polluted this and I cannot allow him to eat it.'

She then went to their cow, tethered in a corner of the courtyard, and put that chapatti into its mouth. I could not comprehend about what mistake I did by picking up and handing out the chapatti to the boy, but a sense of culpability had undoubtedly enveloped me numbing my whole body. Her behaviour had utterly confounded me.

Back home, I related the incident to my mother. My mother's simple reaction was that I should not have touched their chapatti as they belonged to a higher caste. Although not completely grasping the import of the incident or the advice of my mother, I found something repulsive inside me about it.

11

Persecution at the High School

I had passed the 5th Grade and looked forward for admission in the higher secondary school for further education. Registration process for admission had begun. To complete formalities for admission in the 6th grade, I walked on foot with my father to the school.

Atmosphere here in was almost the same as in primary school. Higher caste students- mostly belonging to the landed propertied and business communities - called the shots here. Almost all the teachers came from upper castes such as Brahmins, Thakurs and Kayasthas. It was a private school owned by a local zamindar. He had picked up all schoolteachers from families, well known to him. Casteism and untouchability were commonplace. Prominent local landlords and big farmers had great clout in the management of school. The local rowdy elements always plagued the school atmosphere by incidents of infighting, stabbing, groupism and hooliganism. I disliked the ambience there. However, in view of constraints flowing from my family's economic backwardness, I had no choice but to study there. In classrooms, the domineering upper caste students would always humiliate Dalit students by calling the names apart from intimidating them on one pretext or the other. If they ever attempted to ask questions, the upper caste students would shout them down. Interestingly, the teachers never intervened in such situations. Emboldened by the teachers' apathy towards Dalit students, they would create further troubles for them. Thus, Dalit students could hardly participate in the classroom discussions.

Aware that I was an ordinary student, I always kept a low profile. Only brilliant students – either at study or at sports –were teachers' favourite and popular among the students. I had no such talent to be popular. It was therefore amazing to see that most of the teachers and students with whom I had never earlier interacted, knew me well. A more astonishing thing was that they knew even my grandfather, father and uncles.

One day immediately after entering the class, the math teacher announced, 'today I am going to conduct a test for you, I will give everyone an opportunity to pickup a sum of his choice to solve on the blackboard. Turn by turn, I will call you to come up here to solve the problem. Yes, when the chosen one from amongst you is solving the problem, you all are free to ask him any doubts.'

I was not good at Mathematics. I therefore, did not expect an invitation to the blackboard to solve any problem and take queries from other students to clear doubts.

To my bewilderment, the math teacher Phundan Lal invited me first to the blackboard to solve a problem he had already chosen for me. I was least prepared for the assignment. However, I walked to the blackboard, my feet and hands trembling.

The teacher asked me to solve and explain an equation. Despite my best efforts, I failed to do it and returned to my desk. After this, the teacher called no one to the blackboard. Instead, he suddenly flared up using all kinds of invectives against me. To my dismay, in front of the entire class, he said, 'Boys, do you know who this boy is?' he continued. 'Let me tell you. He is grandson of that Dhyani *Chamaar* who, in his village, always keeps fomenting troubles to the upper castes.' Unable to comprehend, I tried to stretch my mind to guess as to why he was referring to my grandfather in front of students.' Summoning up courage, I asked, 'Teacher, how does my grandfather concern with it? If I am weak in Mathematics, how can you be abusive to my family?' Hearing this, the teacher swiftly rose from his chair and rushed angrily to the rear row where I sat. He stopped at my desk, held me by collar of my shirt and dragged me to the blackboard.

Presenting me before the class, he said, 'Look at this duffer, untouchable boy, he has the temerity to open his mouth before me. Do you think he is fit to continue in the class?'

The teacher then dealt me heavy blows with his fist knocking me down to the ground.

Walking back to my desk, I tried to stretch my mind to figure out why the teacher was doing all this to me. Then what struck my mind was revealing.

Thakur Makhan Lal Singh, one of the teachers in school, was from our village. He was a very shrewd man. Politics interested him more than his real occupation - teaching. He would always engage himself in the village-level party politics. That time, Makhan Lal Singh was president of village panchayat. Misusing his position, he grabbed illegally several bighas of village community land. Grandfather was the only one to oppose him, inviting his animosity. Phundan Lal was a close friend of Makhan Lal who through the former, wanted to settle his scores with grandfather by forcing me to drop the school. Therefore, as Makhan Lal's proxy, Phundan Lal under some pretext or the other was tormenting me.

Atmosphere in the school had really become very suffocating and dreadfull. On occasions, I felt like setting the school ablaze and gun down all teachers. However, I fully understood the impracticability of putting such bizarre ideas to fruit. Notwithstanding, these odds, I continued to hold on to my studies as I realized that I now had Hobson's choice only. Within village also, atmosphere was quite hostile towards our family. Even students from our own community avoided me - some by choice and some under pressure from Thakur Makhan Lal and Durganand. Both Thakurs' agenda was to make grandfather cringe at their feet – something quite unacceptable to a proud man like him. Situation, both within village and in the school, was so appalling that it created in me a sense of fear, frustration and detachment. It felt extremely miserable to be there.

I had no interest left in my studies. In the morning when I would start for the school, my feet refused to move ahead.

12

Thakur's Annoyance

Thakur Makhan Lal Singh's term as *sarpanch* of the village was almost over. Elections for the Gram Panchayat (village assembly) were approaching. In order to win over the voters, various aspirants for this post had already begun canvassing by organizing meetings on caste pattern. Thakur Makhan Lal Singh too wanted to be re-elected. He sought grandfather's support for his candidature. In view of his strained relationship with the Thakur community, grandfather, however, gave cold shoulder to his overture. Hurt and annoyed at grandfather's gall to say no to him, Makhan Lal joined hands with Thakur Durganand. Holding a commond grudge against grandfather, they decided to teach him a lesson.

In order to mobilize public opinion against grandfather, Makhan Lal launched propaganda against the former. They fabricated all sorts of false stories about grandfather to spread among the villagers. Soon, all castes, including Dalit turned against him. People began to view him with a great suspicion. Certain that grandfather had now become a sort of outcast, Makhan Lal added fuel to the fire by leading a group of dominant villagers to take up arms against him. He exhorted them to decimate grandfather's family.

Because of his quarrelsome nature, grandfather had had clashes and skirmishes with almost all communities, though, not for his personal gains. His sole aim was empowerment of Dalits in the village. At times, he even manhandled several Dalits to force them to fall in line with his way of thinking. Against their will, he had coerced them to remain united and fight against the upper castes' domination. Undoubtedly, an ambitious man to create a status of equality for himself and his community, he, however, never indulged in any criminal activity while waging his struggle against the upper castes. However, he had the galls to stand against any injustice. As a far-sighted man, he wanted to forge a unity among Dalits to enable them to fight for their rights.

Thakur Makhan Lal systematically poisoned all villagers' ears against grandfather by telling them, 'A single individual like Dhyani should not be allowed to insult and humiliate each and everyone in the village. He is a curmudgeon and petulant, always hell bent upon insulting all castes, including Dalits. His wings need really to be clipped to prevent him from flying too high.'

Through his shrewd and cunning maneuvers, Thakur succeeded in creating such a hostile climate against grandfather that irrespective of their caste or religion, villagers began to bay for his blood. Grandfather's over-arching stance on a particular contentious issue, which had recently taken place in the village, was the immediate cause for villagers' belligerence towards him. Citing that incident as an instance, Makhan Lal had succeeded in instigating the whole village community.

13

Trader's Subterfuge to Trap Grandfather

The year was 1966. After a gap of nearly five years, grandfather was beginning to heave a sigh of relief as family's overall economic condition had started improving. Apart from a bumper production from the wheat and paddy crops, sugarcane - a cash crop- was now ready for harvest and was likely to yield a substantial income. Now, there was an abundance of food-grains in the household. Having a penchant for agricultural land, grandfather was now planning to increase his holding by purchasing more lands, most of which he had lost in the protracted litigation with Thakur Durganand. To recover it was his topmost priority to re-establish his position in the predominantly upper caste village community. His second priority was to construct a concrete house, a privilege so far enjoyed by the higher castes only.

When grandfather was very much within the reach of achieving his goals, a cunning trader suddenly trapped him. He began cozying up to grandfather by taking advantage of his gullible nature. After winning over his confidence, the trader cleverly started poisoning his ears against Thakurs with whom he wanted to settle his personal scores. He needed someone like grandfather as a tool to achieve his objective.

He would tell him flatteringly, 'Dhyani Singh, you are the only one in the village who can stand up and challenge the supremacy of these Thakurs. It is not me alone; several others also feel the same way.'

Cunning and jealous, as he was, the trader could never bear with anyone doing well, especially a Dalit. Grandfather's re-emergence on the social scene had greatly disturbed him. He feared that after stabilizing his family, grandfather would resume meddling in the community affairs. This had so far been the prerogative of the upper caste men like Shambhu Ram. To provoke grandfather, he would concoct false stories to misinform him about a select group of people. Believing Shambhu Ram, grandfather, without verifying the facts, began displaying his belligerent behaviour towards them. In the process, he annoyed almost all major communities, particularly Brahmins and Thakurs. Thus, he fell easily into trader Shambhu Ram's trap of conspiracy.

To vitiate the atmosphere further, Shambhu Ram brought another family into the game. There was a backward caste family consisting of three brothers. Economically, they had done extremely well. Shambhu Ram was never comfortable with their progress. He, with a pre-meditated plan, instigated the three brothers to occupy someone's plot of land in their neighbourhood. In view of their economic prowess, they assumed that no one in the village would dare encounter them. However, they were highly mistaken. Soon, almost the entire village was up in arms against them.

Shambhu Ram had also swindled them for a hefty amount under the garb of shielding them from angry villagers. Unable to stand the villagers' ire, Shambhu Ram and the three brothers came to grandfather.

It was a cold wintry night. Wrapped in his quilt, grandfather was fast asleep, when Shambhu Ram flanked by three Saini brothers entered the chaupal.

Standing near the door, he called out, 'Dhyani Singh, have you gone to bed?'

That time, I lay on a cot, close to grandfather. I rose to wake up grandfather and informed him about Shambhu Ram's arrival.

Grandfather at once sat up and asked, 'Shambhu Ram, what brought you here at this time of the night?'

'Dhyani Singh, Sohan Saini and his brothers are here to have a word with you,' said Shambhu Ram.

Sohan, the eldest of the Saini brothers, appeared before grandfather from behind and said, 'Chacha (uncle), we are all in real danger. I have come to know about a plan by the villagers to publicly rape our women and kill us all. Now we are at your mercy. You have always protected the weak and helpless. We are unable to stand the combined wrath of the villagers. Therefore, we have come to seek shelter from you. Please save us.'

Without brooding over the matter even for a second, grandfather, a self-announced saviour of the oppressed and weak, spoke up:

'There is no bravery in killing a small family of three brothers, their women and children. The whole village, it seems, is full of cowards and impotents.'

In an attempt to provoke grandfather further, Shambhu Ram said, 'That is why I have brought them over to you. No one wants to antagonize the villagers by siding with them. If you stand with them, I am sure, no one would dare harm them.'

Grandfather right away announced, 'Don't worry, Sohan. I am with you. Let me see, who has the audacity to harm you or any member of your family. Anytime you perceive threat around, just come here with your family.'

Obviously, grandfather had invited great trouble for himself and his family by putting his weight behind the beleaguered Saini family. This amounted to throwing an unveiled challenge to the combined might of the village community. Once assured of grandfather's shield, the Saini brothers had become regular visitors to our chaupal.

Doing a somersault, Shambhu Lal rejoined the rest of the villagers who uptil now were angry with him for supporting Sohan Saini. Washing off his hands altogether, he was now hobnobbing with them. His plan was to bring Sohan Saini back into the village fold by making him apologize to the prominent villagers. Accordingly, Shambu Ram roped in Sohan Saini making him agree to tender his apologies to the villagers. After he toed the line set by the villagers, they let him go unpunished. Soon, Sohan Saini joined them. The entire village had turned against grandfather in this background. This was also the main reason why the entire village conspired to wipe out his entire family, after outraging the modesty of his women in his very presence.

14

Conspiracy Against Family

Fully convinced about villagers' belligerence towards grandfather, Makhan Lal convened a secret meeting of Thakurs at his chaupal. After a lot of confabulation, they planned to wipe out grandfather and his entire family.

Apprehensive of otherwise dominantly belligerent Dalit community's support to the killing of one of their own caste men along with his family, some upper caste elders advised Makhan Lal to take Dalits on board first before going ahead with the plan. They feared that the very thought of killing of one of their kinsmen's entire family might inflame Dalits' sentiments against upper castes, leading the former to burry their mutual differences and join hands against them, and if that happens, the whole plan would boomerang. They knew that blood is always thicker than water.

Acting on this, Makhan Lal decided to send feelers to those Dalits who had long been nurturing a grieving sense of grudge and revenge against grandfather because of his forcing them in the past to stand by him in opposition to the upper castes. As a result, the upper castes had stopped providing many Dalits employment. After loss of their jobs, they were finding it difficult to earn livelihood for their families. Consequently, it generated in their hearts an ill feeling against him. Teacher Makhan Lal and his cronies knew that support of such aggrieved parties from amongst Dalits was very essential to give the whole plan a colour of popular resentment against him. Dominant upper castes were quite clear in their thinking that once Dhyani crushed, no one thereafter would ever be in a position to challenge their hegemony. As he was the only one who, after consolidating his socio-economic condition had begun to take up cudgels on behalf of the whole Dalit community, annoying all upper castes that somehow wanted to rid of him.

The disgruntled Dalits, through a little cajoling, fell easily in line, giving an assurance to help Makhan Lal execute his plan. However, there was one Dalit who, despite having a grudge against grandfather, refused to join in the plan. In protest, he said, 'I do not agree with your plan, as there may be other ways to humiliate him. We can excommunicate him, a step, I think, will certainly have a demoralizing effect, compelling him to behave himself; he hasn't done any crime to be punished like this; and who knows that this is not a conspiracy by the upper castes to remove a mouthpiece of Dalits from the way. Dhyani may be my enemy, but we should not forget that he always came forth helping me and other Dalits whenever we needed him. So, I will not be a party to any such plan.'

Uneducated, gullible and largely dependent on the landed-propertied upper castes for their livelihood, Dalits, many by choice and some under duress, fell in line with Makhan Lal. After mobilizing majority support to his designs, he organized another confidential meeting at the residence of Pandit Yagya Dutt Sharma, the only Brahmin in the village. In the meeting, elders and headmen of all castes participated. They placed a pot full of water in the middle of the ringed meeting. Then all of them, turn by turn, put a pinch of salt into it with a pledge that no one would disclose the secret of the plan and all present would ensure participation of their caste men in the combined assault against grandfather.

Nihari, a backward caste man was extremely shocked at villagers' decision. At the meeting, he writhed a lot to express his resentment over the plan, but he could not summon up enough of courage to go against the majority will. After the meeting was over, Nihari, not being at peace with him, clandestinely came to grandfather late night when the entire village had gone into deep slumber. I had my bed placed in grandfather's room at the chaupal. When Nihari entered the chaupal gasping hoarsely, I was awake that time. 'Who is there?' asked I, looking at his shadow in the thickly dark and dreadful night.

'Arrey beta, dheere bol. (Oh son, speak slowly)', said he whisperingly. He continued, 'Oh chacha, main Nihari hoon (Oh uncle, it is me Nihari here).'

By now, I had identified him. Meanwhile, on hearing someone whispering, my elder uncle, who was asleep at another cot in the chaupal, woke up. At this hour of the night grandfather was fast asleep. I tried to wake him up by tucking away his quilt. I shook grandfather twice-thrice. He then woke up asking, 'What happened?' 'Grandfather, Nihari uncle had come to see you,' I replied.

'At this late hour, Nihari, here, why?' asked grandfather.

Nihari by now had recovered from his uneven breathing.

'Uncle, I know you would be very upset to hear what I am going to tell you,' replied Nihari.

'What is that, Nihari? Tell me right away,' asked grandfather.

Composing him, he said, 'Today, villagers held a meeting in which it has been decided to publicly outrage your women and then kill your entire family.'

'But why,' demanded grandfather.

'I do not know the immediate reason for their provocation. But I guess that since you have always spoken for the weaker people in the village, the upper castes have begun to take it as a challenge to their domination,' replied Nihari.

'Who are those bastards who dare think like that?' demanded grandfather in his familiar loud-mouthed style.

'Uncle, please don't speak loudly; first you listen to me,' pleaded Nihari.

'OK, OK. Tell me about all those who are involved in this plan', asked grandfather lowering his voice.

'Uncle, I cannot tell you about who are the real plan-makers. The only thing I know is that the entire village seems to have turned your enemy. Surprisingly, your own Dalit army has joined hands with the upper castes.'

'Who are these Dalits, by the way,' asked grandfather.

'Almost all of them,' replied Nihari.

'Are you sure,' asked grandfather.

'Of course,' he continued, 'I am a direct witness to all what transpired among the villagers in the meeting organized at Pandit Yagya Dutt Sharma's Chaupal.'

'What! The meeting took place at Sharma's chaupal? I can't believe it!'

'In fact, Dalits are going to lead the combined attack on you. For execution of the plan, they have selected the day after tomorrow,' informed Nihari.

'Uncle, I tell you honestly that per force I have also given my consent to the plan. However, mentally I was not at ease and I thought of cautioning you immediately. Uncle, I am a poor man. Please do not allow anyone to get to know that I have revealed all this to you. I have cautioned you. It is now up to you as to how to deal with the situation,' pleaded Nihari with folded hands.

On hearing this, grandfather first pulled a long breath and then said, 'Nihari, I really feel indebted to you to let me know about this conspiracy. You can go now and sleep. I assure no one would ever get to know that you leaked this information to me.' Nihari walked out silently creating an atmosphere of gloom around us. For a few moments, grandfather remained quiet.

Then, calling out us - my uncle and myself - he murmured, 'man is born once and he dies once. If things have come to such a pass, I am not going to sit quiet. I will teach those bastards a lesson that they will never forget in the rest of their life. They will rape my daughters-in-law and kill my children!'

Grandfather was more peeved to know that Yaggya Dutt Sharma's chaupal was the venue for the conspiracy against him. Even in his wildest dreams, he had never thought of Sharma going against him.

Sharma had been involved in several criminal activities like robbery, heist and murders. For this reason, all villagers hated him. On several previous occasions, castes like Rajputs and Kayasthas tried to teach him a lesson by publicly outraging the modesty of his grown up daughters. Each time, he sought protection from grandfather who shielded him by throwing behind him the weight of entire Dalit community. Despite this, Sharma had a grudge against grandfather wielding enormous influence upon Dalits and other weaker castes. He himself wanted to be an unquestioned leader of them to put up a front against the combined might of Thakurs, Kayasthas and Baniyas.

Sharma was no one's friend. His sole aim always remained to fullfil his own interest. For that, he could go to any extent. With all villagers, including Dalits, turning against grandfather, the atmosphere had become hostile towards him. By convening a meeting at his chaupal to hatch the conspiracy, Sharma wanted to play a lead role in the situation to win over the confidence of all villagers. His eyes were set on the ensuing panchayat elections in which he wanted all villagers to support his son's candidature for the post of president.

Remembering his long list of obligations towards Sharma's family, grandfather said to himself:

'I rue the day when I shielded this treacherous man from the combined wrath of Thakurs and Kayasthas. I protected him at a time when everyone was baying for his blood. By doing this, I unwittingly antagonized all other upper castes. I am still not prepared to believe that he is also part of this conspiracy! Neither do I have a reason to disbelieve an honest and innocent person like Nihari. If all what he said is true, what a perfidy!'

15

Murder in the Village

It was a cold rainy day of December 1966. Early morning, villagers heard wailing sounds coming from Pandit Yagya Dutt Sharma's next-door house. Soon, people gathered there, enquiring of each other about the cause of howling. One of Sharma's five sons had killed their uncle, an immediate cousin of their father. No one, except deceased's family, was witness to the murder.

This incident had inflamed villagers' passions further as they were already sick of Sharma's involvement in numerous crimes, inviting them lot of troubles. Imagining that what would happen to others if Sharma could be so cruel and ruthless to his own blood relation, villagers at any cost wanted him and his murderer son to be behind the bar. Several senior residents even volunteered to stand witness in the case.

To find no way to stave off the situation and sensing real danger to his survival in the village, Sharma now looked desperately for someone who could protect his family from the combined rage of villagers. He now remembered grandfather who was away that time to attend an event at one of his relatives' family. After obtaining the address of the place, Sharma at once scurried his two sons to bring grandfather back to mediate on his behalf in the matter and prevent the case from going to the police. In the meantime, he along with his family took shelter somewhere else to resurface only after grandfather had arrived.

Swallowing his caste pride, Sharma cringed at grandfather's feet. With his wife on his side, he pleaded, 'Chacha (Uncle), I confess my son's serious mistake. It all happened unintentionally. In a fit of anger, he fired at Mittu Lal to scare him away. Who can avoid mishap if it is bound to happen? Chacha, you have always protected me against the offensive of Thakurs, Kayasthas, Baniyas and Muslims who are hell bent upon lodging an FIR. If that happens, my son is bound to land in jail. You know it will ruin me. I beg of you to please do something to save my family.'

'Chachaji, I respect you more than my own father-in-law; you have always been so kind and protective towards my family. I touch your feet; please save my child,' said Mrs. Sharma imploringly putting her saree's border at grandfather's feet.

Being in the throes of a crisis, Sharma, by resorting to this kind of pretentiousness, somehow wanted to get out of the difficult situation. Otherwise, a Brahmin touching an untouchable's feet! Unimaginable, unthinkable and heretic!

For grandfather, a Brahmin bowing in front of him along with his wife, was a great thing. Putting his hand on Mrs. Sharma's head, he said, 'Oh, beti (daughter), you don't worry at all. My all caste men would be with you. That is my promise. Meanwhile, I will talk to other villagers to prevail upon them not to approach the police. I am confident no one will go against my wishes. However, I am a little apprehensive of Muslims who may see in this murder a good opportunity to settle scores with your husband because of his anti-Muslim stance in the past on several contentious issues.'

Grandfather then asked Sharma to leave his family in our custody and rising from his cot, he headed straight towards the centre of the village. Reaching there, he took a seat on the muddy platform ringed around a mammoth Banyan tree, which had been a witness in the past to the settlement of several other contentious issues. He then sent for the senior most members from all communities.

Mian Habibullah, an orthodox and pious Muslim who held sway over his fellow brothers throughout the area arrived there first. No dispute could be settled without taking him on board for arbitration. Pointing to a site next to him, grandfather asked him to take his seat.

'Yes, tell me Dhyani why you have sent for me. By the way, where were you? We had been looking for you since yesterday. Do you know that scoundrel Sharma has got his own cousin killed by his criminal son? He needs to be put in his right place; a case under IPC 302 should be registered against him and his son. In the village, there are several persons, who are ready to stand witness in the case against his son. After all, we all have to show our face to God.'

Within a short time, many other people from various castes arrived there. Giving vent to his anger, Amba Lal Bhatnagar, a leader of Kayasthas, said,

'This Sharma is a modern-day Ravana. If we do not stand up against him today, he would commit many such murders. He is certainly crossing all bounds of tolerance. How can we allow a man like him to continue in this village? There is no crime he has not committed – theft, dacoity, arson, rape and now murder. It is horrific to see his children picking up from him the same traits. How can villagers feel safe with his continuous living in here?'

Leaders of all castes unanimously voiced their concern over highhandedness and haughtiness of Sharma's son. Meanwhile, Durganand Singh, the then village landlord appeared there.

'This is the first time that a murder took place in our village. With this murder, all residents are feeling unsafe and insecure. Now is the time to do something serious to deter this Sharma from moving ahead on the path of crime. I think, he and his son should at any cost be in police custody without further delay,' said Durganand Singh, adding his weighted and powerful voice to an already predetermined move.

Grandfather was listening quietly and intently to them all. For a few moments, after everyone of substance had expressed his opinion, there was absolute silence among the gathered arbitrators.

'It appears you people have already passed the judgement against Sharma. However, I would like to ask if anyone of you is a direct witness to the murder. I agree with you that if he has really killed Mittu Lal, he deserves punishment; however, police would ask for clear evidence. Tell me, how many of you are going to stand witness to the murder?' asked grandfather in an attempt to measure the depth of their resolve.

Hearing this, all arbitrators bowed down their heads in ambivalence. Sensing that there was no direct witness to the case, grandfather asked bystanders and onlookers, 'has anyone of you seen Sharma's son firing at Mittu Lal?' No one came forward as a direct witness. Observing silence writ large on their faces, grandfather resumed, 'If you are really serious to punish Sharma, you will have to produce concrete evidence in front of police.' He continued 'Meanwhile, I came to know that neither Sharma nor his son were at home at the time of Mittu Lal's murder.' said grandfather adding the last sentence deliberately to know arbitrators' reaction.

Upon this, Habibullah flared up and said, 'For God sake, don't say this. The whole village knows that Sharma's son fired at Mittu Lal, killing him on the spot. Yet, here you are, giving a new twist to the incident. Both Mittu Lal's wife and daughter have seen Sharma's son firing shots. So please, don't try to delude the villagers by concocting another story about the murder. Dhyani, you must be scared of God's rage while saying such sinful things. You are obviously trying to protect Sharma, which is more sinful. I warn you that God will never forgive you for such a heinous act.'

All gathered there, raising their voice in unison, stood up shouting and pointing their fingers at grandfather, 'This Dhyani Chamaar always does such things deliberately. Certainly, Sharma must have given him different version of the incident. May be, that black Brahmin has bribed him, but let us see how this time he is going to save him. We will ensure his arrest by the police even if we all have to stand witness in the case. Oh God! What a sinful act! Dhyani, you are bound to rot in hell, if you side with this criminal.'

For a few moments, grandfather remained quiet. Looking at Habibullah and others, he said, 'So, you all people are going to stand witnesses to the murder. Could you tell me who of you is going to be the first one to tell the police truth? If you have all seen Sharma's son killing Mittu Lal, how did you let him go? You should have caught him and handed over to the police. Instead, you are still waiting for the police to visit you to record your statements. I am sure police will ask you about what you did after you saw him committing the murder.'

Hearing this, villagers began looking at each other's face in bewilderment.

A few residents still had sympathy for Sharma - the only Brahmin. However, sensing the mood of the majority, they were per force supporting the move against Sharma. Aware of this fact, grandfather said:

'You know if police descends here in the village, the responsibility of producing concrete evidence would be on those who wish to stand witnesses in the case. I do not think anyone of you would be able to reply to all questions police might ask you. It is, therefore, better to resolve this case within the village' suggested grandfather.

Upon this, a group of arbitrators began whispering with one another. After a while, Sukkhan, headman of Saini community, said 'I think Dhyani is right. It's in the interest of all residents to resove this matter within the village.'

Seeing this, grandfather called that group aside. After discussing something in whispers, they soon returned to their seats. After a little pause, looking towards Habibullah, grandfather asked, 'Do you know what others want to do in the matter?'

'No, I don't know,' replied Habibullah.

'Would you like to hear?' asked grandfather.

'Ok, go ahead please,' replied Habibullah.

On learning what Sukkhan Saini had told grandfather, Habibullah swiftly stood up at his place and flinging his hands, he said angrily, 'Dhyani, you are trying to falsify the truth. By doing so, you are not helping Sharma but creating a Frankenstein monster for yourself. Remember, you will rue this day. This Sharma is nobody's friend. He is just using you to save his own skin. You will soon realize your blunder. Never be sure, this rogue will not create trouble for you in future. By then, it will be too late for you to do anything but to feel sorry. I don't understand what you exactly want.'

'Habibullah, you are a wise man. You know what I intend. I am in favour of resolving this case within the village. We should not allow the matter to go to police at any cost. If that happens, things will thereafter not be normal' said grandfather.

'You are asking me to do something which my *deen* (religion) does not permit. Now it is up to Mittu Lal's widow and daughters to decide if they concur to what you are proposing. If they want to resolve the case within the village, I have no objection but their consent is essential,' said Habibullah in a mollifying manner.

'Why don't you all go and convince Mittu Lal's widow for this?' asked grandfather imploringly, looking towards Habibullah, Durganand Singh, Makhan Lal Singh and Amba Lal Bhatnagar. 'Listen, Dhyani. I am not going to ask Dhatri Devi to tell police something against her wishes nor will I ask other villagers to persuade her to do it. If you have made up your mind to help that criminal, you ought to approach her and advice on what you want her to do,' said Habibullah unequivocally in front of the gathering.

Turning to Makhan Lal Singh, Durganand Singh and Amba Lal Bhatnagar, grandfather asked. 'Do you also think similarly?'

'Dhyani, you want us all to condone Sharma's son's crime? Habibullah is right you are playing with fire which one day will burn you too. We will never advise Dhatri Devi to keep her mouth shut against Sharma and his son,' said Amba Lal, flanked by Durganand Singh and Makhan Lal Singh.

They added, 'Since you have taken up cudgels on behalf of Sharma and his family, better you approach and plead for Sharma's reprieve.'

'Ok, if you people insist upon me to carry out this responsibility, I will certainly do so. But it would be weightier had we jointly tried to convince her,' replied grandfather.

Meanwhile, Sukkhan Saini stood up and said, 'Dhyani you go ahead; we are with you. We all authorise you to convince Dhatri Devi for resolution of the case, within the village.'

Hearing this, grandfather rose from his seat and headed towards Dhatri Devi's house. Reaching there, he stopped by the door and called out, 'Oh beti (Daughter-in-law) Dhatri, it is me Dhyani Singh.'

Assisted by a woman, Dhatri Devi, still crying uncontrollably, dragged herself to the door to see grandfather. She said lamenting, 'Chachaji, my family is now completely ruined. I don't know who would now look after my two grown-up daughters' said Dhatri Devi gesturing to grandfather to sit down on a sting cot.

Having taken his seat, grandfather remained quiet for a few moments and then said, 'Dhatri, we are all very sad at this happening. All villagers want to report the matter to the police to have Sharma and his son arrested. I also do not want the culprits to go scot-free after such a heinous crime.'

Dhatri Devi listened to grandfather patiently and then she said crying, 'Do you think that with his son imprisoned,

Sharma would allow me to live peacefully. I do not know what to do; I am confused. Neither I have ample money to pursue the case in the court nor can I confront them in other ways. My life is absolutely in ruins. I am now more worried about my daughters. '

'I do understand your predicament. That is why I am here to help you. I will not advise you to get embroiled in the court case which, if you persist in will devastate your family further', said grandfather to Dhatri Devi.

Hearing this, her elder daughter approached grandfather saying 'Dadaji (grandfather) at the moment, mentally and physically shaken, mummy is not in a position to say anything in this regard. Let me tell you. Although we are unable to pursue the case in the court, we are not prepared to forgive our father's murderers. We, therefore, look towards villagers for justice', said she looking towards her younger sister.

'You are truly very wise, my child. You understand well the consequences of indulging into such a cranky issue. You don't worry; we will get you justice. You will be reasonably compensated for the loss of your father; Also, we will ensure your safety so that you could all live peacefully in the village,' assured grandfather.

'Be bold, now. Take care of your mother and sister', he added consoling Dhatri's daughter.

After this, he returned to the meeting to inform the arbitrators that Dhatri Devi was not prepared to forgive her husband's murderer. He had not even finished his talk, when several hands – mostly in the camp of Durganand Singh, Makhan Lal Singh and Amba Lal Bhatnagar and Habibullah - rose up together. They shouted laughingly, 'we knew this. How could she let her husband's murderer go unpunished? Now that she has conveyed her decision we should immediately report the matter to the police.'

'You are still repeating your same old stance. I have not yet completed my talks. What Dhatri Devi told is that she does not want police involvement in the matter, as she is not in a position of pursuing the case in court. However, she seeks justice from villagers in the form of financial compensation to enable her to look after herself and two grown-up daughters. She has therefcre agreed to my proposal to resolve the matter within village.' informed grandfather further.

On hearing this, Durganand Singh, Makhan Lal Singh and Amba Lal, at once stood up and began heading towards their houses, whispering among themselves: The whole game is over, now. Again, this scoundrel got off the hook.

Habibullah still sat there along with headmen of other castes. With his head couched in between his legs folded up at the knees, he appeared to be in deep thoughts. 'Humn, Dhyani, you are doing great injustice to that poor woman and her two daughters. I doubt they will forget this trauma so easily. I think you made her agree to your proposal under duress. We, the villagers, have now nothing to do with this case. We wanted to secure justice to the grief-stricken family, and if they themselves do not want this, it is up to them. We disassociate ourselves with this whole drama', said Habibullah frustratingly, taking a long breath.

After Habibullah left, grandfather sent for Sharma who immediately appeared there. For a few minutes, they discussed the amount of compensation for Dhatri Devi. Grandfather took upon himself the responsibility of arranging all this.

By using grandfather, Sharma had succeeded in staving off the greatest crisis of his life.

16

Grandfather Retaliates

Until grandfather served Sharma and Makhan Lal's interests, they remained happy with him. Now that he was not prepared to support their candidature for the post of village sarpanch, they were annoyed and joined hands to decimate him. Sharma had been nursing his ambition to rule over the village for several years. He had tried his luck earler also, but failed, as Thakurs and Kayasthas never agreed to support him.

Grandfather was unable to digest the fact that Yagya Dutt Sharma had joined in the conspiracy hatched to eliminate his family. Deceived and stabbed, as he felt, he was determined to teach Sharma and his compatriots, including Makhan Lal, a great lesson. He thought of a plan to precipitate the situation by preempting villagers move against him.

Grandfather hurriedly convened a family meeting. In his address, he continued at length: 'my children, human life is available only once in the cycle of births and deaths. This is worth only when one lives with honour and dignity that come only through economic freedom and equality, two important aspects of human life. I have always stood against oppression to uphold these values. Throughout my life, I have struggled hard to carve out a respectable position for my family, my community, and myself. I had reduced my dependence upon the upper castes, as I too was holder of a sizeable agricultural land. They are now jealous of our economic freedom, as they know that I am able to resist their oppresive acts only by the strength of my land holding. They also understand that they cannot succeed in their designs of enslaving us until we have this land. They therefore are hell-bent to render us landless. So far, they had failed in their efforts to make us succumb to them. They, therefore, have now hatched a bigger conspiracy and succeeded in taking even Dalits with them. As you heard, their plan is to debase us publicly by outraging our womens' modesty through gang rape. As a matter of dignity, I cannot accept it. I would prefer killing myself to witnessing all that happening. One should rather die fighting as a brave man than surrendering like cowards to the enemy. Now the choice is yours. If you want to flee, I will take you to some distant safe place where you can restart again; but, to me, it would also be pusillanimity, which is no less than humiliation.'

This was his style of testing his family's morale and courage. After listening to him, for a moment, all fell silent. Then father and two uncles said in unison, 'No one can debase our father until we are alive. We will prefer death to disgrace. To save our honour and especially that of our women, we will fight out these demons till death.'

After hearing these brave words, grandfather heaved a long sigh, and then said, 'So, listen carefully. I have a plan to pre-empt the dirty game of our enemy. Now do what I say. That bastard Abhijit Singh, assigned with the responsibility of leading Sharma and Makhan Lal's henchemen to attack us, returns everyday late after dusk passing by our chaupal. Next time, when he passes, we would waylay him, drag him into our Haveli and thrash him in a manner that thereafter he would think twice before daring to lead a combined against us. The act would also send a clear message to Sharma and Makhan Lal who chose him leader of the group to rape our women.'

It was the month of October. Harvesting for rice crop was in full swing. Farmers and labourers would return home late at dusk after working in the fields. One evening, when Abhijit was passing our chaupal, my younger uncle and a cousin waylaid him and swiftly tumbled him down to the ground. They then dragged him to the Haveli and began thrashing with staffs and bamboo-sticks. On hearing his shrieks, villagers rushed helter-skelter towards our Haveli. Whoever tried to approach us, our uncles, father and the cousin immediately razed them down with heavy blows of *lathis* (bamboo sticks). As the feud was on, my three-year-old cousin came in the crossfire and received a *lathi* blow on her head from someone. She collapsed on the spot and died a few minutes later.

Suddenly, fighting stopped and all our aunties, uncles, father and mother were crying loudly on her body. Meanwhile, a large number of people had gathered in front of our haveli. There was utter confusion with no one able to understand what was going on. People gathered there took Abhijit quickly away. A few enterprising people tried to galvanize the villagers to launch a collective attack. However, given that grandfather had now started apportioning the blame for my cousin's death to Abhijit and other prominent villagers like Makhan Lal, Sharma etc., no one could dare reattack us. Rather than seeking revenge, they were now more concerned for Abhijit since he needed immediate medical care. As the neighbouring town was only three kms away, the village *Chowkidar* had since informed the police station about the murder case. Within half an hour, police had arrived on the scene. By now, the situation was totally under control; there was no one to come near the haveli. Everybody appeared to be saving his own skin.

After recording statements from both plaintiff and the respondent(s) and that of the witnesses, the police registered a murder case against Makhan Lal, Sharma and Abhijit and others u/s 302 of the IPC. After two-three hearings into the case, the court awarded the accused a sentence of twenty years each.

With precipitation of the situation leading to imprisonment of Sharma and his cronies, grandfather had undoubtedly succeeded in protecting his family's honour. However, the family had once more plunged into the sea of another era of depravity, misery and helplessness closing all doors to prosperity. Grandfather's dream of purchasing more land and constructing concrete house had shattered. Now, he felt that Shambu Lal had done him in.

Poverty resulting from litigation had gripped the family to the extent that even arrangement of two squares meal had become difficult. Once, we proceeded towards the fields early in the morning to work. That day, no one from amongst women – mother or aunties – turned up in the fields with food. When we asked our father about the delay for food, he avoided direct answer and just said that maybe your mom was not feeling well. After returning from fields in the evening, we first rushed to the community bore well, and having finished our bath, we came home eagerly waiting for dinner. Mice were gnawing in our stomach. We saw our mother sitting silently in a corner near the kitchen and she was obviously avoiding facing us; there was nothing to eat in the kitchen. Then, suddenly she started crying. We were unable to understand as to what was going on. Then standing up, mother walked up to us.

Putting her hand on our youngest brother's head, she said crying, 'Today, this is first time in life that my children would go to bed hungry. Bad times are here as a result of this bloody litigation.'

That night, all of us went to bed without meal. Sitting beside me on the string cot, I lay in, and ruffling through my hair mother said, 'My son, this is a bad phase for us all. You are the eldest of your siblings; all my hopes are pinned at you; when you are educated and suitably employed, I would wish that you leave this village along with your siblings for ever.'

My brothers soon fell asleep, but with pangs of hunger, I could not sleep at all. I saw mother sitting beside me through out the night with tears still streaming down her cheeks. Early morning, father left home and returned with a bundle in his hand after about an hour or so. He handed it out to mother. I saw mother taking out jaggery from the bundle along with handful of rice. Immediately, mother placed a kettle with water on the stove and added all jaggery into it. Then she dropped rice into it. After cooking meal, first she went to our youngest brother who was still sleeping. Caressing his head, she awakened him and then splurged his face with water when he still had his eyes half-shut. Then she woke up other brothers and my only sister. Mother then filled a bowl with pudding she had prepared with rice and jaggery. Obviously, she served first my youngest brother as well as the only sister. I was the last being the eldest.

The accused subsequently approached grandfather requesting him not to pursue the case in the higher court, where they had filed a mercy petition. Intervening in the matter, some local influential leaders devised a method whereby the accused would publicly apologize to grandfather for the mental agony, physical torture and financial losses caused to him and the latter, in return, would pardon them on his part and no longer pursue the case in the upper court.

Given that without interaction and socialization with the village mainstream during the litigation period, grandfather was feeling greatly isolated and lonely. He, therefore, considered the mediators' proposal a good opportunity for his reinstatement in the mainstream society as well as reclaiming his place in the leadership. Public apology by the culprits was a good deal to satisfy his battered ego and restore his pride and honour.

The arbiters, accordingly, convened a meeting of the prominent villagers and chieftains of various communities. At the meeting, all the under-trials tendered apology to grandfather. Yaggyan Dutt Sharma with folded hands walked up to him and embraced him confessing, 'Chacha, I really feel ashamed of being part of the conspiracy against you. Anyway, you have won again. Now save us from ruination.We are bound to perish if you continue to pursue the case in the higher court. You and we have all suffered equally due to our ego-clash. We promise not to hurt you in future by our inflated egos. Please show mercy and forgive us all.'

Hearing this, grandfather's eyes welled up. Putting his hand on Sharma's shoulders, he said, 'I had never expected you at least to be part of a conspiracy contemplated to outrage the modesty of our women and killing of my sons. It really hurt me deeply. It is I, not you people, who is ruined. You were jealous of my farmland, half of which I had to sell out during legal proceedings. You all wanted to see me a pauper and by entangling me in this case, you have succeeded. Nevertheless, I am not like you. Despite so much loss in terms of money, respect and position, I still have enough of courage left in me to forgive you all. After all, I am a Dalit, who is accustomed to swallow this kind of insult and humiliation again and again.'

Soon, the situation normalized in grandfather's favour. As a result, he recovered his place and position in the society.

17

Frequent in Fighting in the Family

The worsening economic condition led to eruption of frequent clashes between father and two uncles, even on triffle matters.

Grandfather held my parents responsible for any trouble in the household forgetting that all quarrel in the family had arisen from the scarcity of resources. Whenever I tried to argue with him, he would say, 'I know, protracted litigations have led to our economic deterioration; however, I preserved family-honour by foiling my enemies' conspiracy to disgrace me.'

On one occasion, when he was in light mood, I asked, 'Grandfather, don't you feel that had you not annoyed a select group of people in village, you would have avoided litigation leading to overall prosperity of family? Did you ever realize that a few upper caste men, who show theatrical respect towards you, always try to poison your ears against some villagers just to fulfill their own interest? Have you ever thought over how Shambhu Lal, by taking advantage of your gullibility, pushed you into confrontation with the whole village leading us all into a serious crisis?'

When I was saying this, grandfather, looking at me, listened attentively. After a little pause, he said, 'my child, you are now educated and understand things well. I confess this time around, it was rather my mistake than anybody else. Taking advantage of my credulity that bastard Shambhu Lal trader made me agree to give shelter to Sohan Saini. Villagers, of course, took it as a challenge to them and turned against me. Now I realise that had I not listened to him, I would not have seen this day. You all are suffering because of me. Henceforth, I will be more careful and not allow anyone to take advantage of my hot temperament,' he continued, 'however, let me tell you that this was the only time that the situation was precipitated because of my foolhardiness. All throughout my life, I received systematic harassment and persecution at the hands of these dominant upper castes. They did not miss any opportunity to target me; this is not the first time that they turned against me. When your father and uncles were still young, I had to run away from this village to avoid their continuous oppression. Grown up and educated, as you are, you would understand this better while dealing with them.'

'But why have the villagers been so deadly against you?' I asked.

'My child, if you hear the story of my life, you won't even believe how much suffering and persecution I had undergone.'

'Why did upper castes single you out for persecution?' I asked.

'It had to do something with my nature. I committed no crime in my life but I had the guts to oppose the wrongdoings of upper castes. I was never comfortable with their domination over our people who for centuries remained under their subjugation, suffering all sort of humiliation and abuse. Upper castes, against our own wish, forced us to do menial jobs and they could not tolerate to see us prosper by owning agricultural land or taking up employment outside the domain of their influence. As I was the only Dalit to rebel against their hegemony and make efforts for upliftment of my people through reforms, they turned enemies. Not only did I refuse to do menial jobs myself as per their dictates but also made other cobblers not to succumb to the pressure to do jobs like removal of dead cattle and skin them. Alike, other Dalits also began taking up jobs as daily wagers on the sites of railway tracks, mini sugar plants, brick kilns, road construction etc. With the income, they purchased agricultural land becoming gradually independent. This did not go down well with the upper castes that now looked for one pretext or the other to teach me a lesson. Soon, they implicated me in a series of false cases like robberies, arson and other petty crimes.'

Continuing our dialogue, I asked, 'If you have done so much for Dalits; how come the whole community of cobblers stands against you, today?'

'My child, untouchables are always victims of their own credulity and innocence. They never tried to realize their real worth. Intrinsically, they are susceptible to the clever maneuvering of upper castes, who very easily poise them against each other, including those fighting for them. In my case also, it has happened on similar lines. I liberated them from bonded labour; encouraged them to take up new occupations for livelihood; exhorted them to own at least some piece of land to be independent of the mercy of the landed property class, apart from asking them to get their children educated,' said grandfather narrating a part of his life's story.

'Despite doing so much, Dalits hardly recognize your struggle towards their upliftment. What I see today is that they are more belligerent towards you than many upper castes. Why is it like this?' I asked.

'Today, they don't recognize my struggle towards their welfare. But I am sure in future they will,' said grandfather.

'By the way, would you tell me what great struggle you had waged on behalf of your Dalit brethren to get them a respectable position in the village society?' I insisted.

'My life is a long history of struggles that I made for the upliftment of Dalits. Are you interested?' he asked.

'Yes, I would like to hear that saga,' I insisted.

Grandfather began to give a detailed description of the struggles he made for the upliftment of Dalits throughout his life:

'There was a time when Dalits and other lower castes were not allowed by upper castes to take water from the same well in the village. They per force had to place their pitchers and pots for water on the muddy ground below the raised concrete ring around the well. I used to feel very angry to see this segregation. Therefore, I began to make my people understand that it was humiliating on their part to put up with that kind of animal-like treatment at the hands of upper castes. As natural, they were hesitant in the beginning to climb up the well to draw water. After a lot of persuasion and repeated reminders of their united strength against all upper castes put together, they finally agreed to fight for the cause. We anticipated a stiff opposition from other communities. However, all cobblers, including their women and children, now treated it a matter of self-respect and were prepared to make any sacrifice to reclaim it.'

I convened a secret meeting to discuss the modalities of our plan with other elders in the community. Following a lot of deliberation, a day was fixed to go to the village well to draw water. On the appointed day, Dalits along with their young folks gathered around the well right in the morning. Taking lead, women climbed up the platform, put their pots and pitchers there and began drawing water. Within no time, the entire village community, including the upper and backward caste Hindus and Muslims, appeared there. Instantly, they began smashing our pitchers and pots with sticks and staffs. The situation soon became so tense that a bloody feud between Dalits and the rest of villagers appeared imminent as the youngish Dalits were flexing their muscles, prepared with traditional arms like axes, spears staffs and sticks, to trade blows with them.

Realising that the fight between Dalits and upper castes in the village could lead to eruption of violence against them in the neighbouring areas too, I decided to withdraw from there along with my people. However, my struggle did not stop there. I continued to wait for the right moment to exercise our right to pull water from the same well. Those days, *Arya Samaj* movement was spreading fast in northern India with a message of equality among the Hindus. A group of the *Samaj* happened to visit our village. First, they organized a meeting for the upper castes only. Addressing the meeting, *Arya Samaj* leaders stressed the need to grant the so-called untouchables equal rights in order to forge unity among all sections of the Hindu society. They called upon them to embrace '*untouchables*' as their brothers and sisters and allow them to enjoy equal rights as far as the practice of religion was concerned. In order to purify the untouchables, Arya Samaj had been organizing *Shuddhikaran* (purification) ceremonies in which they were handing out to untouchables a *janeoo* (a sacred thread) after putting them through some rituals and allowing them to learn and enchant *Gayatri* mantra. This was hitherto the monopoly of upper castes.

Utilizing the Arya Samaj visit to our advantage, I decided to take up with them our problem. *Samaj* leaders soon granted us an audience. Narrating to them the pathetic story of cobblers, I sought their intervention in allowing them to take water from the commonly used well of the village. Arguing my case, I said if they considered untouchables part of Hindu society, why then they were forcing them to drink dirty water and live like animals. *Samaj* leaders gave me a patient hearing on the matter and then convened a meeting of prominent persons from upper castes to take up the problem with them. After a great deal of persuasion, they agreed, though reluctantly, to allow cobblers to take water from the only village well. After another ritual, performed by Samaj leaders involving both the cobblers and upper castes, was over, they allowed me to climb on to the well platform to draw a bucket of water, as a symbol of assimilation of Dalits into the mainstream. As I was doing this, a few dominant persons were still raising their eyebrows.

For a few following days, everything appeared to be normal. Cobblers were taking water from the well along with other communities. Suddenly, there were whispers among the upper castes with regard to this unusual development. Highly incensed at the happening, a village trader instigated the upper castes to oppose this newly introduced practice and prevent cobblers from coming to the well to take water. He created great ruckus in the village over the issue. A few persons, who had earlier participated in the purification ritual, also fell into his malicious propaganda. Led by the trader, they began to prevent cobblers from pulling water. On the other hand, Dalits, who had obtained a religious sanction for collecting water, were not prepared to relent. They were willing to make any sacrifice to protect this right. There continued a tussle between them and us for several days. Finally, I had to galvanize the cobblers for a do-or-die battle in defending their right reasoning that if they succumbed to the vehement opposition from upper castes, they would not get second opportunity to jump off this barrier. Therefore, they needed to face the challenge with all their might.

Showing unprecedented courage and unity, all cobblers decided to move towards the well, holding in their hands traditional arms like axes, spears etc. We all male members surrounded the well from all directions waiting for the upper castes to approach close by. Then, around 60 young women of our community, each with a staff in one hand and pitcher in the other climbed on to the platform. Having placed their pitchers and pots, they began to draw water. Reacting to our move, upper castes gathered swiftly on the spot. They started fiercely smashing our pots and pitchers. Enraged at their behaviour, our women immediately came down upon the attackers heavily. So ferocious and brutal they were that without caring for their female modesty and inferiority, they were trading bloody blows with the enemies. In the gory feud that followed, our women crushed heads and hands of several attackers. In the aftermath of this incident, no upper caste dared come near the well for several days. However, our women without a mark of fear continued to visit the well to pull water. Obviously, there was a sense of deep hurt and humiliation among the upper castes. They were unable to digest the insult at the hands of women and that too from cobblers.

In the village history, this was an unimaginable, unthinkable and unprecedented incident to have ever taken place. For several subsequent days, we all cobblers continued to rejoice the exemplary courage and boldness shown by our women. In fact, I myself was amazed to see that kind of bravery in our women. Until now, I had the impression that I was the only one who could have diced with upper castes, but what our women did that day was unparalleled in the history of cobblers' community, not within our own village but in the neighbouring areas as well. This incident worked as a watershed in the village history, emboldening Dalits a great deal. Thereafter, they never looked back when it came to fight for their rights. The incident also proved a great booster to the morale of other weaker sections in the village. Inspired by cobblers' community, these marginalized castes and sub-castes began coming together to assert for their natural rights and looked towards me for leadership.

Ashamed of their thrashing by Dalits, the upper castes were seething with anger and an intensive feeling of revenge was brewing up among them. They were now exhibiting greater intransigence, intolerance and orthodoxy in their behaviour towards the lower castes. With passage of time, however, most of the Brahmins and Thakurs began reconciling to the new arrangement for Dalits sharing village well with upper castes. Not comfortable with this, the trader, however, continued to provoke both the upper and intermediary classes against the understanding. Despite his manipulations, when he could not succeed in enlisting support of all dominant castes to his scheme of things, he fell silent for some time. Frustrated, angered, and annoyed, he decided his own course of action to fructify his dirty plan.

In hobnob with a few men of his ilk, he brought a carcass in the dead of night and dropped it into the well. For several days, villagers kept pulling water in the normal way and no one could spot the carcass as it had sat down in the bay. Within a week, a foul stench emitting from the well filled the air. However, nobody could make out the reason for it. Meanwhile, when some women drew water from the well to fill their pots, they noticed reddish longish worms floating on it. Villagers were confused to find worms in the water. Immediately, all residents stopped drawing water. They then decided to clean the well by draining out all water. A team of upper caste divers descended into the well in hammocks made of gunny bags. Landing on water ring below, when they dived into it, they stumbled upon a large mass lying at the bottom. On pulling it out, people were shocked to see a buffalo's skeleton. Air filled with unbearable stink, residents were unable to breathe. This was an unusual incident for everyone to see. Stunned and dismayed, raising their hands upwards in the sky, all residents spoke up unanimously: 'Oh God! Who is that sinner who did such a heinous crime? May he suffer from leprosy!'

Meanwhile, the trader spread the rumour that I had thrown the skeleton into the well. Not surprising, villagers easily believed him, leveling all kinds of allegations against me. Soon, people began to look at me suspiciously. In fact, most of the residents had already declared me a culprit. Police came. Several residents, of course, at the behest of the trader, testified against me. Fortunately, police in the British period were impartial and without proper investigation and concrete evidence, they never arrested anyone. In this case, also, police did listen to all the so-called witnesses against me, but in the absence of clinching evidence, they left without arresting me saying that the matter needed further investigation to bring the real culprits to book.

For several days, no one went near the well to take water. As a cleaning drive, villagers once again cleared the well by taking out all its water and even the mud inside. No one had yet started pulling water from this well; they were visiting a neighbouring village to fetch water.

A few days later, holy water from the river Ganges was brought and after performing a community puja it was mingled with the water in the well. Then only people resumed pulling water from it. The bitterness and heartburn in the minds of upper castes over Dalits sharing water from the same well also washed away. The well now became a common property of the villagers. In the whole process, Dalits had now become 'touchables' by wearing ceremonial thread and chanting Gayatri Mantra.

It was a golden time for Dalits as they had succeeded in claiming their fundamental rights. I, however, became an eyesore for the upper castes. They were now looking for one pretext or the other to teach me a lesson for my temerity to challenge their authority.'

18

Continuous Victimization at the School

The news of Yagya Dutt Sharma, Makhan Lal Singh and Amba Lal's imprisonment spread fast throughout the nearby areas, including my school. Highly humiliated, they were unable to digest the fact that a Dalit had caused the upper caste men such disgrace. As narrated in the preceding chapters, Makhan Lal had a huge circle of friends and sympathizers, with Phundan Lal being one of them.

After coming out of jail on bail, Makhan Lal, Sharma and other co-accused had reached an understanding with grandfather not to pursue the case in the upper court where they had filed an appeal. Tendering their apologies to grandfather, was just a theatrics on their part. At heart, they were still remorseless and wanted to retaliate in some manner. As far as overall atmosphere was concerned, it had become quite normal and many of the villagers had now begun to visit grandfather to discuss with him other petty issues concerning the community. Now, no one wanted to have direct tussle with him at the behest of Makhan Lal and Sharma.

At the school, Phundan Lal, a proxy of Makhan Lal inflicted a systematic torture upon me. He gave me regular thrashing on some pretext or the other. The whole plan was to force me to drop out of school. Despite undergoing a great deal of persecution, I never informed my family about it. As, somewhere in my mind I had the fear that once I drop out I had no other place to study. Our increasingly deteriorating economic condition had further demoralized me. Therefore, enduring all persecution and torture at the hands of Phundan Lal, I held on to school. However, given the suffocating atmosphere there, I was unable to focus on studies, particularly on Mathematics taught by Phundan Lal.

Phundan Lal and his three brothers, who migrated to the town from Lahore during partition, had established a big business empire. Local residents would say that they had established that empire through suspicious and surreptitious activities. Because of their money and muscle power, they had easy access to the local administration. Hindus in the town respected them a lot, as they considered them as shields against Muslims whom they considered a threat to them. Phundan Lal and his clan members had deep-rooted hatred towards the local Muslims. Some peace-loving people in the Hindu community blamed Phundan Lal and brothers for vitiating the town atmosphere by creating mistrust between Hindus and Muslims.

Phundan Lal, having received proxy from Makhan Lal, decided to fix me to take revenge of grandfather. At any cost, he wanted me out of school. To terrorize and frighten me, under some pretext or the other on trifle matters he would exclusively target me and thrash in front of the whole class. I held great hatred in my heart towards him. Among students from the rich farmer community, he was a highly respected teacher. There were reports suggesting that he would take bribe from them to allow them cheating in the examination, particularly in Mathematics to help them secure high marks. There were also rumours that he himself would solve the question papers for the subject and send it to the examination hall for distribution among all those students who received tuitions from him. No one from the school administration dared question him on this.

It became a regular practice on Phundan Lal's part to punish me physically. His continous thrashing had a debilitating effect on my health. Psychologically, I was terribly devastated and would always be forlorn in the class. Despite knowing that I had committed no mischief in the class to invite punishment, I never opened my mouth to protest against this torturing. Aware of my family's miseries resulting from protracted litigation, Phundan Lal was taking full advantage of my helplessness. Once, rising suddenly from his chair and pointing at me, he asked me to stand up. I looked around thinking he was addressing someone else.

Meanwhile, he walked up to me yelling, 'you rascal, bastard, a low caste always disturb peace in the class.'

Holding me by my neck, he dragged me near the blackboard and doffed violently the muffler wrapped around my head. Grabbing my head in his both hands, he hit me against the blackboard hurling simultaneously filthy abuses. I was unable to understand why he was doing all that to me. My head had swelled up, and my cheekbones turned reddish due to repeated beating against the board. Meanwhile, I felt something trickling down my temple. I was bleeding. Still, I somehow stood on my feet touching my temple with forefingers of my left hand.

Shocked, terrorized and feared, I remained grounded there without uttering a single word. Seeing me in this condition, a student stood up and asked Phundan Lal, 'Sir, I fail to understand why you always target this boy singling him out for punishment even though the mistake is done by someone else?'

I walked back to my bench and sat there with my head, drooped down at the desk in front of me. I felt extremely pained and sad. I attempted to control my pent up emotions but to no avail. My eyes welled up and I began sobbing.

I heard the boy was still saying to Phundan Lal, 'Sir, it seems you have some old enmity with this boy.'

Hearing this, Phundan Lal got quiet and walked out of the class. After the class was over, the boy, namely, Rasool walked to me.

'Why don't you protest against this teacher? Supposedly, he is doing all that under an impulse of vindictiveness. He seems to be doing this to you at someone else's behest. I don't know why you bear with all this especially when you didn't do any mischief. One should never feel afraid of such a rascal whose family amassed huge wealth through illegal and suspicious methods. Do you know all his brothers behave like mafia in the city? It is these bastards, who since their arrival have been vitiating the social harmony in the city by creating discord between Hindus and Muslims. They never miss the opportunity to instigate Hindus who before their arrival had long been living coordially with Muslims, Jains, Sikhs and Christians. You don't try to understand his real intention behind all this tormenting of you. He somehow wants to force you to abandon your studies. I advise you to write to the District Collector about this prejudiced, hateful and cruel treatment meted out to you in the class,' asked he, putting his comforting hand on my shoulder.

I listened to that boy attentively and thanked him for his sympathetic and consoling words. With classes over, the school closed for the day. At 4 pm, I left for home. I was feeling excruciating pain in my head; and my face bore puffed up marks all over. While walking back home, I kept thinking about the possible steps to be taken against the teacher. Soon, the fear that any action against him could possibly ruin my educational career gripped my mind, holding me back to initiate any action against him. As I knew that once I got entangled in a case against the teacher, I would not be able to continue my studies at the school. One or two such dreadful thoughts restrained me from approaching the local administration for an action against the teacher. I didn't even report the matter to my father or grandfather let alone approaching government authorities. Aware of my helplessness, Phundan Lal along with other two teachers who by now had joined him, continued to inflict his frequent and relentless torture on me.

With each passing day, I was getting weaker and weaker and was unable to focus on studies. If Phundan Lal missed a particular day to thrash me, another teacher would take his place, often asking me,

'What are you going to do with studying English?' The teacher would single out Dalit students and tell many bizarre things by cracking jokes targeted at them. He would say, 'Dalits are not born with mental faculties, required to learn languages such as English and Sanskrit. Only Brahmins and upper caste students can learn these languages.'

After putting forth his arguments, he would say, 'Why do you waste your time on learning English? You should learn Hindi well, and that is enough for you.'

The teacher Vimeshwar Tyagi would always ask questions in English and exclusively compel me to answer in English. Alike many other students, I was unable to reply in English. The school was located in a rural backward area where no one, except one or two teacher spoke English. Most of the time, the teacher himself explained lessons in Hindi. I was a good student at languages. However, to speak English was a tough task for me as for others. Despite this, Vimeshwar Tyagi would always single me out and compel me to reply in English only. Other students enjoyed seeing me in this torturing state. Although, none of them ever spoke English, they, at my inability to express in English, made fun of me. Meanwhile, Vimeshwar Tyagi, finding me unable to express in English, would pick up a broken chair leg and start hitting me on back, legs, palms, shoulders – any part of my body he lay his hands on. He would not stop thrashing me until I took to floor.

Life at school had become hellish. I had lost my interest in study as well as in the educational system itself. These were the worst days for me in school, driving me to a state of introversion. Neither I was courageous enough to abandon the school nor was I able to tell my parents about the ordeal I was undergoing there. Entirely indecisive on what I should do, I remained in this frame of mind for a long period. Nevertheless, grandfather's dictums kept me inspiring to continue my struggle to achieve my goal. He would say that one should not stop one's struggle until one achieves one's goal even though one may face insurmountable difficulties. Grandfather, however, was not aware that I faced a rather peculiar situation. Within the village, he managed to face all challenges, with great amount of courage and determination as he and his family members were second-to-none in physical fighting with traditional weapons like staff, axes and swords. At school, there was no one to have a physical fight with the teachers on my behalf. At times, I felt like having fallen into an abyss where I found no support to climb out.

Lying in my cot and covering my face with a sheet, I would lock myself inside the muddy thatched house with no ventilation and cry for hours. Continous persecutions in school drew me eventually to disillusionment. Many weird thoughts like taking up arms to wreck vengeance upon all my tormentors now dominated my mind, keeping me awake through out the night. I knew such bizarre thoughts were flowing from my pent up emotions and I could do no such thing in reality.

Seeing no let-up in my torture in school and no support coming from any corner, I became withdrawn. On trivial matters, I would be angry and start crying. My hunger and thirst had disappeared. Nothing interested me now. Physically, I had become a skeleton. Laughing at my miserable condition, English teacher Visheshwar Tyagi would make fun of me by cracking dirty jokes. 'Look at this Majnoo here.' He would comment while drawing other students' attention. Then walking near my desk and looking into my eyes, he would say to me whisperingly 'are you in love with some Laila of your village!' At this, all students in class would guffaw.

Meanwhile, household ambience once again had become rather quarrelsome leading to recurring brawls between father and uncles. These were my formative days. I was unable to cope with the horrible situation exisiting in both family and school. I wished to live in solitude by renouncing all worldly matters.

At this juncture, a hermit, having a gravitational personality visited us. Our family had the tradition of obtaining '*Guru Deeksha*'. In keeping with it, my parents and I took *Deeksha* from that hermit, becoming his disciplines. He gave us all a particular incantation to invoke. He had no belief in traditional Brahmanical system of devotion. At long sessions of spiritual talks and meditation at night, he would sing devotional songs. His simple talks appealed me a lot. He never worshipped any idol and would sit quiet in lotus posture at dawn. His routine consisted of early morning bath after ablution, watering and tendering plants and flowers around his hermitage and then setting out for alms. Seeing him do all this, visitors would offer their voluntary services to assist him. He would very gently decline to accept their services, just asking them to take their seats under the thick leafy trees in the front yard. Having finished all his work, he would contribute his bit to preparing food for visitors and serve them food himself. After lunch, he would sit in a specific posture under a *peepal* tree talking intermittently to visitors. He never asked for money, food or clothing. However, people voluntarily brought to the hermitage grains to cook food for the visitors. Love, affection and equality towards all were his main teachings. No talk about any religion or caste, he wished good for everyone and equality towards all without consideration of one's status, emphasizing the purity of body and soul. By nature, he was reticient. Although he ate very little, his body looked like that of a wrestler. There was a halo of unusual glow on his face. In many respects, he appeared to be different from normal human beings. His name - Baba Magan Das, one who is always blissful - was very much in keeping with the narrated characteristics.

In him, I saw a new ray of hope to help me get over the tormenting phase I was going through.

19

Employment as Daily Labourer

Aware of father's economic hardships, I had to take up employment as a daily wager, on a project for construction of a canal to channelise water to a far-flung area for irrigation purposes. At the workplace, my job was to carry stones in an iron basket on my head. It was terribly painful and hard to carry weighty stones on head. With unbearable heavy load on head, my feet would tremble unsteadily while stepping upward a steep climb. I did not have enough of physical strength to do this kind of job. However, I had to do it to help my father to enable him to provide subsistence to family. As they say, human being is a slave of circumstances. My contribution to family's livelihood was very significant, as without it, family would be at the threshold of starvation. I did understand father's limitations to feed seven souls in the family.

One day the contractor, looking at me, called us workers to his makeshift barrack. Looking towards another co-worker and pointing at me, he enquired, 'How old this boy is? He appears to be a minor; he is too slender to do work equal to an adult worker. Therefore, I will not pay him full wage as for others.'

'He must be around 14 years old. For you, he appears to be physically weak, but he does as much work as any other worker,' replied the worker the contractor was talking with.

'No question of paying him full wage! He is still a minor, and he will get only half wage.' retorted the contractor with sternness.

On hearing this, I felt sad. I had already put in 16 days of working at the project, and accordingly made my calculations to receive a certain amount of money on the payday. All my calculations now seemed to be going wrong. My eyes welled up and I could utter nothing. I had worked according to my full capacity contributing as much as any other worker. The contractor, however, was unwilling to accept me as an adult worker basing his judgment about my physical ability on my sleek appearance only.

Next day, when I, along with other co-workers, arrived at the site, the contractor, with his supervisor, was already present there. Before assigning us job for the day, the contractor, reiterating his earlier stand towards me, said, 'This boy is not a full man, so I am not going to give him full wage.'

Upon this, one of the workers spoke up, 'Sahab, what do you want this boy to do? He has been working here for the last seventeen days, but you never earlier informed that he would not be paid wages entitled for an adult worker. You are telling this now that he has already worked for so many days. You should have told that on the first day itself when he was brought to the site for work. Sir, you better don't look at his body. He can work as hard as an able-bodied man.'

'How can you say that he can do the same amount of work as a fully-grown up and healthy man can do? Can he carry this stone on his head?' asked the contractor stamping his foot on a stone lying nearby.

'Yes, he can. Will you pay him full wages if he carries that stone.' responded the worker and turned towards me looking into my eyes confidently.

'Yes, I can do it', I assured him.

On hearing me say so, the contractor commented, 'I very much doubt you can do that.' He then started moving away looking at me simultaneously.

'Wait, wait, Sahab,' the worker called out.

Then turning to me and pointing towards a heap of stones at the upper side of the bridge, he said, 'Listen, take courage; you have to carry this stone in the basket on your head up to there.'

Confused and unable to decide as to what to do, I remained silent for a few moments. Then without much thinking, I accepted the huge challenge. The contractor was still looking towards me. Walking up to me, he called two workers. Reaching there, he said, 'Look, you have voluntarily agreed to do this. I am not forcing you. If something happens to you, I will not be responsible. Yes, if you successfully carry this stone up there, I would pay you full wages for the entire period you worked here.' Overlooking first part of contractor's statement, I just paid attention to his last sentence, which I felt more encouraging. The contractor stayed there to see if I would really be able to carry that heavy stone on my head to the point indicated.

Immediately, two workers came forward. They stooped to roll the stone into the iron basket. Having placed it onto basket, we all three (the two co-workers and me) lifted the iron basket jointly to put it on my head. The moment the iron basket was rested on my head, the small cloth cushion wrought in ring shape, which I had put on to protect the skull from direct contact with the carrying object, seemed to have disappeared as it felt that the iron basket was crushing deep down into my head. My body was screeching and feet were trembling like date trees in a whirlwind. However, despite that, I carried that heavy object up to the destination. At once, the contractor walked up to me and putting his right hand on my shoulders, he said, 'Bravados! I never thought a boy your age might be capable of carrying such a heavy load on head. Anyway, you will now be paid full wages.'

With stone emptied out of the basket, I felt immense relief, as if resurrected from the dead. I was extremely happy to have won the condition and challenge put up to me. The contractor granted me leave for the rest of the day with full wage. Having put off my worker's cloth, I happily rushed towards home.

On a visit to the village those days, Baba Magan Das was staying with us. On reaching home, I found father sitting beside Baba Magan Das. This time I was supposed to be at work place so father thought that I shirked from work. Standing up and approaching me, he asked, 'How come you are here! This time you should have been at the barrage – your work place.'

I had not yet uttered a single word, when Baba Magan Das, sitting on his asana, told father smilingly, 'He was let off early today for doing a nice job.' I hardly paid attention to what Baba had just uttered. I customarily bowed to him and took a seat nearby. After a few minutes, he asked me almost in murmurs, 'How do you feel now? It must really be painful, my child. Anyway, you did a good job.' Suddenly it struck me that Baba was infact talking about the situation I faced at the workplace. For the next few days, it baffled my mind to think as to how he came to know what transpired at workplace.

Baba Magan Das would enquire of the well-being of all family members when he came to visit us. On another occasion, when he descended to visit family, after checking for the well-being of each and every member, he enquired of one of my cousins who was at that time visiting his sister. When my uncle informed Baba about it, he remained quiet for a few moments and then said, 'Humn, I hope that by the grace of God, he must be safe and fine. The time today was really tragic for him but God is very kind that he survived the mishap.'

Having uttered these words in a low voice, he again got quiet. My uncle would always give credence to what Baba used to say. Hearing him say so, my uncle, touching his feet, asked, 'Baba, why don't you say clearly what happened to my son?'

'There is nothing to fear. God is great, and you must be thankful to Him that your son is safe.'

Uncle's worry, after hearing Baba, was clearly writ large upon his face. For a few moments uncle remained mum, and then stood up saying, 'Baba, I am feeling restless. I am leaving for my daughter's house right away to find out what really happened there.'

'No, no, you need not go there. Your son would return by the evening,' said Baba Magan Das.

As my cousin returned home in the evening, all family members rushed to him to enquire of his well-being. We were shocked to hear from him that he had a miraculous save as the autorickshaw in which he was traveling met an accident killing other five co-passengers save him.

My family members, including me, had unwavering faith in Baba Magan Das's words. Except long twisted plaits on his head and half grey beard and moustache on his face, he was like any other human being. However, everlasting quietness, chearfullness and effulgence, always reflected on his face, made him appear somewhat different from ordinary human beings.

All interest in study was lost. I began leaning more and more towards spirituality. Day and night, I would meditate and try not to engage myself in any work concerning family affairs like agriculture, employment of father and uncles, cousins' marriages and so on. I wanted to run away from social life. For, I now considered myself a free bird, ready to fly as far and high as I wished. In the class at school, I was completely oblivious of proceedings there. Thrashing and spanking at the hands of teachers was still continuing but without any effect on me. I had resigned to this reality there, and everything had become sort of a routine for me.

Meanwhile, summer vacation began. During this period, I felt quite relaxed. After vacation, I was unwilling to rejoin the school; however, I had to succumb to father's dictates.

On the very first day, the English teacher welcomed me by making the following remark, 'you wretch, you don't obey me. I told you that you should not try to become an Englishman.

In India, English is for certain classes only. How the hell you don't listen to me and still trying to become an upper class?'

With my head bent down, I just listened to the teacher without any expression.

My ordeal at the school was increasing immeasurably with every passing day. The two teachers were determined to force me to abandon the school. The more resilience I exhibited against their violence, the more cruelly and fiercly they were thrashing me. Feeling quite lonely, secluded and sad in a class of over 40 students, I always lived in a distressful state. I felt like leaving the school forever and resign to some unknown desolate place where nobody could know about my background, particularly my caste; the sole cause for my never-ending woes. In those depressed moments, I felt like setting the whole village, school and those two teachers ablaze.

Disenchanted with everything – education, food, sleep, talks, socialization, I confined to myself. Nothing interested me, and on trivial things, I would lose my temper. Seeking liberation from the bonds of family, school, religion and society and, above all, the caste I was born in, I wanted to run away from home.

20

Days in Ashram

It was a bright moon lit night of Vijayadashmi day of October 1972. That time I was standard X student. In the evening, we all family members had returned home late from the neighbouring town after celebrating the festival of Dussehera. Back home, I realized that I had forgotten my umbrella somewhere. When father came to know about it, he flared up angrily hurling dirty abuses at me. Pushing me violently aside, he said, 'Bastard, you nowadays appear to be lost in a different world. I am the lone earner of bread and butter for you; and here you are hell bent upon ruining me. I thought you would be a great support for me to earn livelihood for the family. Instead of helping me financially, you keep doing something or the other, which causes losses to me. We would be better without you.'

Continuing his tirade, he said, 'I do not know what sort of son you have given birth to. He is good at nothing, he will be a parasite on me; being the eldest of his brothers I expected him by now to be an earning member; but he is always in pensive mood; I don't know what is wrong with him; most of the time he is lying alone in a dark corner of the house.'

Mother showed no reaction. However, to see father fulminating and condemning me this way, I felt shocked and sad.

'Where have you left that umbrella I had bought you just last week?' he asked furiously.

I said nothing, as I did not remember where I had left it. My silence further enraged him. He kept looking at me angrily awaiting a reply. I was still quiet with my head down looking at the feet. At this, he rushed towards me and catching hold of my neck, he stamped two, three slaps on my cheeks and left remarking, 'I wish you were not my son.'

Hearing these words from father, I began crying. I thought I was of no use. I had never imagined this kind of reaction from him at the loss of a small object like an umbrella. Also, from very young age I had started supporting him economically even by working as a daily wager. He, however, did not appear to be satisfied and expected some big earning from me. He felt happy when I would bring him money by working out. He, however, could never bear anything on my part, which caused him any loss. I could understand the reason for his frustration and anger. However, I was in no way responsible for his family's destitution.

With father's unexpected reaction, my belief that everyone in this world, including parents, was selfish got crystallized. Being already highly distraught due to the hostile atmosphere at school, his attitude over such a trifle matter drove me further away from him. Viewing his hostile temperament, I never mentioned to him about my problems in school. Had I told him, he would have got an easy pretext to withdraw me immediately from the school forcing me to take up some petty job. Such ill-treatment from father, and that too, for an insignificant item, caused me tremendous mental agony. That day I did not have my dinner. I straight went to the Chaupal to sleep.

Still awake, grandfather was sitting on his charpoy with a quilt wrapped around him. He had heard father shouting at me as the house was just a few yards away from Chaupal. I at once reclined quietly into my cot. To find me silent, grandfather asked, 'Why was your father shouting at you?'

'Because I lost an umbrella in the festival,' I replied.

'Your father is rather selfish and he is in hurry to see you earn money and share family responsibilities,' remarked grandfather.

'He also mentioned to me you are not serious about your studies. May be he is more perturbed at seeing you withdrawn,' added grandfather.

After learning from grandfather about father's concern about my studies, I got more careful not to bring to his attention the harsh conditions I was facing in school. This could have been an easy excuse for him to force me to drop out of school and take up some petty employment. This thought, coupled with the fact that father had his own scheme of things and expectations that he wanted to realize at my cost, sent shudders down my spine. I was least prepared to compromise with my own ambitions in life. I was not doing well in studies due to unfavourable conditions in school; however, I did understand the value of education. Father never cared to know why I was not doing well. He was interested only in seeing me mobilize resources for himself and his family's comforts at any cost. Traditionally, the eldest son in a household had to discharge responsibilities towards both parents as well as his younger siblings. This was not in keeping with my temperament. I was dead against such tradition but, at the same time, I was aware of my limitations.

Without any further talk with grandfather, I covered myself with a quilt and tried to doze. Unable to sleep, I asked myself 'What is the purpose of life if one has to per force do things that one doesn't like?'

My suppressed emotions were now bursting out. Lying in cot, for a few minutes, I sobbed. Grandfather had now fallen asleep. Suddenly, the thought that I am of no value to anyone in family or society overcame me. Many other bizarre things flashed on my mind and heart, pushing me into anguish.

Around 9.30 P.M., I came out onto the street running past the Chaupal to pee. As I gazed up at the sky, it looked tranquil and beautiful with glittering stars. It fascinated me so much that for several minutes I continued to look up at the twinkling stars. Then I went back into the Chaupal and reclined into my string cot. Feeling philosophical, I continued to contemplate many things. Meanwhile, something peculiar was happening within me goading me to leave for some unknown destination. Putting off all my clothes and with a single loin on, I set out westward.

There was complete serenity all around. Nothing - human, dog, cat or animal - was visible in the streets. About one kilometer to the north, there was a railway track leading westwards to the states of Punjab and Kashmir. Reaching there, I began walking along the track, further towards the west. Up above in the sky, the moon, amidst the drifting clouds, looked like playing hide and seek with the stars. While treading along the track, lined up on both sides by the thick and large trees of Jamun, Neem, Sisham and Babool, it felt the moon was following me as it now hid itself behind the tall trees and it now re-appeared. There was tranquility everywhere. I kept walking along the track until I reached a concrete road leading to the town where Baba Magan Das was presently camping. During this time of the year, he would invariably visit his Guruji's hermitage. I had never earlier been to this town but had heard its name. I continued to walk in the direction of my destination, reading and looking at the signboards to convince myself that I was on right path. I kept on moving until I saw a milestone on which engraved was the name of the town I was heading to. The town, as indicated on the milestone, was still 15 kilometers far from there. In this stretch, on both sides of the road, there were thickly dark mango groves making the night appear more dreadful. From different directions, howls of jackals were coming in. Meanwhile, many wild animals were crossing my way. I could see only a few of them and many others remained invisible to me. Only glowworms intermittently were guiding my path as if they were my torchbearers in this dark, frightful but divine night.

I was indeed getting a unique feeling that night. Being in that state, I experienced a transcendental joy, difficult to describe. It felt as if all my worries in life had disappeared. I felt free, fearless and happy. No animosity, bitterness or hatred towards the teachers, who caused me continuous physical and mental suffering, was left in my heart. The same degree of indifference I had towards my parents and other members of the family – no attachment and no affection towards anyone. No anger, no sense of revenge against oppressors of my family in the village either. Now, both my mind and soul focused on something inexplicable as I felt several unusual things. However, a human body with its limitations does experience the effects of nature. Likewise, I felt severe pain in my feet, when, walking in the darkness, I hit them against some hard objects like broken pieces of bricks or pebbles. Being bare body, I was feeling cold too. I began to run to ward off the cold. I felt a little warm. Sometimes I had to stand under the trees to protect my body from the fiercely blowing wind. At some distance along the roadside, I noticed some blaze. As the violently blowing cold wind was making me shiver, I could not help rushing there to warm myself up. On reaching there, I discovered that it was a crematorium and the blaze was of a pyre on the bank of a rivulet to burn some dead body. Though I had realized that the fire was of a pyre, I could not restrain myself to get closer to it. I sat near the pyre to warm myself up. After about fifteen minutes of chafing before it, I stood up and began to move fast towards my destination.

I was still about two kilometers away from the city, when I heard the sound of playing a musical instrument. I realized that I was quite near my destination, but the place of Baba's hermitage was unknown to me. After entering the city, I kept moving into the direction from where the sound of musical instruments was coming. Then, I noticed some people coming towards me from that direction. I took the street leading towards that. After arriving there, I realised that it was an organization of Ram Leela. By that time, most of the spectators had already left and a few others who stayed behind were about to leave. Seeing me without clothes, people were gazing at me but said nothing. Meanwhile, a group of young people, walking up to me, started hooting and laughing but they soon left the place reveling. I hardly took any notice of their behaviour. In a few moments, the ground was empty, and no human figure remained in sight. At the back end corner of the ground, there was a makeshift tea stall. I walked up there and found some hot place, supposedly a hearth. I also found a gunny bag spread over the ground. On one side of the hearth, there was a small heap of coal. I picked up a few coal pieces and put into the hearth. Soon, the coal started burning and throwing flames. In one corner of the stall, there was a bundle of old newspapers, which I spread over the ground near the hearth, and sat on them with my back towards the hearth.

It was warmly soothing; I kept turning sides to warm me up sufficiently. After a while, I fell asleep. I had gone to sleep thinking as to how to find out Baba's hermitage. Then, a dream occurred to me in which I found Baba calling me. In the midst of my dream, I suddenly woke up asking, 'Yes, my master, did you say something?' He at once started moving towards a direction waving at me to follow him up. After this, I truly woke up and found nothing around. Yet, I remembered very vividly the direction and path where Baba had walked on in my dream. I at once stood up and without second thought, took the street connecting to the main road that led to another town. On the road, I must have walked only a few minutes when I heard sound of conch-blowing coming in from the other direction.

It was around 4 A.M. I must have walked only a few yards when I noticed a dim light in a hut enclosed by a cluster of thick tall trees. I guessed it was my destination. I stopped in front of the hut, overlooking it from the main road where I stood. Then I walked down another few yards towards the thicked, where I saw a white-colour tomb outside the wooden gate through which one has to pass to reach the mainstay of the hermitage. I sat down on a corner of the tomb with my back towards the wooden gate so that someone coming out could take notice of me. It felt very difficult to sit there, as the surface of the tomb was extremely cool. Being bare body, I was shivering with cold. To keep the body warm, I began to walk in the orchard at the front yard of the *Ashram*. Sound of the chirping birds was creating a divine music in the atmosphere, soothing my mind, heart and soul. Now Sun had started rising in the East. I, facing the East, was just looking at the rising Sun when someone called me out from behind. I turned around to see a hermit behind me just near the wooden gate. The hermit, walking towards me, stopped short and asked me,

'Who are you maharaj, and where have you come from?'

I looked at his face and at once identified him. He had once visited our family along with Baba Magan Das. Since then, I had changed a lot physically making it difficult for him to recognize me. In keeping with the family tradition of showing salutation to spiritual gurus, I walked up to him to touch his feet. The sadhu, Baba Shyam Das, first looked at me and then, putting his right hand on my head, asked, 'Who are you? Why have you smeared yourself with ashes? Today, it is very cold. Are you not feeling cold, being barebody? What brought you here?' I kept quiet. For a few seconds, he stood still and then he walked back up to the mainstay of the Ashram. I overheard him saying, 'Oh, sadhus, there is some mystic outside sitting near the tomb; he is smeared with ashes; he looks highly spirited.' Saying this, Baba Shyam Das came back to me. Pointing towards the wooden door leading up to the mainstay, he waved at me to follow him up. I pursued him, and soon found myself in the main muddy hall of the Ashram where over a dozen sadhus were sitting on mattresses of palm leaves spread over the floor.

I was still looking around when, in one corner of the hall, I noticed Baba Magan Das sitting in his familiar posture. I straight walked towards him and bending on my knees, placed my head on his feet. He was supposedly still in meditation. With the touch of my head, he gently opened his eyes. Seeing myself seated in front of him in salutary posture, he lifted his right hand and putting it on my head he said, 'Be glorious and noble.' Then, pointing to a mattress spread nearby on the ground, he asked me to sit down. I took my seat in front of him. I was still shivering with cold. Seeing me in this condition, he took out a sheet from his Jholi (bag), and putting it on my bare body; he said, 'Why did you run away from your family without informing them? You should not have come like this. Your parents must really be very worried not to find you there. You appear to be shirking your responsibilities.' He then took out another sheet and holding it out to me said, 'My child, it is very cold; you are doing a penance by keeping yourself uncovered in such a severe cold. Wrap it and sit comfortably.' I at once wrapped myself with the sheet.

To see me squatted in front of Baba Magan Das, other sadhus first looked at each other and then turning to him, asked in unison, 'Magan Das ji, it seems you already know each other. Who is this boy? Is he your disciple? You never told you have someone like him as your disciple.'

'Yes, he is my disciple; but I have not yet formally initiated him into *sanyas* (renunciation). He is still studying. Last month, when I visited their village, he was normal. His visit in this form indicates that something strange has happened to him,' said Baba.

Having said this, he stood up from his hay bed and walked into a hut adjacent to the main building. Constructed in a traditional way of Indian sainthood, the hut was made of mud and had a thatched roof. Sitting outside there, I overheard him talking to someone inside the hut. Meanwhile, calling me out, he emerged from the hut. On hearing him calling me, I had already stood up on my seat and started walking towards the hut. Seeing me proceeding towards the hut, he stopped midway. Then turning back, he asked me to follow him into the hut.

On Entry, I saw an old grey-haired *sadhu* sitting on a string cot. Baba Magan Das signaled me to touch his feet. I instantly bent on my knees to perform my salutations. Then, Baba Magan Das introduced me to the grand old sadhu saying, 'Guruji, he is my disciple from Bhagwan Puri. He is still studying. He was quite normal until my last visit to his village. Today, he appears to be a matured *sanyasi*. He is bare-bodied even in this severe cold. You may like to ask him as to why he has come like this.'

By now, I knew that the grand old saint was my grand guru. His name was Baba Santosh Das. The grand Baba first provided me *Prasad* (sweet of offering), and then waving at me to sit down he asked, 'My child, why did you leave home? Your parents will be crying for you. You should not have come like this. The path you are choosing is not as simple as people think. Asceticism is not a joke. Nowadays, people have made it a profession to earn money by duping innocent people. In asceticism, one has to suffer from all sorts of pains, which, not everyone can simply bear. Therefore, I advise you to return home to be with your family. You won't achieve anything here in the *Ashram* by becoming a sanyasi.' He told me many other things, which I could not comprehend.

'Guruji, what you are saying may be right, but I don't want to go back. I want to live here in the *Ashram*, or I will go elsewhere if you don't allow me to stay here. I certainly do not wish to go back to my parents. After coming here, I am feeling happy and free from all those pains and sufferings I had been undergoing while being with my family. Please don't compel me to leave this place. Whatever responsibility you assign me here, I am prepared to do that, but I don't want to return to my parents. I want to die here in your service,' I requested.

On hearing me say this, the grand Baba said, 'Oh my child, listen, I am not going to send you back right now. We will call your parents here and talk to them. If they have any problem to finance your education, we will help you - to enable you to continue your studies. You can stay here as long as you want, but I do not want you to initiate into asceticism (sanyas). You are not for this. You have to educate yourself and do something good for the society.'

Upon this, I became sad. Grand Baba also got quiet. This while, Baba Magan Das, sitting in a corner, still, kept looking at me smilingly. Grand Baba now seemed to be contemplating something. Breaking his silence, he said, 'Okay, you can live here, we will not force you to go, but you will have to do all those rituals that other sadhus in the *Ashram* do. You have to get up early in the morning before 4 A.M., and among other things, have to perform the morning ceremony of conch blowing. After this service, you need to sit in meditation for an hour or so, and then set out for alms from the neighbouring villages. Can you do all this?'

'Yes Babaji, I will do all that,' I replied.

'We are not here to sit idly. Sadhus also have their own routine that is far more difficult than the routine of businessmen, bureaucrats, advocates and military men. These people do their duties for payment. We, on the contrary, do them without expecting remuneration from anyone. Our activities are no longer appealing to people. Of course, a lot of rich people, officers, and businessmen do visit us here every day seeking solace. They are dissatisfied with themselves. Their power, authority, wealth – nothing - provides them mental peace. Despite having plenty of them, they seek more power, authority and wealth. Peace cannot come, through wealth, power and/or even spirituality. You will see even Sadhus are not at peace with themselves.'

The grand Baba tried to dissuade me from staying at the *Ashram*. His main point was to knock into my head that there was no difference between sadhus, mahatmas and common people. I had left home to take shelter here on the belief that I would not be facing day-to-day humiliation and insults, as inflicted upon me in school, because of my being born as untouchable. Bearing this in mind, I submitted, 'Guruji, while living here in the *Ashram*; at least, I would not suffer from the torturous situations I have been subjected to so far. Right now, I am at complete peace with myself and the surroundings.'

At this, the Grand Baba said, 'My child, you are naïve to think that in asceticism and sainthood there is no discrimination of caste, creed and colour. I indeed do not want you to have future shocks. You had better return home, to lead a normal social and married life. Hermits and priests, who have taken a pledge to observe celibacy, abstinence and renunciation, do exactly opposite things. Sometimes they even indulge in the things, which even ordinary people avoid doing. Whatever they preach for others, they hardly practice themselves. During my long sojourns in the country, I met only a few saints who were above the considerations of casteism and untouchability. Seats of the so-called high priests are all dens of corruption. These so-called priests, their disciples and devotees indulge in acts that are heinous crimes in society. Womanizing, sodomy, pedophilia, molestation, boozing, you name anything, are widely rampant in such places. There is as much demonstration of wealth and power in these places as in the business world. In order to make people believe in that they have celestial powers, they do public affectations like remaining naked, standing in cold water, sitting in front of fire etc. They want people to remain superstitious so as to keep their religious seats, that bring them name, fame, wealth and power, intact.'

I kept listening to this lengthy discourse and said nothing. I was so happy in the *Ashram* that his long discourse just passed over my head. He continued with many other things to persuade me to leave the *Ashram* and go home, but nothing was going into my head.

He continued, 'You would experience in life ahead that the chief priests of all temples, Gurdwaras, churches and mosques keep their blessings reserved for big industrialists, businessmen, politicians and administrative officials only. Poor people hardly have any place in their hearts. Their spiritualism has certain pre-conceived notions, and the clever priests have dragged God into their spun network. Pandits, pastors, granthis, maulavis, and saints and sadhus are all in competition with each other to establish their centers of power, authority and wealth. They have nothing to do with the welfare of common people. I do not understand what knowledge you will gain here in this *Ashram*. Proper education will provide you knowledge through which you can get everything of happiness – power, prestige, wealth. How pitiful! When our society needs educated people to lift it out of the morass of casteism, untouchability and blind faith in fate, our youths tend to turn to spirituality, which amounts to shirking their duties towards society. Having practised spirituality throughout life, I know its realities.'

Having listened attentively to Grand Baba's lengthy statement on the hollowness of spiritualism and asceticism, I had the feeling that Baba was perhaps disillusioned with the very life he led with unwavering commitment so far. I was wondering that if Baba did not realize truth in his ascetic life, how he remained in it for so long. I wished to ask him about that, however, I remained quiet. After this, Grand Baba never asked me to return home.

By now, Sun had wrapped the whole sky in the lap of its boundless light. Sadhus in the *Ashram* had spread their palm-leaf mattresses in the open sky under the sun. Weather was bright, beautiful and still. Everyone in the *Ashram* appeared to be in a blissful state.

I was now spending my time happily in the *Ashram*. Getting very early in the morning, taking bath, blowing conch, sitting in meditation for an hour or so, sweeping the front yard of the *Ashram* and then setting out for alms had become routine.

Sometimes, I would accompany Baba Magan Das to the fields near the River Ganges to search for medicinal herbs for the treatment of lepers who would very often visit the *Ashram* seeking Grand Baba's blessings. Early in the morning, several sadhus would grind herbs in the bowl-shaped rocky pots for providing to the patients. People believed that the herbal juice given by the Grand Baba to the leprosy patients had miraculous effect, curing them completely within three-four months. Some believed that it happened due to Baba's supernatural powers. People of all castes and religions suffering from the disease would visit the *Ashram*. Baba treated everyone equally. He had instructed all his disciples not to take any money from the cured patients. However, out of faith and reverence to Baba, families of the cured patients would bring food grains like rice, pulses, vegetables, etc; and submit to the Baba to accept them. On insistence, Grand Baba would allow some of them to leave the material in the *Ashram*. Except this, he did not accept any other offering.

By nature, Baba was reticent. Without speaking a word, he would squat in meditation on his string cot throughout the day. He liked to be alone in his small enclosure. People believed that he was a self-realised person. After spending considerable time at the *Ashram*, I too developed a feeling that the Grand Baba must be a great soul as one experienced total mental and bodily peace in his proximity.

The *Ashram* was set in the mid of thick cluster of mango, *amla, jamun,* guava, *ananas*, orange and lemon trees, but an ancient mammoth *peepal* tree, standing in the front yard, around which there were tombs of several heavenly departed saints, always served as a place of shelter for the visitors during the daytime. At night, no one dared go near it, as it appeared extremely dreadful that time. However, a few saints used to sit under it in meditation even at night. The tranquil atmosphere of the *Ashram* had provided me boundless psychological solace. I always felt like being in the state of beatitude. I had now made up my mind to spend rest of my life in the service of Grand Baba and Baba Magan Das. After my arrival here, my whole world had changed.

By now, parents were in the knowledge of my staying at the *Ashram*. On a few occasions, I even visited my village along with Baba Magan Das. However, I never met my parents and other family members during my brief stay there.

My grandfather would complain to Baba Magan Das, 'Baba, you should have shown mercy at our family. Being the eldest grandchild, I had certain expectations from him. All my dreams for uplifting my family through this child by having him educated seem to have shattered after he left us.'

My mother would invite me over lunch or dinner but I never went. Once she herself brought me food. Placing the plate, loaded with rice, chapatti, dal, veg currie, ghee and curd, in front of me, she first looked at me and then asked crying, 'Do you ever remember me, your father and your sister and brothers? You don't even feel like visiting your house. How can you be so cruel? Have you ever thought of what all we endured after your departure? Did I bring you up to see this day?'

Her words had hardly any effect on me to change my mind. My father during his visit to the Baba at Chaupal would cringe at his feet crying and requesting him, 'Babaji, please have mercy at us. You know he is our eldest child. Being so, I had pinned all my hopes on him. Had he not left home, he by now would have become my great support to help me bring up my other children. With his departure, our life is devastated. I consider myself responsible for all this. I pushed him into this state. I never took the trouble to find out as to why he used to be so sad all the time. Instead of talking to him, I always expressed my anger at him making him further sad, thus compelling him to run away. Although, I am happy to see him cheerful, I cannot bear his separation from the family. Every member of the family feels peeved to see him in this form.'

On hearing this, Baba Magan Das said, 'We all, including Grand Baba repeatedly advised him to return home.

It has had no effect on him, and he is still insistent upon initiation into asceticism. We tried our best to make him understand his responsibilities towards family but he is not willing to come back. I have not yet initiated him, and I will wait further to see that he finally comes home. Let him spend some more time at the *Ashram*. May be, he will change his mind.'

After spending a few days in the village, I alongwith Baba Magan Das, returned to the *Ashram*. On return, Baba Magan Das related all what had transpired between him and my parents to the Grand Guru.

For a few days after my return, Grand Baba did not talk to me. Then I observed him showing his increased affection towards me. One day he called me in his hut and said, 'my child, if you continue here, your mission of life will remain incomplete. You are assigned with certain responsibilities, which you would not be able to fulfill as an ascetic. Therefore, I want you to be equipped with the weapon of education. If you are unwilling to return home, we would arrange for your education in the neighbouring town, but you must go to school.'

On hearing this, I felt crest-fallen. I had thrown the idea of education out of my mind. I kept mum. Grand old Guru continued, 'I do not want you to waste precious years of your life. As an educated person, you will do a great good for the society. As an ascetic, you are not acceptable as equal to others. You would see for yourself while interacting with hermits that they would first enquire of your caste background.'

Unconvinced by Baba's discourse and advice, I took his words as a deliberate attempt on his part to make me feel disillusioned about spirituality and asceticism so that I would return home to resume my studies. He persisted in his efforts but I was determined not to budge from my position. On another occasion, Grand Baba cited instances from the medieval history of India about how great Dalit saints like Ravi Das and Nabha Das were mal-treated by the upper castes. They ridiculed and jeered at them and harassed at every step of life. All such instances were passing over my head and I was still not prepared to give up my present status.

21

Prejudice Amongst Sadhus

The year was 1974. Pilgrims from all over the country had begun congregating at Haridwar – a venue for *Kumbh* Fair – to participate. The Grand Baba, alongwith his disciples, decided to go there. After a two days walking journey, we reached Haridwar (abode of God). Several million believers, sadhus, saints, priests and religious leaders belonging to different *akharas* (sects), sub-sects of Hindu saint-tradition like *Nirmal, Sanyasi, Vairagi, Udasi,* and *Nath* had pitched their camps on both sides of the river, occupying miles of grounds. This was my first exposure to such a large spiritual gathering where great saints, ascetics, mystics, seers, priests and preachers had gathered at one place at the sme time. To my great astonishment, here too, I witnessed a great division among the communities of saints and seers. Even for 'Holy Baths' in the sacred river on this occasion, separate dates / times for various *akharas* had to be fixed on considerations of high and low order.

On the date, fixed for Udasi sect for a sacred dip in the holy Ganges, Grand Baba, alongwith his disciples, gathered on the bank. Our group, with him in the lead, had stood in the queue to move towards the *ghat* (bathing place in the river). Meanwhile, a sadhu just behind me in the queue tried to go ahead of me by pushing me aside. On my resistance, he flared up and yelling at me, threw me out of the queue. On seeing me falling on the ground, one of the sadhus from our group, standing ahead of me in the queue, rushed back and tried to intervene but the sadhu refused to vacate my place. When our sadhu tried to reason out with him, telling him how he could behave with another Udasi like that, he said, 'Here in the queue, everyone is Udasi; but all those standing in the queue are not equal, as some of them are Brahmins while others are *Khstriyas, Vaisyas and Shudras*, by birth. Do you know I am a Brahmin? Now, tell me, who are you? In which caste are you born?' We could have lied to him by telling that we were Brahmin or *Khstriya*. However, we told him the truth by revealing our caste in view of Hindu classification of society.

We had not even finished talks that the sadhu, summoning blood shots in his eyes, started screaming and asked us to get out of the queue immediately. It was shocking. It at once reminded me of all what the Grand Baba was trying to push into my head over the last two years. Meanwhile, some other sadhus behind us in the queue joined that sadhu and our entire group including Grand Baba was forced to move out. Insulted, humiliated, dejected and disappointed, now we all stood out of the moving parade of Udasi sadhus. However, this incident did not appear to have had any effect on both Grand Baba Santosh Das and Baba Magan Das.They still maintained their steady silence.

Grand Baba and Baba Magan Das alongwith other sadhus of the group stayed behind waiting for their turn to take dip in the River Ganges. I, however, left the place and started walking alone northward on the right bank of the Ganges. I continued to walk on and then reached a desolate place full of bushes and cedar trees. Tired, I sat in the shadow of a thieves of trees and soon fell asleep. About two hours later, when I woke up, I felt quite relaxed and light. I stood up and walked on a pathway leading to an empty *ghat*. There were only a few people around taking dip in the Ganges. Reaching the ghat, I put off my knee-deep *lungi* and dipped in the river. Having finished my bath, I sat there on the bank for some time thinking of so many bizarre things. All joy and happiness I had so far experienced in the *Ashram* with Grand Baba and Baba Magan Das had disappeared. I then left the place and walked back to the tent we were camping. On my return, I saw both Grand Baba and Baba Magan Das squatting on their seats on the ground. On entering the camp, I saluted both of them in customary fashion.

'Oh, my child, where were you all this while? You vanished without telling any one. Tell me, did you finally take your Holy Bath or not?' asked the Grand Baba.

'Yes, I had gone far away northward and had my dip in the Ganges there,' I replied.

I then went inside the tent, covered myself by a sheet and lay down on the ground to sleep. Both Grand Baba and Baba Magan Das were still squatted on the ground. A little later, Grand Baba called out, 'Oh my child, have you gone to sleep? Come and sit here.' I still lay silent and said nothing.

Finding me quiet, Grand Baba called out, 'My child, you appear to be sad today. It looks strange to see you so silent. Are you still thinking about that incident that took place earlier in the day? They barred all of us from moving in the same queue towards the ghat. We managed to reach there much later to take a dip. But I don't take these things to heart.'

Confused and hesitant to tell him about my predicament, I remained silent for a moment. I was indeed highly agitated at the behaviour of that Udasi sadhu, who had pushed me out of the queue just because of my caste. However, at the same time I was trying to pacify myself by arguing that that was the reality of life, where millions of Dalits including me were bound to face this everyday. There was no escape route in sight for them. At every step in life, they had to swallow this bitter dose of untouchability and casteism. A few minutes before, I was about to burst out with anger, but had now become calm. However, the condescending manner in which that Udasi sadhu treated me had made me fully aware of the false veneer on the face of Indian asceticism.

Its hollowness was now quite clear to me. Lofty talks of ideals, like '*Braham Satyam Jaganamithya*' and '*Eko Braham Dwittiyo Na Api*" oft-repeated by these saints and sadhus about God, Soul and Religion proved not only empty but also belying. For them, caste was still a divine fundamental principle to determine an individual's station in the mundane life.

All this while, Grand Baba perhaps was reading my mind. Suddenly, he spoke up, 'I know, my child, you are not yet able to digest the incident. That is why I always keep telling that you are not made for ascetism.'

'Yes, Babaji, I am still agitated at the treatment meted out to me. I no longer see any truth in this kind of asceticism,' I continued, 'If God has created us all equal, then why that Omnipotent God does not destroy all such Sects and their Chiefs who hate and discriminate against their own fellow followers. Or does God connive with them in their acts of thuggery?' said I venting my anger and frustration.

With Grand Baba smiling gently, there held peace in the tent for a few moments and then he said, 'So, now you have got to know the realities of asceticism. My son! My disciples and I are living with this truth for several decades; and just one bitter experience made you disillusioned about it. In fact, there is nothing wrong with asceticism. Great philosophers, seers and saints of the world, through realization of truth, have contributed a lot to the ocean of knowledge from which the entire humanity has benefited. Here in India, everything is fine except this unique, unrivalled and unparalleled system of caste and untouchability, which is plaguing the society.'

He continued, 'Yet you cannot discard the entire system of asceticism simply because people do not understand its essence. I lived with this, I am living with this, and I will die with this. I do not mind people discriminating against me. Let them do it. This is their way of thinking. Maybe we old Dalits have resigned to our fate and do not dare oppose such things. Being a literate, you could not tolerate insult at the hands of that sadhu. That is why, I advise you to get good education and do good service to a larger number of people in your family, neighbourhood, village, society and country.'

I was trying to hear Grand Baba with attention, but my mind was transfixed and faces of my tormentors in the school were now crossing my mind. Soon, ambivalence gripped my mind. I was not able to decide on whether I should continue in the *Ashram* or return to school.

Meanwhile situation in the *Ashram* was changing fast. Most of the sadhus had left on long sojournes. Several of them had taken flight to their heavenly abode during their pilgrims. So, they never returned. Only Grand Baba, Baba Magan Das, two other sadhus and I resided there. Suddenly, Grand Baba stopped taking food. For two weeks or so, he survived on fruit juice and water only. Now, he never came out of his hut and remained all the time seated on his bed. Twice or thrice in a day, he would call me in his hut and reiterate all that he had so far advised me from time to time. My mind had gradually begun deviating away from the *Ashram.* The process had indeed started with the incident in the Kumbh Fair. State of peace, joy and happiness was surely vanishing.

One night, around 12 p.m. Grand Baba called me in. Reaching there, I found Baba sitting in his familiar yogic posture, perhaps in meditation. Taking my seat on the floor beside his cot, I asked, 'Yes, Babaji, please let me know, why you sent for me?'

'Look, my child, I have many times told you that here in *Ashram* there is nothing worthwhile for you. This is the last time I advise you to return home, educate yourself and proceed ahead in life. My blessings will always be with you. Now, go and take rest and ponder seriously over what I told you. Hereafter, you would have no one around to advise you,' said Grand Baba.

His all previous advices and suggestions had fallen on my deaf ears, but this time, his words seemed to be having great effect on my mind. After going back to my asana (seat), I kept thinking throughout the night of what he had told me.

It was 4 A.M. when Baba Magan Das, still in his meditation, suddenly rose up from his seat and walked straight towards Grand Baba's hut. Seeing him leaving his seat so suddenly and walking into Grand Baba's hut, I at once sat up. A little later, he came out of Grand Baba's hut and called out, '*Arrey* listen, awake, *Babaji* has passed away.' All sadhus present at the *Ashram* woke up.

That morning, Baba Magan Das finished all morning rituals rather quickly. By sunrise, a large number of people from the local town and neighbouring villages had gathered at the *Ashram* after hearing the news of Grand Baba's heavenly flight. With all rituals and rites, essentially performed for the cremation of saints' mortal remains, he was buried in a grave prepared specially for him. With Grand Baba's departure, the *Ashram* no longer looked lively. There was lifelessness and desolation all around. Baba Magan Das had now formally succeeded him to look after the *Ashram*.

22

Disillusionment Against Spirituality

It was the month of June. During this time, hermits would usually take their seats on palm-leaves mattresses spread over the ground under the shade of a giant peepal tree standing at a corner of *Ashram*'s front yard. After daylong rest, all sadhus had rolled up their mattresses and moved to their seats in the mainstay. One of the sadhus, after despositing his mattress inside, came out and kept wandering idly in the front yard looking towards a culvert on the main road passing in front of the *Ashram*. One part of the passages under culvert was open towards the *Ashram*. There existed a thick cluster of bamboo trees, covering the culvert and its passage towards the *Ashram*, making it imperceptible. Coincidentally, I came out into the frontyard and noticed sadhu Akshay Das walking into the passage under the culvert, waving at someone invisible to me because of tall bamboo trees in between.

Curious to know where he was heading to, I tiptoed behind him. Reaching there, I noticed some other human figure standing inside the passage. Hiding myself behind the bamboo trees, I leaned out my neck to know what sadhu Akshay Das was doing there at dusk with the other person. Extending my neck a little further from behind the bamboo trees, I peeped into the passage and noticed that standing there was a woman facing Akshay Das with her both arms around his neck. Holding Akshay Das in her arms, she stepped a little back to the wall of the passage and slouched against it. Akshay Das was now smooching passionately over her lips and cheeks with one of his hands on her blouse to unbutton it. Having opened her blouse from the front he moved his mouth to her breasts and began sucking them madly one by one, simultaneously inserting both of his hands into her sari to lift it up. The woman, with her sari pulled up to her waistline, began to sit down bending backward. Soon, she lay on her back on the floor with Akshay Das leaning over her. Untying his *lungi* and throwing it aside, Akshay Das, swiftly pulled out his erected penis from his loin and positioning himself in between her legs and lifting them up over to his shoulders, began pushing fiercely back and forth. Now, both were embracing each other tightly in their arms moaning and making sounds of 'oomph, oomph' breathing ferociously. It lasted about six-seven minutes. Disengaging themselves, they sat up and again kissed each other. Then they arose to leave. Holding her hand in his, Akshay Das said to her whisperingly, 'You come here every third day.'

At this, the woman said, 'No, no, I cannot come here every day because it is too far from my house. During day time, under some pretext, you can come to Junia ka Tilla (name of a local place) around which there are thick bushes behind which we can meet and make love quite safely away from peoples' eyes.'

'Humn! I think, you are right, that is much safer place for our meeting,' said Akshay Das putting a ten-rupee bill on her palm. Seeing him coming out of the passage I quickly turned around and walked towards *Ashram*'s gate.

I told no one about what I had witnessed happening between Akshay Das and that woman. I noticed that hereafter;

Akshay Das at some pretext or the other would go out any time of the day. One day when he left the *Ashram*, probably to meet his lover, I heard Baba Magan Das talking to himself saying, 'Where does this Akshay Das go every day? He never brings alms for the *Ashram*, then why does he go regularly out and come back just like this?'

When he was back in the *Ashram*, Baba Magan Das asked him casually, 'Hey, Akshay Das, where do you disappear regularly now days?'

'I just go to the school playground. I love to watch children playing hockey, cricket and other sports,' said Akshay Das confidently.

'But children normally play in the evening and you leave any time of the day. I never saw children playing during the time you leave the *Ashram*. Are you hiding something from me?' Baba Magan Das asked him pointedly.

Hearing this, blood drained out of Akshay Das's face. 'No, no, sometimes I go to the nearby river also, where I enjoy watching fishermen catch fish,' said he nonchalantly and pretentiously. Thereupon, Baba Magan Das looked askance and made no further query. Akshay Das, however, did not halt his daily outings.

One fine morning, on getting up early, we noticed that he was not in his charpoy (string cot). We thought he must have gone for walk. Meanwhile, one of the sadhus noticed that all his personal belongings were also missing. When we were still talking amongst us about sudden disappearance of Akshay Das, a man from the neighbouring *basti* (colony) came to visit the *Ashram*. After paying his obeisance to sadhus and looking towards Baba Magan Das, he said, 'Babaji, have you heard what happened yesterday night?'

No, we didn't hear anything, what has happened?' Baba Magan asked the visitor.

'You know that Sadhav, mansion in our *basti*, who is away to work most of the times at the construction projects in the district headquarters, his wife ran away with someone yesterday night,' said the visitor.

Baba Magan Das said nothing, but deep furrows on his forehead were clearly indicative of what was going on in his mind. He was almost sure that Akshay Das had eloped with the woman in question. Throughout the day, we waited for Akshay Das to return but there was no trace of him anywhere. He had gone forever. Hereafter, we heard zilch about him. Meanwhile, I was fast losing interest in spirituality and nothing interested me in the *Ashram*. I had made up my mind to return home and resume my studies.

It was an evening of July 1975. Baba Magan Das, sitting in front of the thatched kitchen, was peeling off potato. Seeing him do that I left my asana (seat on the ground), and walked up to him. Sitting beside him, I picked up the basket of potato and began to peel them off, requesting him to allow me to do so.

'Okay, my child, do it, if you wish so; chop off two pieces of cauliflower also,' he stood up saying so.

Having prepared the vegetables to cook, I went in the kitchen to make fire in the earthen oven. Meanwhile, Baba Magan Das joined me there.

'My child, I no longer feel peaceful here after departure of Grand Baba. This Akshay Das brought us bad name. Now basti people look at us with suspicion. Never before has any sadhu from this *Ashram* done so.'

'Guruji, I also don't feel good here. I feel like going back and resume my studies,' said I intentionally to probe him.

'O, my child, you have snatched words from my mouth; I wanted to tell you about the same. Grand Baba always exhorted you to get educated. I am glad your mind is returning to this idea. I will take you to the town school tomorrow for admission. I am not yet very old, and can continue to support you financially until you finish your schooling. Educated, you will be much better off in your worldly life. I am truly very pleased at your decision to resume studies. Today, Grand Baba must be very pleased in his Heavenly abode. He always wished to see you an accomplished man, capable of doing something substantial for the betterment of yourself and the society you are born in.'

'Guruji, if you permit me, could I request you something?' I asked.

'Yes, my child, tell me what you want.'

'Guruji, if you approve, I wish to go back for continuing my study in my previous school.'

'It would be better if you stayed here to study in the local school, but I will not force you. Wherever you are my blessings will always be with you.'

Hearing this, I put my head at his feet respectfully.

'Be noble, happy, and glorious in life,' he blessed me shuffling my head with his hand. He continued, 'My child, get up early in the morning, I have to perform a *puja* for your wellbeing. May evil eyes not cast on you! It was really good to have you here as you were great support for me. I don't know how long I am going to be alive after your departure as I no longer feel happy and peaceful.' His eyes were watery while saying so.

Next day, I finished all my assigned duties quite early. Seated on his asana in front of the sacred fireplace, Baba Magan Das was still chanting his mantras. After his puja, he got up and came to me enquiring, 'So, my child, are you ready for your journey back home?'

'Yes, Gurjui,' said I with folded hands.

'Well, you came alone here, but I will accompany you to your parents,' said Baba Magan Das.

Then calling a visitor, he asked him to warm some milk. Meanwhile, he kept collecting and packing some articles to take with him. Now, I was all set to embark on my journey back home. Holding me out an earthen cup filled with milk, Baba Magan Das said, 'my child, here is some milk for you, drink it as we have to walk a long way.'

While drinking milk, I looked around on various objects and articles placed here and there in the *Ashram.* Most of the items like wooden sandals, sacred tongs, and begging bowls for alms, *ektaras* (single wired guitar), bundle of plaits, conchs, and rosaries, belonging to both living as well as departed sadhus, had special significance in the ambience of *Ashram*. Since they had been associated with ashram's most spirited saints, it was auspicious for it to retain them as antiques.

The thought that I had myself been associated with these sacred articles deeply touched me. Despite this, I felt now happier with the idea of returning home. All my earlier resolve and determination not to ever return home had now been overtaken by the new thought. I had to start afresh from the point I had given up. I had mixed feelings for the future. Somewhere at the back of my mind, there was an anxiety sending shivers down my spine. I was troubled to think as to how I would cope up with the situation at school, if everything were the same as it was when I left. Simultaneously, I was not sure of my ability to meet the expectations of both my parents as well as Gurus who had been consistently goading me to rejoin the school. Of course, the decision to return home was mine. Education, as emphasized by Grand Baba and Baba Magan Das, I could obtain even while living with them. Perhaps, my infatuation towards my parents, siblings and other loved ones in the family had driven me to take this sudden decision to head back home.

Before departure, both Baba Magan Das and I walked to the Sacred Seat of Grand Baba in the hut and touched our heads against the ground in front of it. After this, we took leave of the other three hermits then present there.

Having traversed a journey of nearly two hours by bus, we reached the village. After hearing the news of our arrival, many people gathered at our Chaupal.

For the first few days, I did not visit my parents at home. Then one day, Baba instructed me to see my mother. He himself took me to the house. Once at home, my old memories, though mostly bitter ones, quickly flashed on my mind. Nothing had changed in here. It was still in the same half-dilapidated condition.

As we entered through the gate, my sister, Salesh, noticed us first. She immediately ran inside, perhaps to announce our arrival to mother. We were still standing in the middle of the foreyard when mother emerged from the house. She paid her obeisance to Baba Magan Das by bowing her head. Then, turning towards me, she looked at me. I could observe a glint of happiness in her eyes.

'Guruji, it is so kind of you to bring him over. For several months, my eyes have been yearning to have a glimpse of him. He seems to have forgotten us all. He has had several visits to the village, but he remained confined to the Chaupal and never bothered to see his father, brothers, the only sister and me. He has become stonehearted. Do I need to remind him that I am his mother who gave birth to him in this very house? It is now over a week since he is in the village, but he never felt like visiting us.' With this, mother, unable to control her emotions, burst out crying. My sister also joined her.

'O, *Mai* (mother), why are you crying? You should not be sad now. I have brought him back to you, and henceforth, he will remain with you. Don't cry; he will not become sadhu. Now, you must take care of him', said Baba Magan Das consoling mother.

On hearing this, mother stopped crying. Turning to Baba, she said with tearful eyes, 'No, no, Babaji, you are just making us believe that he has come back forever. He has indeed turned cruel and has no affection for his younger siblings. Most of the boys his age have got married. I also had some wishes to fulfill by him. I must be the most unlucky mother who could not hold her son back. Certainly, in our love and affection there was some deficiency that drove him away from us.'

'O, *Mai*, don't be so distressed, keep patience. Henceforth, your son will be with you.'

'*Guruji*, if what you are telling is true, we are really grateful to you.'

'Yes *mai,* this is true.'

Now, Mother appeared much relieved as if a heavy burden removed from her chest. Our house had become crowded, as a number of men, women and children had gathered there. Mother really looked happy. She kissed me many times on the forehead as if she had found her lost precious thing back. It felt as if I had returned here after centuries. Entering the room where I used to sleep in, I roved my eyes around and checked every corner of it. Pegs on the wall of the house, where I used to hang my satchel, my shirts and pantaloons, were still in the same place. The bed I would sleep on was also in the same position. Books in the open wooden almirah, totally covered by cobwebs were lying in a similar condition.

After leaving me with mother, Baba Magan Das walked out towards the Chaupal. My grandfather and other elders of the family were now waiting for a confirmation from him about whether I had really come back to stay with them henceforth permanently. All were delighted to see me back and rejoin them. A few minutes later, I also joined the Baba at the Chaupal. Showing his affection, my grandfather held me to his chest. Father surprisingly expressed no overt feeling of happiness. By nature, he always appeared to be hard-faced. Even in his happiest moments with his children, he never exhibited expressions or gestures like kissing, caressing or holding them to his chest. His being an exception, the whole household was full of joy, witnessed in a family only on rare occasions like birth of a baby boy, marriages, etc. The night passed with a happy note. Next morning, Baba Magan Das performed a special puja at our house. After that, all family members alongwith several other persons from the community dined together. There was joyous atmosphere all around. I, however, was having mixed feelings about my future. Traumatized, scared and confused, I began to worry if I would be able to prove myself and achieve something worthwhile. I asked myself, 'What would happen to my dreams if I don't do well in studies and contribute something substantial to transform my family and the community, as that was the motivating factor of my coming back.'

Two days passed and so did the nights. Third day morning, everyone in the house, except me, had got up. I woke up only when someone shook me by shoulders. On opening my eyes, I found mother sitting beside me on the charpoy with her one hand caressing my head.

She said, 'My son, everyone has taken bath; you also get ready quickly to join for puja.'

Saying this, she left to attend to the household chores. For a few moments, I remained on my cot looking up at the ceiling and thinking about the discipline and regime with which I used to start my day until only three days ago. Things like rising early, taking bath, blowing the conch, meditating etc. were no longer part of my routine now.

Pushing these thoughts behind, I somehow left the bed. Immediately, I picked up a metal pot full of water and walked towards the jungle to ease myself. Having relieved myself near a rivulet flowing past the village, I rushed back to a tube-well to have a quick bath. Within a short while, I got home, where everyone was waiting for me to join in the puja. I hurriedly took my seat on the ground near the altar. Baba Magan Das was chanting *shabar* (self-created) mantras of Kabir, Ravi Das and Nanak. Everybody present listening to him with concentration. I had been hearing and chanting these mantras for over two years. Guru Magan Das then recited *Guruvani* (words spoken by great Gurus). At the *Ashram*, on umpteen occasions, I had heard Guruvani from the Grand Baba and several other saints. I was skeptic about that the *Guruvani* would have any impact upon persons present there. Even many saints and priests hardly conducted themselves according to them, let alone the ordinary people. That became obvious to me at the Kumbh Fair. I sat transfixed near the *Havan* (Altar). After the ceremony, *Prasad* (offering to the Lord) was distributed, first among the participants and then to the passers by. Now was the time to have meal. During the feast, someone made a mention about my admission in school. Thereupon, Guruji said, 'My real purpose of bringing him back is his schooling. So, take him there today itself. I will stay put till he settles down.'

I left for the school soon after breakfast-cum-lunch, without waiting for anyone to accompany me. By the time I reached there, the school had closed for the day. I happened to know one of the teachers, close to Makhan Lal Singh, the teacher from my village. Notwithstanding his proximity to Makhan Lal, this teacher had never shown any apparent bias against me. I decided to visit him at his residence, next door to the school.

Chaudhry Bagendra Singh was the senior-most teacher in the school. Several teachers, currently teaching in the school, had been his students. Reaching his palatial house, I knocked at the door. A domestic servant, unlatching the door from inside, peeped out and asked, 'Who are you and whom do you want to see?'

'I am Preet. I am from Bhagwan Puri. I want to meet Chaudhry Sahib in connection with my admission,' said I requesting the servant to allow me to see the teacher if he was around.

'Please wait, let me find out if Sahib would see you,' the servant said closing the door on me and walked inside. Within a few seconds, she came back. Opening the door, she asked me to come in. Stepping in, I stopped short of the porch where Chaudhry Sahib, presently Vice-Principal, was seated in his comfort chair, clad in the white *Dhoti* and *Kurta*. He was an orthodox Gandhian. Though he himself was a landlord, his mother and wife used to weave daily on the spinning wheel. That day also, both of them were spinning. Seeing me in the porch, Bagendra gestured me to come in. Pointing towards a stool standing next to him, he asked me to take the seat. To know the purpose of my visit, he asked, 'Tell me what brings you here?'

'Sir, I seek re-admission in your college, I pleaded.'

'Why re-admission now? You already wasted two long years. Where have you been all this time? I heard you had taken Sanyas. Is that true? How will you now be making up for these lost years? I do not think you will be able to pass high school, as you have been out of touch with your studies so long.'

'Sir, please grant me admission, I will try my best to make up for the lost time and catch up with other students,' urged I.

For a while, he remained quiet and then asked me, 'Have you brought along some papers like old report cards?'

'No Sir, I don't have any paper with me, and I really don't know if there was any available at home too. Sir, I was X standard student of your college until two years ago. You can find out my personal particulars from the school archive. But please grant me admission,' I submitted.

Then, I waited for a response. His eyes still glued to the newspaper, he said, 'Okay, come tomorrow around 8 A.M. and do not forget to bring your fees.'

On hearing this, I was greatly relieved. In these two years, all my contemporaries had left the school after passing out. My juniors were now in the same class in which I was going to sit! A feeling of guilt, of course, overcame me for a moment, but soon I somehow managed to free myself from it. On way back home, the same very thoughts about my plans, dreams and ambitions kept dominating my mind. Now, my greatest worry was about my ability to adjust in the changed atmosphere.

Back home, I went straight to the Chaupal to inform Baba Magan Das about my admission. There was no one at the Chaupal. My mother, who was tending to she-buffaloes in the backyard, noticed me searching for Guruji. She walked up to me and said, 'My son, after you left for the school, Guruji also left for his *Ashram* saying that he would visit us only during the paddy harvest.'

Disappointed, confused and saddened by his sudden departure, I kept mulling over as to why he had left in this manner without meeting me for the last time. Now that he had left, I could do nothing.

Next day, I got up quite early. Having finished all my daily activities like bath, meditation, a little walking, as I used to do in the Ashram, I left for the college sharply at 6.30 AM. At first, I visited vice-principal's office. Handing out an application form to me, he said, 'Fill in the application form and deposit it, along with fee with the clerk in the administrative department.'

Without any delay, I completed the necessary formalities and after submitting my application, I went back to inform Chaudary Saheb about it. He asked me to sit in his class.

Teaching sessions were in full swing. Despite my best efforts, I, however, was not able to focus on studies. High school exams were drawing closer. I made all possible efforts to focus on my studies but to no avail. I did not want to waste another year as I had already lost two precious years while professing asceticism. Fear of failure in the examination had gripped my mind. In school, preparatory leave had been announced. My classmates, however, were regularly visiting the school to clear their doubts with the teachers. One day, I also went to the school to meet my maths teacher for the purpose. Although, not a good student in maths, I was trying hard to clear my high school. While the maths teacher was solving the problems of other students, he asked me to wait. When he finished with them, I walked up to him with a request to clear my doubts about a few problems. Suddenly, the teacher, for reasons best known to him, giving vent to his anger hurled my notebook upon me. I was stunned and could not make out as to what had gone wrong. He then stood up and walked out of the classroom giving a bad look to me.

Crestfallen, frustrated and depressed, I returned home. I appeared in the exams with full preparation with all my ability. I did quite well in other subjects; however, I failed in mathematics, my Achilles heel.

On seeing my result, I again ran away from the college and returned to it only a few days later to see that I was not able to focus on studies at all. Reading the tension reflected over my face, my father had probably guessed my difficulty. However, he forced me to continue to attend the college regularly. There was no interest left for studies.

In the meantime, a new mathematics teacher joined the school. Fortunately, our class got him as Math teacher in place of Phundan Lal. He was a far cry from the latter. Within a short period, Hastendar Tyagi, the new teacher, made his observation about me. He called me aside after the class was over and asked, 'I notice your mind is not in the class. What is wrong with you? Are you scared of mathematics? Or you have no interest in studies at all?'

'Sir, I really want to study. However, I have lost interest because of my weakness in mathematics. Honestly speaking, I haven't yet learned anything in this subject. I have serious difficulty in grasping mathematics. If, somehow, I overcome this problem, I am sure I will be doing well in my studies overall,' said I opening my heart to him.

'By the way, Phundan Lal is a good teacher. Since you have been attending his class for so long, how come you have not been able to learn mathematics?' demanded Hastendar Singh.

'Sir, if you permit me, I wish to confide into you about the background and reasons as to why Phundan Lal has been harassing me in his class.'

'Well, don't be sacred, treat me like your brother and speak your mind. I will try my best to remove fear from your mind to help you focus better on your studies,' said he very affectionately.

On hearing his sympathetic words, I narrated all that I had undergone through all these years. After hearing about my ordeal, Hastendar Singh said, 'It's not yet too late. You have nearly three months to go for your annual examinations. I can see you have no problem barring mathematics, and I take this responsibility to make you prepare in a manner that you pass mathematics without difficulty. I advise you to come to my residence from tomorrow for extra tutoring.'

Upon receiving such assurance from him, I felt much relieved. However, somewhere at the back of my mind, I was still skeptical about my ability to hone my skills in such a short time to the extent that I would be able to score passing marks in maths.

'Yes sir, but what time I should come to you?' I enquired.

'It is up to you to decide. As for me, I have no problem. You can come anytime after the school or early in the morning at 7 A.M.,' suggested Hastendar Singh affectionately. I chose the time immediately after school hours.

First day, Hastendar Singh gave me lesson in geometry. He broadly explained how to solve the problems and then gave me a few ones to test me. As I had focused well on the solution methods explained by him, I easily solved the problems by quickly applying the right formula. It helped me in regaining my self-confidence. Teacher also had now got an idea about the level of my skills. Having finished geometry, he then shifted to trigonometry, algebra and then pure arithmetic. Within a short span of one month, I was feeling very comfortable with the subject. The phobia I had developed in it over the last three-four years appeared to be fast evaporating. With my progress, Hastendar Singh was more happy and satisfied than me.

Annual examinations for class X were now round the corner. One day, Hastendar Singh called me in his office and said, 'My dear, the exams will begin in a month from now. You should have no problem in clearing your maths paper. So, you better prepare for other subjects.'

By now, I had developed so much interest in mathematics that in the days left before the examination, I wanted to learn more and more.

'Sir, I am quite confident in other subjects. My only worry has always been this mathematics. I want to make sure that I clear the subject comfortably. Therefore, I do not want to take a chance and would like to continue receiving tuitions from you. My preparation in all subjects is progressing well, along with mathematics,' I insisted.

'Well, I can see you have improved a lot in maths and your confidence level appears to have made you more ambitious. Anyway, it is good. I have no objection to your continuous tuitions, particularly when you are at ease in other subjects,' said Hastendar Singh.

Examinations came. I performed far better in all subjects including mathematics than my own expectations. When results were out, I was amazed to see my marks in mathematics. I had scored 60% – my highest score in any subject! Hastendar Singh was very happy with my success. When college re-opened and I went to collect my mark sheet, Hastendar Singh, presenting me to other students, said, 'Look here at Preet, who was so scared of mathematics. But within a couple of months, he picked up so well that now he has emerged the second-highest scorer.'

I thanked Hastendar Singh from my heart for my success. Students were looking at each other, gaping. Holding my mark sheets when I came out, some of them even asked me, 'How could it be possible for you to score so well in mathematics especially when you were too weak in it?'

Telling them the truth I said, 'It is all because of Hastendar Singh, our teacher. He provided me with tuitions for a couple of months before examinations. During this short period, he was able to instill in me a great amount of confidence enabling me to grasp the subject fast. It really helped me in honing my skills in a manner that I began to find the subject truly very interesting. What I could not learn in ten years, Hastendar Singh has taught me all that within a couple of months. So what I have achieved in this unique subject is all because of his genius and not mine.'

Meanwhile, all students and teachers in the school came to know about my unexpected success in the maths. Given my previous record of performance in the subject, all teachers, except Hastendar Singh, and students were puzzled at my success and made all sorts of speculations. Overnight, Hastendar Singh became the most popular and sought-after commodity in the school. Parents whose children were going to appear for the high school examination soon began thronging his residence in large number with tuition requests for their wards.

My performance in mathematics was truly a miracle for me. It changed my world altogether. I had never even imagined doing so well in this otherwise boring and scaring subject for me. After passing High School, all my dreams appeared to have come true. Now the way up for my higher education was quite clear. My success worked like a great booster, encouraging me further to strengthen my resolve, determination and will to do even better in my higher studies. After this, I began to focus on my studies with full perseverance and dedication. I continued my education in the same school for another two years to clear my XIth and XIIth grades.

With Hastendar Singh's reputation rising up as a far more intelligent and competent maths teacher, Phundan Lal, my tormentor in the school for over three years, began getting heartburns. His tuition business, over which he had so far enjoyed monopoly, had almost collapsed, as over eighty percent of the students who earlier took tuitions from him, had moved to Hastendar Singh. Phundan Lal would make sarcastic remarks at me whenever I happened to pass by him. He would say, *'Humn, ab to tu bara sahib banne ja raha hain. Tumhara dada, Dhyani Chamar to tumhare baare mein bare bare sapne dekh raha hoga.'* (Humn, now you are going to be a big officer. Your Grandfather, Dhyani Cobbler must be having big dreams about you.) On another occasions, looking at some other student but targeting me obliquely, he commented, 'I know how one or two students cleared their maths papers last year. I fail to understand how a student, who could learn nothing in three years, was not only able to clear his maths paper so easily but with flying colours.'

I knew his comments were directed at me. However, ignoring him I just walked past him. Unable to digest my success and because of his deep-rooted hatred and jealousy towards me, Phundan Lal was drawing altogether a different meaning from it. There was no more any opportunity for him to persecute me persistently. His evil-designs had failed to force me to abandon the school. Interestingly, he continued to evince interest in knowing about my performance in studies through other teachers even though I was no longer his student. I was now doing quite well in studies. My bad days now appeared to be ending. This was my last year in the college as I was going to appear for my Intermediate exams (12th Grade). My spectacular success in the Intermediate examination further dampened Phundan Lal's enthusiasm to crush my resolve.

After a tumultuous period of 8 years, I was now all set to leave the school. There were many sweet and sour memories to carry along. During this period, many funny things took place at the school. It still makes me laugh when I remember the incidents occurred at the school during that period.

Although most of the students hailed from rural areas, a sizeable number, however, was from town's trading community. Boys from farmer families hardly paid any attention towards studies. Most of their time, they spent on teasing the whitish color boys with cherubic cheeks and well-shaped and rounded buttocks. There were rumours about some of the adolescent boys in the school that they were after certain boys. On a few occasions, their involvement in sodomy cases had come to the knowledge of principal and teachers. However, the school management, in view of their family influence and position, could not summon courage to take any stringent action against them. Interestingly, most of the students they chased belonged to the trading community.

According to the rumours, some boys of the local traders would themselves invite the tough looking boys, mostly from the rural areas, to their homes over tea and snacks to seek sexual gratification. I considered them just rumors as adolescents were always in the habit of enjoying themselves by spreading these kinds of unfounded rumors during school days. However, my perception about these boys changed when Jeetu, a boy from neighbouring village, who used to commute with us to and from school, revealed an interesting story about a boy of his class. Jeetu said, 'Oh buddies, do you know what happened yesterday? Listen yaar, Nitish, that boy of a cloth merchant from my class invited me to his house for lunch after school at 12:30 hrs. After lunch, he insisted to spend the afternoon at his residence. His father at that time was at the shop. After feeding us, his mother took lunch for his father at the shop and while leaving she asked me to stay with Nitish for the noon until her return. After she left, both Nitish and I, stepped on to the double bed in Nitish's bedroom. For a while, we kept talking bizarre things about school, teachers and other students. It was summer time. The room was very cool. It had beautiful drapers on the windows and a pedestal fan in one corner. The bed had very good linen spread over it. In the cool breeze of the fan, I fell asleep. I then felt somebody fondling my crotch. I woke up and found that bloody Nitish had turned his back towards me with his trousers down to his knees and his ass completely exposed. Pretending to be asleep, he at the same time was trying to unbutton my trousers. Lying still, I made no movement; by now he had unbuttoned my trousers. Having done this, he held my dick in his hand and started massaging it. Within a few seconds I felt intense hardness in it. Nitish then held it and put into his asshole. Having done so, he began to rub against it moving slowly back and forth. Instantly, I found myself on top of Nitish who lay on his stomach. I wildly gave a few hard pushes into his back and then collapsed aside gasping to breath. I then hurriedly put on my trousers and left his house. Arrey yaar, these shahri (towny) boys are great gandu. They can be easily bugged for no price. Instead, they would feed you and pay too for doing it!'

Jeetu was a loose-mouth. Within a couple of days, everybody in the school had got to know about the incident.

After what Jeetu revealed, we also began to believe that it was not an isolated case and that the practice of homosexuality was widespread in the school. Subsequently, similar stories about boys from rural background engaged with several boys from the town also came to light.

As far as homosexuality was concerned, even fourty years ago, India was much ahead of many developed countries in the world! That people never admitted it to be prevalent in society was an all together different matter.

23

A Girl in the Village

There was a beautiful girl with heavy bosom, cherubic cheeks and well- rounded derriere, provocative enough to attract young boys of the village. She was unusually liberal in all respects. A very good thing, which I liked the most about her, was that she never believed in castcism or untouchability that was so common in the village society. She would mix up freely with girls and boys of all castes. In fact, she would gather titillating information from girls her age about their crushes towards young boys. Elders always used to point their finger at the free and frequent movement of this girl throughout all communities. For three to four years, the girl played a postwoman for carrying love-letters exchanged between young boys and girls and kept the young village community fully informed of all that was going on among young girls and boys of various castes and blocks.

Preparations for Ram Lila (a stage show based on the life of Lord Rama) were on. All the young girls and boys in the village would look forward eagerly to this annual event lasting for a fortnight. For the show, villagers brought artistes *from eastern UP to play various characters from Ramayana. While elderly viewed it as a socio-religious organization, for the youth, it was an occasion purely for entertainment. They would utilize this fortnight as an opportunity to keep their promises they had made with each other for several months during the year.*

There was a place in the village earmarked for Ramlila show where residents erected a stage and decorated it with colorful and glittery curtains and multi-hued tiny electric bulbs. The entire Ramlila period was indeed a great fun. The annual show had become the most longed-for occasion for the young boys and girls to meet each other. However, as explained elsewhere, the basic purpose behind organizing *Ramlila* was that of social engineering and strengthening moral value system. Alas, it was not so. To the best of my mind, the show played an altogether different role insofar as my village was concerned.

One day, when the show was on, this girl brought a letter from an upper caste girl to deliver to a friend of mine. Coincidently, my friend also belonged to an upper caste. What the girl wrote in the letter was unthinkable. The letter gave us a shock of the day, as we even in our wildest dreams never thought that a girl from such a wealthy family holding high reputation through out the area could be so frustrated. She had expressed fearlessly about her suppressed sexual urges. What the girl wrote in Hindi, its rough translation is below:

'My dear Anand, Preet and Vinod,

I wrote this letter surreptitiously last night when all our family members had left for Ramlila. I stayed at home with my mother under the pretext to complete my homework. In fact, I wanted to deliver this letter personally to you threesome, but I am sending this to you all through Munia. Please remember, nobody should get a wind of all what I am saying and writing herein. This should strictly remain a secret. Munia, of course, knows about it.

Now read carefully. Tonight I plan to come down to Ramlila. A little later when Ramlila begins, I, under some pretext, would come back home along with Munia. My youngest brother will escort us up to the wooden gate of our haveli. You three just wait in the adjacent cattle yard and when my brother has gone back after leaving us there, both me and Munia, will come over to you there.'

Initially, we were not prepared to believe that a girl like her whose voice we hardly ever heard earlier could write such kind of letter. Our hearts kept pounding with excitement throughout the day. However, we also feared that it could be a plan to trap us. Nevertheless, we were waiting eagerly for the evening and then beginning of Ramlila. Meanwhile, spectators from village and neighbouring areas had begun to throng the venue. By 9:30 pm, all visitors and members of the organizing committee of Ramlila were in their place.

Standing in the last row of the audience, we were roving our eyes around focusing mainly at the rooftops of the houses, lined along the main street of the village, where female spectators used to sit, but found *Munia* and this girl nowhere in sight. Around 10:30 hrs, one of us noticed *Munia* waving at us overlooking from one of the rooftops. Seeing her signal, Vinod and Anand immediately headed towards the place the girl had indicated in her letter. I stayed behind. I then noticed Munia and the girl climbing down the bamboo stairs put up along the wall of the houses. After coming down on to the brick road past the house, Munia called one of the *Rajput* boys, who at once appeared there asking, 'what do you want, *Munia*?'

'Actually, she is not feeling well and wants to go home. Could you please call her brother to accompany us back home?' asked Munia, pointing to the shy looking girl.

'OK, wait here', said he, and went to inform he girl's younger brother. Within a couple of minutes, her brother came to escort them to their house. I kept waiting there for another couple of minutes after their departure. Meanwhile, chairperson of the Ramlila committee appeared there and engaged in talks with people watching the show from the last row. I also kept listening to him nonchalantly without paying any attention to what he was talking. I somehow wanted to escape from there to join my friends. However, that bastard man—this is what I was thinking that moment—kept me bound to his weird talks and I saw no chance to escape. After one hour or so, under the pretext of emptying my bladder, I got up to leave. After walking a few steps further into the direction where viewers urinated, I took a turn into the opposite direction. Panting, I reached the place where my friends should have waited for me. On reaching there, I looked around, but discovered that no one was there. Then, I heard some whispering sounds coming from the cattle-barracks. By the time I was moving towards cattle yard, I noticed some figure emerging from the yard gate. I swiftly moved towards the gate. It was pitch-dark. Then I heard someone calling me. I turned around and saw Munia standing at the other end of the door. I asked her in a whispering voice, 'Where are Anand and Vinod?'

'They have already left after doing', said she whisperingly.

'Where have they gone? I did not find them there', asked I.

'No, no, baba, they left nearly one hour ago', said she.

'Both of them did with us turn by turn and we both are still waiting for you, please come', Munia said.

I for a moment was motionless. I was unable to decide whether to go ahead or not. Then within the next few seconds, although fearful, I wished to go ahead. I had just moved a few steps ahead when I heard some people approaching us. It felt, my feet had frozen and my body numbed completely. Then Munia warned, 'You run away, they are coming this way'.

Having said this, she herself rushed towards the yard, and disappeared. I quickly took the opposite direction towards our chaupal where grandfather would sleep. Luckily, that time, grandfather was in deep slumber. Silently, I stepped into my cot and soon fell asleep.

Next morning, on way to school when I met my friends, I did not talk to them. Breaking the ice, my friend Anand asked me, 'Where had you gone last night, yaar? We waited for you for nearly an hour but you did not turn up. We thought something must have happened. One of us came out twice to check if you were around, but you were nowhere in sight. After having finished, when we were still looking for you, the girls advised us to leave saying they will wait for you. We hope you met them. They were scared that if they did not entertain you, you might disclose it.'

Amazingly, I was not even thinking about all that transpired the previous night and I let it go.

In the evening, when I was taking bath at the tube-well owned by Munia's family, I was amazed to hear the news she brought to me from Bela. Munia arrived there under the pretext of conducting a pair of buffaloes for drinking water.

Leaving the cattle near the water tank, she walked up to me and said, 'Bela is scared that you might tell out all that happened yesterday between your friends Anand, Vinod and us.'

Despite my assurance, she said, 'No, no, Bela is really scared and does not believe you. We, therefore, offer to entertain you during one of the nights till Ramlila session goes on.'

I was a little puzzled to give a firm reply. To find me quiet, she said, 'Your silence indicates that you would definitely spill the beans.'

I tried my best to assure her, but the girl was not convinced and persisted with her proposal. From her behaviour, it was clear that the girls were very scared and wanted their sexual escapades to remain shrouded by bringing me on their side. It was astonishing to note that the girls from such conservative families could indulge in such adventures despite living in the secure and protected environment behind the four high walls of their havelis.

On Munia's insistence, I agreed to meet them on one of the following days. The very thought of Bela's reticient and over shy nature confounded me a lot. However, after the incident, I knew about the real self behind the veneer of her façade. Surprisingly, her behaviour towards me had now changed. Earlier, while going to school, she never looked towards boys, who funnily chased girls. All that had changed now! She would now always look for an excuse to talk to the boys.

A few days remained for Ramlila to be over. One night, when Ramlila was on stage, Vinod left the venue with the excuse that he was not feeling well. Both Anand and I sat there throughout the show. Next morning, there were whispers all around about Munia and Vinod. After leaving us behind in the show, Vinod had straight gone to the cattle yard where Munia, as per their prior arrangement, was already there waiting for him. When Vinod, with his one hand wrapped around Munia's waist, was conducting her into the cattle yard, a Rajput boy from neighbourhood saw them. Hiding himself behind the wall of the yard, the boy waited there to see what was going to transpire between them. Once inside, Vinod soon got engaged with Munia. Meanwhile, the Rajput boy tiptoed to the yard and lifting himself up, he peeped in through the half-broken wall window. Although, unable to see clearly and completely in the dark, he heard them moaning and groaning. It did not take him long to comprehend as to what was going on between them. He swiftly rushed back to the Ramlila venue to break the news to the chairperson of the organizing committee. In view of the sensitivity of the matter, the chairperson waited for the Ramlila to be over to discuss the matter with his community persons. Meanwhile, he sent two of his men along with the Rajput boy to check the veracity of the information. The threesome reached the cattle yard soon as it was only a few yards away from the Ramlila stage. That time, Munia and Vinod were coming out of the yard after the act. Realising that some persons were approaching them, Munia and Vinod hastily parted ways. Vinod moved fast in the direction of his haveli without looking behind whereas Munia quickly vanished into her chaupal just adjacent to the yard. The two men sent by the chairperson returned, confirming what the Rajput boy had reported earlier. They said that they themselves witnessed the boy and girl coming together out of the yard.

As it was late night, management committee members decided to discuss the matter next morning with the parents of Vinod and Munia. Accordingly, the chairperson and village sarpanch together held a closed door meeting with both parents. Ofcourse, the the boy and girl were also present.

When confronted, instead of confessing, Vinod retorted, 'I was not alone; there were two others also before me.'

'But we saw you only', said one of the witnesses.

'No, no, they had already left', snapped Vinod. All this while, Munia was standing in a corner with her head bowed.

'Who were the other two you are referring to?' asked the chairperson.

'Anand and Preet', replied Vinod.

'Oh! Now I understand why you three are always together. You are indulging in these heinous acts during this sacred period of Ramlila. We will take care of you later, but first let us talk to that Dhyani Chamar about his grandson. A Dalit boy having affair with an upper caste girl! Unbelievable! Unthinkable!'

Suddenly, girl's father, rising from his seat and summoning blood shots in his eyes, rushed towards Munia. Hitting her on the face, he angrily said, 'Haramzadi! You have become so insolent that you are not even afraid of coming out alone in the dead dark night. You have defaced us. How long you have been blackening your face?' tell me.

Leaving them behind, the chairperson, alongwith the village sarpanch went straight to our chaupal where grandfather was engaged in discussion with some other visitors. The sarpanch signaled grandfather to come aside. Following the sarpanch, Grandfather asked him, 'Sarpanch, what is the matter you want to talk about privately?'

A little away from the chaupal, they walked into the backyard. Taking grandfather into a corner, the sarpanch said,

'Dhyani, we know you consider yourself at par with upper castes. We have been putting up with this misplaced notion for decades; but now you tend to cross the threshold. We will not permit you and your grandchildren to trample upon our honour. That is why I am here to inform you about an incident involving your grandson. He deserves severe punishment to educate him about the consequences of dicing with us. We advise you to control him; otherwise he might pay for it with his life.'

'Sarpanch, are you not aware of my temperament? Come on! Tell me clearly the crime you think my grandson is involved in. If you don't, I am not going to accept this non-sense any more.'

Getting a little closer to grandfather, he whispered something into his ears. Grandfather was listening to him, gaping and nodding. A little later, grandfather said, 'If that is the case, I am not going to defend him. However, you need to verify the matter thoroughly before jumping to a conclusion. Given the recent background of his life spent in the Ashram, I firmly believe my grandson will never indulge in such things. We, therefore, need to interrogate the other boy named in the case.'

That time, I was away in the fields. Anand was very much at his home. Therefore, he and his father were sent for. After some grilling, Anand revealed that he and I were present at the Ramlila throughout. He named a few villagers as witnesses with whom we were sharing the seats. The villagers confirmed to the sarpanch and grandfather that Anand and I were present throughout the show, whereas Vinod had disappeared within half an hour.

Hearing this, grandfather flared up and said, 'Sarpanch, you should be very careful in a serious case like this. Without verifying the facts, you very easily dragged my grandson into the case. I know he keeps company with those two boys but that does not mean that he would be involved in every activity of theirs. Now it is quite clear to you that neither my grandson nor that boy Anand is involved in this. May be, the other boy is deliberately trying to pass the buck by involving others. Nevertheless, I would accost him. I would advise him to keep from such characters. Now go and control that silly girl.'

The sarpanch left without saying anything further. I had returned from the fields. I had a bundle of fodder on my head when I entered the courtyard. Without waiting for me to unload, grandfather said, 'You have come to make me see this day. I have never bowed before anyone in my life but you are bound to bring shame on me if you keep company with those blithers. I can put up with any mistake on your part but not like the one brought to my notice today. I warn you to be careful in future.'

Dumbfounded, I stood there stretching my mind to make out what mistake I had committed. Summoning courage, I asked grandfather the reason for reproving me. 'Go away and don't argue. You better mend your ways and keep good company. If you don't correct yourself, you would be ruining your life,' said he imperatively. I immediately walked away. Later in the day, when I came to know about the whole story, I heaved a sigh of relief.

Grandfather was in the habit of poking fun at upper castes by citing instances of their sexual adventures, like an uncle having intimate relations with his own niece, a girl indulging in sexuality with her own cousin, a father-in-law having an affair with his own daughter-in-law and so on. While he would narrate these stories, people would listen to him in amusement. No one ever came to know about his own sexual escapades.

Once I noticed grandfather, doing something that left me perplexed and mystified. There was a *Thakurain* in the village who, in relation, was grandfather's aunty. She was a widow and must be one or two years older than him. She was a frequent visitor to him and used to indulge in long conversations with him. Nobody could ever make out the beginning and end as well as the level of their conversations. Out of deference, grandfather would always offer her a seat on the upper edge of the *charpoy*. On occasions, the old *Thakurain* would sit in the charpoy facing grandfather in a pose that her genitals were completely on show. Grandfather never called her aunty, whereas she would always address him by name.

It was the month of April. Harvesting season for the wheat crop was on. During this time of the year, the entire village gave a deserted look as most of the folks were out at work in the fields. One day, the *Thakurain* was on her usual visit to grandfather. No family member was at home. I had just returned from school. I hurriedly hung my satchel on a peg in the wall and settled down for my lunch cooked and arranged by mother for me before she left for the fields. I went straight to the chaupal after my lunch. At this time, grandfather was supposed to be sitting or sleeping on his charpoy in the verandah. Not finding him in the *charpoy*, I looked around. Suddenly, I heard the creaking sounds of charpoy coming from inside the chaupal through the only slightly slammed wooden door. I turned around and peeped into the room. What I witnessed was unthinkable.

Grandfather, lying on top of the old Thakurain, was moving gently and slowly back and forth, making short throaty sounds. I at once stepped back and left towards the fields. Throughout the way, I remained occupied with the scene witnessed a while ago. I baffled more at the thought of whether at the age of seventy plus, one was able to perform this act. Interestingly, the old Thakurain was in her late seventies and it was revealing to see that both of them were enjoying at this age.

24

Fascination Towards the Girl

It was the month of March. Holi, the Festival of Colors, was approaching. Students had begun playing colours with each other. Around this time, an interesting incident involving Bela happened to me. Bela, so far a sheepish and quiet girl had suddenly turned vivacious. One day, she alongwith few other girls, was returning from school. I was moving behind them maintaining a little distance. As their moment was slow, I thought to go ahead of them. I began stepping up. When I approached them, Bela, swiftly moving towards me, pulled out an inkpot from her sachet and before I could react, poured it all over me, wishing me 'Holi Mubarak'. Although taken aback by this kind of unexpected display of playfulness, in my heart, I was delighted to attract the attention of a girl like Bela. Always conscious of their status, Bela's parents were certain that their daughter would never dare to get close to a low caste boy.

At my heart, I was thanking the girl for spraying color on me. Those days, it was no less maddening and an honor to have a high caste girl playing colors with a Dalit boy. I trully felt elated and overwhelmed after the incident!

Next morning, when I was returning from the fields after ablution, I found Munia waiting for me at her tube-well where she would come regularly this time to deliver to her father. She waved at me to stop. I walked to the well pretending as if I was going there for taking bath. I sat down near the pipe and began splashing my mouth with water. After serving her father tea, she walked past me, dropping a piece of paper. I pocketed it immediately and walked swiftly back home. At home, I straight went into the corner where I used to keep my books and sachet. My mother was still busy with preparing buttermilk — my favourite morning drink. Curiously, I hurriedly took out that piece of paper and tried to glance at the message. In the dim light of our muddy house, I could not read it clearly and correctly. In the meantime, mother called out, 'Son, buttermilk (Maththa) is ready; come and drink it'.

I quickly put the paper back into my pocket and came out into the front yard, where mother was waiting with a large glass of buttermilk in her right hand, and a piece of jaggery in the left one. As I was curious to know the contents of the letter, I hurriedly gulped all the stuff down in one go and wiping my mouth, went back into the room. I told my mother, 'Mother, let me arrange my school sachet first, then only will I take my breakfast.'

'OK, arrange your bag soon as you are getting late for school', said mother. Reaching inside, I leisurely took out the letter out of my pocket, and began reading it thoroughly. It read as under:

'Mere Sanware yaar,

Kal holi khelne mein bara maza aaya. Bahut dino se tumse baat-cheet karne ki ichchaa ho rahi thi, Kintu aisa mauka hi naheen mil raha tha. Tum us din Ram Lila ki baat abhi bhoole to naheen. Mujhe vaastav mein bahut achcha laga. Bahut der tak tumhari prateeksha ki, kintu tum naheen ayae. Main chahti hoon ki meri tumhari mulakat jaldi ho. Mera vishwas kijiyega ki us din raat bhar main yeh samajh kar naheen so payi ki tum yeh rahassya kissi se keh na do. Mujhse vaayda karo ki tum kabhi bhi yeh baat kissi se naheen kahoge. Meri taraf se tum kabhi bhi jab kabhi bhi mauka mile, tum wah kar sakte ho. Ab aage holi aa rahi hai. Hamare milne ka is se achcha muaka aur kya ho sakta hai. Main Munia ke haath tumhe suchit karoongi aur us jagah ka naam bhi bataoongi jahaan par hum mil sakte hain. Kintu kripya yeh baat kissi ko batlane ki koshish kabhi naheen karna. Tumko meri kasam.

Tumhari Bela

(My brownie friend,

I enjoyed playing holi with you yesterday. For long, I had been wishing to speak with you, but was not getting any chance. I hope you have not forgotton the incident on that Ramlila night. I really liked it. We waited for so long, but you did not turn up. I wish seeing you soon. Belive me, fearful that you would let out the secret, I could not sleep that night. Please promise that you would never disclose it to anyone. You can have me whenever you want. Holi is around the corner. There cannot be a better occasion for us to meet each other. I will let you know, through Munia about our next meeting place. But, please keep it up to you.

Bela)

Holi was still several days away. However, after receiving this letter, I was feeling excited. My spirits were suddenly high. There was a sense of satisfaction - something incomprehensible. I had never experienced this kind of happiness before. Maybe, this metamorphosis was due to the spring season. There was a belief that youth were more amorous and romantic during this time. No one knew how far that was true, but almost everyone in the countryside thought so. They would say, '*Lagi Chait ki paanche, Aur Mari Gadhiyya nache.*' (At the onset of the fifth day of the month of Chaitra, corresponding to early-March, even a weak she-donkey starts dancing with joy to attract its mate). I thought cupid's arrow had struck me too. I visualized Bela all the time - sleeping, eating, reading, and walking. Even when I was engaged in something very important, she would suddenly appear in my mind, intensifying my passion for her.

One day, while going to school, she walked past me and uttered feebly, 'Tonight, I will come with Munia to meet you.'

'It is okay.' I said.

Meanwhile, residents had begun celebrations. There would be long sessions of drum-beating and singing amorous songs - a feature of Festival of Colors - throughout the night. Most of young boys and girls were enjoying the occasion making great fun. One week passed in waiting but Bela did not appear there. All of a sudden, all the ecstasy evaporated causing a great shock to the whole village community.

25

The Girl Creates Scandal

Through out the village, men and women, belonging to various communities were whispering among themselves. Yet the young fellows had no idea of what so serious had happened that elders were discussing in suppressed voices. Then the rumour, that Bela was pregnant, spread like wildfire through the village. Though Thakurs pretended that there happened nothing unusual in their colony, the news of pregnancy of their chieftain's daughter had shocked and shaken them deeply. They considered their chieftain's honour as the honour of their whole community. Bearing this in mind, an elderly Thakur came out with a face saving formula. He knew an old woman belonging to Dhanuk community (Dalit caste), who in her young days served various communities as mid-wife helping many women in giving birth to babies. In her old days, this mid-wife was living an impoverished life. Moreover, being issueless, there was no one in the family to support her. She lived with one of her castemen. The supporting family had three grown-up daughters, however, due to the abject poverty; it was difficult to marry them off. The head of the family at one point was close to the Thakur, who had illicit relationship with the former's wife. Approaching his old Dhanuk friend, the Thakur said, 'I have a proposal for you. If you accept it, I will help you in marrying off your young daughters. I need your assistance. You have to send the old lady with me to my house.'

'No, no. I have already paid a heavy price for my sins that I might have committed in my previous life. That is the reason why God has pushed me into dismal poverty. To top it all, I have three daughters I am always anxious of marrying them off. This old woman is a great support for my family. It is because of her benevolence that I have somehow managed to bring my children up. We can never forget her sacrifices. Had Chunno not been there to support us, I would have died long back leaving my family destitute. She supported us at a time when my family was in dire need of financial assistance. At that critical juncture of my life, Chunno Maa (Mother) gave me all what she had with her. She is not only playing as mother, but she actually is so for my children and me. She is looking after my daughters as grandmother. She is even negotiating with some of her old relatives to arrange my elder daughter's marriage. Sooner or later, we will find some suitable boys for our daughters,' said Maange Dhanuk.

Hearing this, Thakur remained quiet for a while and then composing himself, he said, 'Maange, I can see your health is deteriorating fast and you also understand it very well. You are aware that you are suffering from chronic tuberculosis. I don't think you would survive to see your daughters getting married. I know you are unable to receive treatment due to poverty. If you don't live long, how you are going to arrange the marriages of other two daughters. If you accept my proposal, your financial problem would be resolved. Two thousand rupees is not a small amount that I am offering you in exchange for sending Chunno to my house. With this money, not only you can marry off your daughters, but you can also have some money left for your treatment. Now, it is up to you to decide, but better you think twice before saying no. You know well even if you don't agree, you cannot prevent me from taking her forcefully. At any cost, she is going with me.'

Maange could notice the threat in Thakur's last sentence. After a little pause, he said, 'Thakur! Please don't force me to do something which spoils my next life too. Chunno Maa is everything for us. If something happens to her, my family will perish. Also, if villagers get to know about Chunno's visit to your house, they will start seeking meanings. You never know, someone can inform the police, and if that happens, police will fleece me. No Saheb! Please don't push us into such a big trouble.'

'How will people of your village get to know what we are discussing here? This is simply between you and me. No one would ever get a wind of it. You bring Chunno to our village after midnight. She would do this in the Haveli of chieftain, Thakur Saheb. Nobody would ever come to know about this. We will receive you at the boundary of our village. Just escort Chunno up to the water-passage between our two villages. I will be waiting for you there. Then I will take Chunno with me to the Haveli of Thakurji. After she performs the abortion, I will leave her back here okay.'

Thus, having fixed the time, day and the site for the reception of poor Chunno Thakur arose to leave. Maange, under great pressure and allurement, agreed to escort her to the agreed place.

As Thakur was preparing to return, Maange said hesitatingly, 'Sahebji, please leave some money.' Aware of Maange's helplessness, Thakur had come prepared to meet this quite expected demand from a poor Dalit. 'Arrey, why are you so worried about money? I say I will arrange this for you. Not only that, Thakur will also give you some reward. However, I do understand your condition. You certainly need some money. Here is your advance,' said Thakur, handing out five hundred rupees to the poor Maange, still unaware of what fate held in store for him.

By now, somehow everyone had come to know about the pregnancy of Bada Thakur's daughter. Despite this, there were some people who were not prepared to accept that any such incident could take place in the family of Bada Thakur. On the other hand, a large section firmly believed that something was definitely wrong with the chieftain Thakur's family and the unusual tranquility and normalcy, displayed by the Thakur clan, was just to create an impression to the contrary. For a few days, people kept discussing about the incident from different angles. After that, everything died down and people stopped talking about. However, a few intelligent and shrewd villagers kept track of everything that was happening in Thakur's block.

There was a mole in the impenetrably fortified block of Thakurs, who, out of compulsion, and for the sake of Thakurs unity, was with them, but in his heart of hearts, he hated Bada Thakur. This man was very outspoken. On several occasions, people found him expressing his outbursts against the chieftain whose criticism was a kind of blasphemy for other Thakurs, who believed that their community reputation was largely dependent upon the image and honour of their chieftain. This man always stood up to challenge Thakur chieftain's wrongdoings. He was comparatively poor than other Thakurs, who would often ridicule him. Whenever he tried to highlight any glaring instance reflecting black shades of Thakur's character, other Thakurs immediately silenced him. Not only was he not listened to, but also declared a lunatic. Even other villagers had begun doubting poor Thakur's state of mind. Whenever he opened his mouth against Bada Thakur's sexual indulgences with boys and girls, most of whom were his own nephews and nieces, people would take this fulmination as an indication of his abnormal mental state. On an occasion, when he was with a group of young boys, he uttered a funny word about Thakur chieftain. He said, '*Oh laundo! Tum jaante ho, yeh jo saala bada Thakur hai, yeh salaa launde-baaj hai*? (Hey boys, do you know this bloody chieftain Thakur, he is a paedophile?) In fact, his manner of talking was such that no one took him seriously. He always remained lost in his own world uttering funny things. People even began to believe that he was mentally deranged. Sometimes he talked in a frenzied manner about chieftain Thakur who, he believed, was the one to spread rumour against him in the community declaring him abnormal. He thought that chieftain Thakur was solely responsible for his present state. Once, when he was taking bath at the village community well, he began shouting.

'Arrey is gaon ko kya ho gaya! Is Thakur saale ko koi naheen rokta. Isne meri behan ke sath ganda kaam kiya, aur jab maine iske baare mein gharwalon se kaha, to meri behan ne bhi mera hi mazaak uraya. Maine khud Thakur ko ganne ke khet mein uske upar chara hua dekha, ganda kaam karte huwe. Yeh dekh kar mujhe ek mansik dhakka sa laga. Mujhse jab yeh nazara naheen dekha gaya, toh main turant ganne ke khet ke bahar nikal aaya. Maine jab yeh baat apne maa-baap se kahi, unhone bhi mera vishwas naheen kiya, aur mujhe bewakoof, pagal kehna shuru kar diya. Meri koi sunta hi naheen. Woh salaa bada Thakur jaisa kehta hai, uski sab maan lete hain. Iske baad maine is Thakur ko apne bhatije ke saath ganda kaam karte hue dekha. Meri us baat par bhi kissi ne vishwas naheen kiya. Is gaon mein aag lag jayegi. Yeh sala sab ki izzat se khilwaar kiya hai aur koi isko kehne wala naheen hai. Khair, maa chudaye gaon, mujhe kya, jab meri koi sunta hi naheen.'

'Hey, what has come over this village? Why does no one stop this rascal Thakur? He screwed my sister. I myself saw chieftain riding over her in sugarcane fields. It shocked me, and when I could not see it any longer, I immediately got out of the place. When I reported this to my parents, no one trusted and even my sister mocked at me and everyone called me fool and mad. Nobody listens to me. That scoundrel chieftain always had his way. After this, I once witnessed Thakur sodomizing my own nephew over a haystack in the fields. Nobody trusted me for this too. Down with this village! This scoundrel trampled upon the honor of the entire village and nobody dared stop him. Anyway, to hell with the village! Why should I care for when nobody listens?'

Seeing him babble like this, several persons collected there taking pleasure in his outbursts. When he was a bit cooler, one of the persons gathered there asked him, 'Why do you keep talking like this and who would believe you for all you were just uttering?'

Hearing this, he collected himself and said very politely, 'Listen brother, first I request all of you not to call me mad. I am within my senses. Unfortunately, you people also go by what that chieftain has spread about me. The words I was using about him are quite true. I get irritated because nobody has ever paid heed to what I try to tell. So if you also consider me mad, then it is up to you, if don't believe me, it is okay. However, if you consider me a normal person, I would give you a detailed account for the last incident as I mentioned before. Believe me; I am not mad at all. To cover up his sins, this chieftain Thakur has cooked up and spread these rumours about me.' To see the poor Thakur talking so sensibly, and all present there suddenely began speaking in unison, 'Arrey he is not mad. He appears to be quite normal. We should trust him, and allow him to speak up. It seems the chieftain has conspired to have him declared mad. He certainly knows many secrets of chieftain's colorful life. Let us ask him to reveal more about what he himself has seen about chieftain Thakur.'

One of the men asked, 'OK, brother! If you know, then tell us about the last incident involving Thakur with your nephew. Where and when this incident took place?'

'OK brothers, I am very happy that today you have at least agreed to listen to me patiently. Now, I will tell you about this incident to which I am a witness', he replied.

The poor Thakur continued, 'The chieftain Thakur was alone at his tubewell in the fields. All laborers working at his farms had gone home for lunch. It was a scorching summer day of May and I was at my field to keep watch over the barn. In order to quench my thirst, I went to Thakur's tubewell. This time, no one was visible in the surroundings. As soon as I entered the verandah adjacent to the tubewell, where Thakur normally used to sit and sleep, I was stunned to see that my nephew lay naked on his stomach and Thakur was riding on his back pushing swiftly back and forth. He could not notice my arrival. Unable to bear the scene, I stepped back. For a few minutes, I stayed out. After a short while, Thakur, lifting and arranging his lungi (Indian shorts), came out. Hiding and walking past the other wall of the verandah, I came to the front. I saw my nephew fastening his pyjamas. I registered a few slaps on his cheeks immediately when I encountered him. Then I dragged him out of the verandah. Meanwhile, on hearing commotion, Thakur arrived there. Finding me at the spot, his face got frozen. I abused him (Thakur) in my full throat, but he laughed me out, saying, 'You are known as mad. No one in the village would believe you if you try to tell about it. To my dismay, at the behest of chieftain Thakur, my nephew told me, 'You are crazy. I had come here only to drink water.'

'Hearing this from my nephew, I slapped my face and sat down holding my head in my hands. Any normal person who witnesses such an act involving his own kins would behave like this. Is there anyone of you who can withstand this kind of spectacle? All this while, to my chagrin, Thakur was grinning sarcastically at me, making me feel more miserable and helpless. When I was still busy in countering the chieftain, my nephew quietly left the spot. My brothers, what my nephew told me, really drove me mad. Else I am within my full senses. And what I am telling you is absolutely true.'

On hearing this, all by-standers began to realize that Ghasi was not mad as he had been made out to be by the villagers. All that he just told appeared to be quite true. As there were already some stories involving chieftain Thakur in such activities, people began to believe what Ghasi had now revealed. In fact, some of chieftain Thakur's contemporaries would call him humorously 'a launde-baaz (pedophile)'. They knew about his fondness for young boys and girls. However, surprisingly, none of his victims ever dared to report the exploitation. All his victims did not talk about their abuse at his hand due to two reasons; first, they would become a butt of laughter; and second, nobody would have believed chieftain Thakur doing them all this. Now with the revelation of this episode, and that too, by someone from chieftain Thakur's own community, people began to pay serious attention to these stories. A few prominent people from various other communities, including grandfather, decided to use Ghasi who was hell bent upon exposing the chieftain Thakur. They gave him a task to spy on everybody living in the vicinity of chieftain Thakur's fortified haveli. They wanted to get down to the bottom of the incident involving Bela to find out if there was any truth in the rumours widespread in the village community about her pregnancy. Ghasi gladly agreed to do this task as per villagers' guidance. More so, as people no longer treated him as mad.

In order to keep a watch on the activities in the neighbourhood of Thakur's haveli, Ghasi began to mix up frequently with all those who he suspected were trying to hush up the incident. At times, he used to act as a crazy person uttering incomprehensible phrases. To get down to the bottom of the matter, he even remained awake until late in the night. One night, during his recce in the block, he heard sounds of shoe-thud. He saw a group of 7-8 persons emerging from Thakur's haveli. Though he pretended to be aslept on the rooftop of his house, he was consciously awake to have a vigil at the Thakurs. When he saw the group moving northwards, he quickly sat up and putting on his clothes, picked up a staff and started into the same direction to follow them. While doing this, he was keeping a little distance so as not to be seen. When Thakur's men reached the pre-determined place, he stopped a few yards behind them. He noticed two figures were waiting for the group at the other end. He swiftly hid himself behind a bush near a divider between the fields. Then, one of the figures was seen moving towards Thakur's men while the other remained standing there. Two of Thakur's men also stayed back with him. After the Thakur's men had gone a distance, two persons, who had stayed back, whispered something to the other figure standing opposite them. For a few seconds, there was a commotion. Then he suddenly noticed that the figure, which was standing in front of the pair from Thakur's group, was no longer visible. Immediately, the duo stepped back and began rushing towards the village. Ghasi was wondering as to where the third figure had disappeared. As soon as they had gone a distance, Ghasi rushed towards the site. He looked about but did not find anyone. Then he walked a few steps ahead and what he saw was shocking. It was body of a feeble person with his head rested on the divider and the lower portion in the field. He at once stepped back; rushed towards the village - he wanted to run for a few minutes to reach there soon. On his way to the village, he spotted Thakur's men were moving ahead of him. He stopped short and followed them up keeping a distance so as not to be noticed. When the group reached near Thakur's place, only three of them were now heading towards the haveli. He tiptoed after them taking cover behind a wall of the adjacent house. Thakur's two men were now escorting a feeble bending female figure into the Thakur's haveli.

In the dead of night, serenity had enveloped the atmosphere. Ghasi kept awake throughout the night with his eyes and ears fixed at Thakur's high-walled haveli. He could hear thin cries coming out of the haveli. Though not clearly audible, Ghasi had a fair idea that it was Thakur's daughter crying with pain. Obviously, Chunno was at work in the haveli. Thereafter, it was all quiet there. Around three in the morning, two men appeared in front of Thakur's house. Then, that frail female body emerged from inside the haveli. Soon, she was joined by Thakur's men. Then all of them began moving towards the north. Ghasi, who was lying on the string cot over the rooftop of his house, swiftly stood up and started climbing down the bamboo ladder put up against the wall of the house. He continued to follow them in the direction of their movement. They again reached the site where they had earlier received the frail figure only a few hours ago. Ghasi was shocked to find that the frail body also disappeared after a few moments of hubbub. Was he witnessing the same drama again? The men then hurriedly moved back to the village. At once, he walked up to the spot and found an old female body lying a few steps away from the other body.

Next morning, when most of the elders were still in their beds pulling at their hukkas (traditional smoking pipe), the sensational news about the discovery of two bodies from the field of a farmer from the neighbouring village had begun doing rounds. However, the situation in Thakur's block was quite normal.

Suddenly, there was commotion when in the afternoon local police descended the village for questioning the chieftain Thakur. Interestingly, Ghasi had become a witness in the case. He was now in his full self to tell things with clarity to the police. When police started questioning the chieftain Thakur and his men, Ghasi stood up, and flinging his hands, said, 'Sahib, nobody would open his mouth against this man; however, I am prepared to tell you everything, not only about the last night incident, but also about his other adventurous and illegal acts of pedophilia. One of the policemen, seeing him coming to them, turned around and said, 'Yes, yes, come forward and tell us all that you know about the incident last night and other such incidents the chieftain has been involved in the past.'

Ghasi then related to the police the whole story of immoral acts involving chieftain Thakur. The police recorded his statement and left without taking further statements from either Ghasi or any other villager.

Surprisingly, when Ghasi was in the course of telling the police about the pregnancy and abortion of chieftain Thakur's daughter, police cut him short. Just when he wanted to give exact details of how the chieftain Thakur was in the center of the last night's incident involving murder of two innocent Dalits, the police as well as all those standing beside chieftain Thakur snubbed him. No one in the Thakur community was prepared to believe what Ghasi had just revealed. In fact, in their opinion he was still a mentally deranged person. They unanimously began to tell the police, 'This kind of behaviour is not new on his part. On earlier occasions also, this mad man has accused Thakur Sahib of such abominable things. We request you, Sir, to not believe all that he claims as evidence against Thakur Sahib's involvement in the murder of poor Dalits.'

The head of the police party looked towards Thakur and started walking towards his chaupal (community sitting room). After chieftain Thakur had left with police party, his men began jeering at Ghasi, calling him all names. Seeing all this, Ghasi, with his dejected face, walked away.

Although other communities were fully convinced about Ghasi's normal mental state, Thakur community considered him an unhinged man or maybe that was a deliberate move on their part to cover up their chieftain's wrong doings. Youngsters from the Thakur community missed no opportunity to harass Ghasi and project him a lunatic person.

26

Thakur's Sexual Indulgences

A year had gone by. Next spring season had arrived. People from various communities had begun celebrations for the festival of colors, normally running through a full one month finally culminating in the burning of Holika (religious bone-fire). On one occasion, Ghasi was given *thandai* (marijuana punch) to drink. Under its influence, Ghasi started dancing and singing vigorously. Suddenly, he stopped and began to laugh uncontrollably. Soon after this, he fell silent for a few moments and then started crying inconsolably. While crying with his full throat, he then started shouting, 'Listen villagers. You all are bastards; all these years you have considered me mad. None of you ever believed me when I told you about that larki-chod (daughter-fucker) chieftain Thakur. He fucked my sister; but my own parents did not believe me when I told them about it. That bastard chief sodomized my own nephew and I saw this myself. Unable to stand that scene, when I accosted that bastard nephew, he also joined Thakur to make fun of me. I have been reduced to a useless and helpless person. Though I know everything about Thakur's history, no one ever took me seriously. I am more a victim of the credulity of society rather than that of mother fucker chieftain Thakur.'

Ghasi continued, 'I know you will never believe me; but I know the whole secret about the incident that took place inside Thakur's haveli. The fact is that his daughter was pregnant and that she cannot be pregnant without someone fucking her. This haramzada (bastard) Thakur, in connivance with his henchmen, has committed three crimes at the same time. He first took Maange Dhanuk into confidence persuading him to send his adopted mother Channo Devi to his haveli to perform abortion on his daughter. Once the job of abortion was complete, he had both of them killed. Do you know how many girls had this man sexually abused and pregnated? I am truly very happy to note that someone finally fucked his daughter and she too became pregnant. He reaped as he sowed.'

Ghasi then fainted and remained unconscious for several hours under the influence of *thandai*. Thakur's men came, lifted him, and took him away. Next day, after regaining his consciousness, when he was standing in front of his house, Thakur's goons approached him with abuses, humiliation and threatened him with ex-communication if he ever again tried to offend the Thakur community.

On another occasion when Ghasi was unable to stand the collective torture, humiliation and isolation at the hands of his own community, he lost his temper completely and began hurling all sorts of expletives upon them. As Thakurs tried to manhandle him, he swiftly got out of their clutches and reached home. There he picked up his *Katta* (country-made pistol), loaded it up with a gun-powder cartridge and presently returned brandishing it in his right hand. Seeing him in this form, onlookers and by-standers started laughing. Furious as he was, he fired a shot and started hurling all sorts of abuses particularly upon those who he considered were close to Thakur. He said, 'You all assholes, sister-fuckers, sons of bitches have allowed this chieftain of your community to behave like a bull among the cows. As a bull keeps riding upon many cows without any obstruction, Thakur has been doing the same over the years. He has raped at least one daughter or sister or mother or niece from each house of Thakur clan. He has spoiled at least one young boy in each family of Thakurs; but you cowards have been hiding all his acts deliberately just to save your false reputation and pride that you hardly have. Your daughters, nieces, sisters, mothers have all been systematically screwed up by this human-bull who has been let loose by you people. And why he should not do all this? After all, he is your leader in whom you see your own honour. At his behest, you all have had me declared a nut. You have given me all sorts of names, but today I am not going to listen to anybody. If anyone of you tries to cross my way, I will kill him.'

Ghasi was in the best of his elements that chieftain appeared on the scene. Now there was a great spectacle ever seen in the village history. With red shots in his eyes, Ghasi appeared extremely fierce and devilish. On seeing chieftain Thakur, his rage, suppressed all these years, suddenly took over him. It seemed he would destroy anyone coming near him. By this time, a crowd of around hundred people including elderly men and women, youngesters and children gathered there. Ghasi's nephew, whom he had caught red-handed with the chieftain, also came by. Ghasi swooped upon him and hit him on the head with his pistol, warning the on-lookers not to move forward. The nephew was now bleeding due to the blow dealt with by him. Ghasi caught him by neck and putting his revolver against his temple, he said, 'Bastard! You also made fun of me. Now tell all these villagers, particularly all these high-nosed Thakurs, if I was wrong. O Harami (bastard), speak the truth or I will not spare you today.'

He dealt another blow to his nephew while saying all this. Now, the boy was trembling with fear but no one came forward to his rescue. Ghasi gave another kick into his back to force him to reveal the truth. The boy was now terribly shocked and shaken. He called for help repeatedly saying, 'Please save me, save me.'

Everybody was stunned at the turn of things. In the given situation, it appeared there was only one man in the entire village and others were cowards. This man was Ghasi Thakur. A few dared to approach him, but quickly withdrew after Ghasi brandished his *Katta* warning them not to come near by. Intermittently, he continued to give blows to the boy. Eventually, the boy's audacity and intransigence gave in. He was crying, 'Yes yes, please forgive me chacha (uncle). I had made fun of you along with chieftain. He truly did dirty thing with me not once but a number of times'.

Referring to his other peers, the boy further revealed that 'the chieftain had been doing this with other boys also. Two days ago, Thakur called me in his sitting room; he gave me some money and then did the same thing with me, offering me another fifty rupees if I brought Usha (a village girl of another Thakur) to his chaupal.'

This was Ghasi's spectacular act. All the Thakurs standing there bowed their heads down. However, no one dared to encounter the chieftain Thakur. With his mouth tight-lipped, the Chieftain stood there, still. He then tried to get out of the site. Now that the boy had revealed the real character of him, Ghasi loosened his tight grip upon the boy's neck and let him go. He then rushed towards the chieftain. Shouting with his full voice at the chieftain, Ghasi said, 'You, daughter-fucker, say again that I am mad as you declared in the community. You have made me a butt of laughter. All these years, you have been fucking the daughters, wives and young boys of the Thakurs unopposedly.'

All this while, he kept his pistol aimed at the Thakur. Ordering the chieftain, he said, 'Tell them, I am not mad. Also, tell that you had fucked my sister; that she had not uttered a word against you out of shame; that your daughter was pregnant; that you got her aborted through Channo Dai, who was forcefully brought over to your house by your goons to perform the job. Bastard! You had both Channo and Maange killed after the abortion.'

Hearing and seeing all this, all present there fell silent. Chieftain Thakur was standing there with his head down. He was no longer in a position of countering Ghasi. Villagers were looking towards him, gaped. His silence was the greatest witness to the fact that he was indeed involved in many immoral and impermissible acts. With this revelation, the enormous influence and fear that the Chieftain Thakur had established over the entire village instantly evaporated.

Meanwhile, the elders from all non-Thakur communities were unanimously not in favour of allowing the case to die down without punishment. However, they wanted to settle the matter within the village without going to the police. As common in the countryside, the issue had become a matter of honor and reputation for the entire village. Community elders therefore decided to boycott the chieftain, forcing him to live like a desolate. His unchallenged dominance, prestige and honor had now taken a deep beating in the society where his words once ruled the roost.

With unfolding of these incidents, it had become quite obvious that the concepts of superiority/inferiority, position, prestige etc. were nothing but means to satisfy the ego of only a few ones for retaining their unchallenged position. This myth about inherent purity, superiority and martiality had just exploded in front of all. These developments worked as eye-opener for everyone underlying the fact that all, irrespective of their status of low or high, had similar natural physical desires and discovered their own ways and means to fulfil them. Not even the impenetrable fortified safe havens could work as a barrier in order to prevent these activities.

However, society's attitude towards Dalits involved in inter-caste relationship was quite different. Sometime ago, an incident had taken place in the neighboring village. A Brahmin boy fell in love with a Dalit girl. Initially, it was one-sided affair. The girl, out of modesty or lower status, did not reciprocate his advances. Nevertheless, the boy continued to pursue her with tall promises. Finally, the girl gave in. The boy was successful in establishing sexual relationship with the girl. As was expected, rumors of their affair began to spread gradually and soon became a public knowledge.

As a result, all upper-castes from the area assembled in the village. They summoned the boy's family also to corroborate the rumour. The boy's father simply feigned ignorance. However, when confronted, the boy boldly admitted his relationship. On hearing this, boy's father flew in rage hurling all sorts of abuses. He said, 'Bastard, you have abased our family. Even in my wildest dreams, I cannot imagine my son having physical relationship with a Dalit girl. You have disgraced us all. You have polluted your body, soul and mind. Tell me, how society is going to accept your relationship. You better leave home and go elsewhere with her. I am not going to allow you to live here any longer.'

Summoning courage, the boy spoke up, 'You people consider youself as superior to the rest of the world. I beg to differ. There is nothing wrong in having relationship with that girl. She is more beautiful than any girl. Do what you like; I am not going to desert her. Moreover, I do not share the belief of higher and lower stratas. She is intelligent, beautiful and has character.'

Gaped, people were looking at the boy. After his fulmination, the boy retreated inside his house. Later, a few men whisked boy's father aside. After hush-hush conversation, they returned to the gathering. Two of the elders stood up at their place and said, 'The boy has been very gentle. He never opened his mouth in front of his elders. His conduct today clearly indicates he has come under an evil spell of that girl. For this, that girl and her entire family need to be taught a lesson so that in future she would not dare cast her evil spell on our boys.'

Upon this, all those present were unanimous in saying, 'Yes, yes, that Dalit family should be taught a life-long lesson to desist them from any such future incursions.'

Immediately, a group of able-bodied men rushed towards the Dalit *basti*. They at once swooped down upon the family like hungry vultures. As the male members of the family tried to resist, they beat them with staffs and threatened to kill if they tried to come nearby. Then they forcibly dragged the girl along with her sister-in-law (brother's wife) out of their house and brought to the gathering. They ordered her to confess that she had taken the initiative in cosying up to the boy and that despite boy's disinterest in her, she kept pursuing him. Expressing her revolt, the girl refused to succumb to their dictat. Infuriated elders then ordered to drag the girl along with her sister-in-law into a nearby cattle-yard. Swiftly, a few youngish men stood up, caught up both the girl and her sister-in-law by hair and pulled them inside the yard, kicking them left and right. Meanwhile, the boy's father and other family members at the instructions of other arbitrators were held up inside the house. In the yard, both the girl and her sister in law were gang-raped. Having subjected to this, they warned them of dire consequences if they tried to report the matter to the police.

This incident caused a great personal shock to grandfather. Though he yearned a lot to take up cudgels on behalf of the inflicted family, yet he could not do so as the family could not muster enough of courage to speak up against the upper castes.

27

Granduncle's Remorseful Love

Granduncle, Praful Singh, was a multi-hued man having various talents like wrestling, weightlifting, singing, dancing. Above all, he was a great hooker and lady-killer. What a fascinating combination of contrasting talents! We, as youngsters, used to hear many tales about his sexual adventures during his youth. Alike grandfather, granduncle had also lost his wife—our grand aunt—in his youth. Most of the times he used to be away from home and appear only on occasions like Holi and Dussehra festivals. Even being present in the village, he hardly stayed with family members, and spent most of his time while working for a widow Thakurain. His visit to the village would coincide with the harvesting seasons to help her. There were rumous that granduncle had sired two children from Thakurain, who had developed extra-marital relations with him during her husband's lifetime.

Thakur, who was suffering from a mysterious disease, had developed fondness for granduncle, and contrary to his Thakur pride, he displayed great liking for him.

Grandunclewas a hardworking and sturdy guy. Thakur would engage him mainly for looking after his farming activities. During his long and continuous association with Thakur household, he somehow got very close to them, and finally wormed his way into his young and beautiful wife's heart.

The young, Thakurain would feed Praful Singh with a great deal of affection and generosity, which was quite unusual in those days for a Dalit, coming, as it was, from an upper caste married woman.

In turn, Praful Singh was fully devoted to the Thakur family. He would be away for a greater part of the year, but definitely return at the beginning of the harvesting season. He was perhaps mindful of the fact that Thakurain needed his services most at that crucial period. People would jokingly remark that there was an implicit understanding between him and the Thakurain.

Thakur Nirmal Singh relied on Praful Singh so much so that when he needed someone to accompany him to the doctor in the neighbouring town or for any other important matter concerning his family, he trusted him more than anybody else. And Praful Singh, in keeping with his total devotion towards the Thakur family, always made him available on such occasions.

After a protracted illness, Thakur Nirmal Singh demised. At the time of his death, Praful Singh was beside him along with the young Thakurain. Before breathing his last, Thakur held Praful Singh's hand and asked him to look after his family. Praful Singh on his part left no stone unturned in fulfilling Thakur's wish.

Granduncle had left his only son in the custody of his elder married sisters (our aunts). Being a widower, he had plenty of time, but he spent this surfeit time at his disposal in the service of the Thakurain and her three young children.

Interestingly, two of the children in the Thakur household had taken after Praful Singh. People in the village would often poke fun at him asking embarrassing questions like when and where he got chance to father these children. Instead, he would be evasive and change the topic. Yet resembling faces of granduncle and the two children revealed everything to give people reason to believe the liaison between the Thakurain and him.

Praful Singh was highly possessive and careful towards Thakurain's family. Whenever someone tried to tease or harass the children, he would pick an easv fight, thus effectively donning the role of a father. On the other hand, Thakurain never gave an air of physical relationship with him. She always conducted herself publicly in line with a traditional Thakurain as an adherent of strict social code of casteism and untouchability. Despite this, villagers never believed this. They knew well that her public distance was only a clever ploy. When they were away from the public scrutiny, distance would vanish, social barriers would crumble and love would blossom between them and they were all for each other.

Whatever the villagers talked about their relationship, things remained always shrouded and never allowed to surface in the open. Granduncle and the Thakurain led their whole life in this manner, caring little for the village talk, and ensuring their dignity as well as privacy. Perhaps, the Almighty had also blessed their love.

We, the siblings, though quite young, had started comprehending stories about granduncle and his ladylove. That time granduncle could be nearly 66; and the woman was around 55. It happened to be the harvesting season for paddy crop. While working at Thakurain's fields, a wild bull attacked granduncle. As a result, he suffered serious injuries and lost his consciousness. When a villager on his way home witnessed the bull hitting him allover, he took him to have been killed. Too scared of the bull to defend him; instead he rushed to the village and broke the news to my grandfather, who immediately scurried some of the family members in that direction. All, present at home, ran towards the site to rescue the injured granduncle.

On reaching the spot, we noticed that the Thakurain, with her back towards us, was bending over granduncle, flattened on the ground. There was no one around in sight as after hooting the bull away, the villagers had left.

Unaware of our presence, the Thakurain was sprinkling water over granduncle's face, crying and talking to herself, 'Oh God! Why has this injustice befallen me? He was a great support to my family and me. Throughout my life, I have been dependent upon him for everything. My lord, please protect me! Please save his life!'

These words from now-old Thakurain were obvious expressions of her deep-rooted love for him. Aware of the prevailing social barriers between the upper castes and Dalits, things were now more than clear to us about the longstanding relationship between them, with Thakurain expressing her deep and intimate concern for granduncle's well-being in this way.

Now we were in front of her. Raising her bent head upwards when she looked at us, she immediately straightened up, wiping off her welled up eyes. We were relieved to find that granduncle was breathing normal. Soon, he opened his eyes after he recovered his consciousness.

Meanwhile, we observed sudden change in her behaviour. She instantly regained her poise and went about repossessing her exalted social status. She apparently wanted to hide her intimacy and concern for granduncle in our presence. We helped granduncle in making him sit up. He was bleeding profusely from several parts of his body. Immediately, we arranged a bullock-cart from a neighbouring field, helped him stand and walk to it, and had him transported home in it.

For several days, granduncle received treatment for his injuries. During his recuperation, we witnessed grandfather hurling abuses upon him. He would complain, 'This swine, slave, and shameless guy has ruined his life. Since his young days, he is in the service of that debauched woman as a captive in her love-net. All these years, he has been totally indifferent towards his four daughters and the only son who has been living like an orphan at his daughter's place. However, when it comes to that wicked Thakurain, he is even prepared to sacrifice his life.'

Ignoring grandfather's blowups, granduncle would just turn away his face from him.

After some time, Thakurain fell seriously ill. Her disease could never be diagnosed even after a protracted treatment. Thakurain, perhaps realizing that she would not be able to survive, informed granduncle through her son that she wanted to see him. Granduncle that time was not present in the village. Our family normally would not have any clue about his whereabouts when he was away. When Thakurain's son approached grandfather enquiring about granduncle, he remarked, 'You and your mother know better than we do. We have no idea where he could be.'

Thakurain's condition had fast deteriorated. To our amazement, granduncle appeared from nowhere in a couple of days. He had somehow come to know about the illness of his Rajput *Malkin*-cum-lover. He immediately proceeded towards Thakurain's haveli to enquire about her well-being. No one could know about what transpired between the two during those last days. The old sick Thakurain died within days, leaving granduncle, absolutely lonely, sad and dejected.

Being reticent by nature, granduncle hardly revealed anything to anyone about his past. However, only a few people in the village could talk to him in a candid and humourous manner. As they knew about his weakness, they would arrange his favourite food and drink (country-made liquor and goat meat) to make him talk. Once he was completely drunk, these people, mostly his peers, would then begin cracking jokes about his relationship with the Thakurain. It would become a funny session to watch him speak. We grandchildren, by now considerably grown up, would also join in the fun. When someone from the gathering joked, 'Uncle Praful, nowadays, you appear to be very sad. And why not? You have lost your great anchor in the departure of that Rajput auntie of yours.'

Although completely drunk, however, hearing the word 'your Rajput aunt' granduncle spoke up as if he were in his full sense, 'She was your aunt, not mine, bastard! She was my wife; I fathered her two children; and bastard, you say that she was my aunt.'

When he revealed this hitherto shrouded secret, everyone burst out with laughter. The cat at last was out of the bag.

All those collected there were rejoicing his revelation. After a little pause, he fell silent. Meanwhile, one of his contemporaries, Hashim, prepared another heavy peg for granduncle and invited him, 'Hey Praful! You are not taking enough of drink today. Let us have one more!'

Holding his tumbler in his right hand, granduncle said, 'Yes yes, today I will drink till you wish.'

He then gulped the full peg in one draught and asked for one more. He was now fully out of his senses. After guzzling down another peg, he sat for some time, transfixed, and then began crying. The mischievous organizers of the party were perhaps waiting for this moment. They were sure that he was now vulnerable to reveal all truth about his relationship with Thakurain. Granduncle had now started crying more loudly and bitterly. He went on talking. The on-lookers were enjoying this candid and fearless talk. He said, 'Yes, yes. After Thakurain's death, I really feel lonely and sad. After my wife's death, she had taken great care of my needs. She gave me everything that a good wife is expected to give her husband; in return, I also gave her and the children everything - love, affection, labour and care. She indeed was a great woman. She remained loyal to me until the last moment. She could have easily picked up a young man from amongst the Thakurs in the village, but she knew that Thakurs were more interested in her land and property than in her. After her husband's death, her immediate family members even conspired to wipe her out physically. However, I was always there to protect them from any possible onslaught. I had given my word to the dying Thakur. And I kept it by taking all care of his family.'

Granduncle then paused. After a few moments, he resumed, 'I gave Thakurain every bit of mine. She too took good care of all my physical needs; but she deprived me of one pleasure and this remorse I still carry along.'

'What is that pleasure?' asked Hashim.

'You see, despite her complete surrender in all respects, she never allowed me to kiss her. I always wanted to kiss her after making love. But alas! On every occasion when I tried, she would push me away with a rebuke saying, 'I will not allow you to kiss my cheeks, you low-caste Chamaar!'

28

An Initiation into Sex

Born and brought up in a caste-ridden society, I had had to experience the bitter taste of discrimination, disdain and hate throughout life. In an environment of such hopelessness and frustration, it really provided great solace if someone, breaking the barriers of caste and untouchability, offered love with open heart. In our village, there lived a beautiful woman who had no belief in the duality of pure-impure, high-low, etc. Neither did she have faith in God. Love for her was both the ultimate truth and the God. She would say that since the dawn of civilization, love had always elevated human souls filling them with compassion, association, integration and final assimilation. She had her own way when it came to love. In her view, 'if love were a sin, it would not have provided us limitless joy. If God had willed caste above love, then lovemaking with a lower caste would not have generated the same level of ectasy as with the higher caste. Therefore, love was nothing but God.'

This lovebird was a chachi (aunty). Coming from an upper caste landlord family, she was a very courageous and bold lady. Unlike other women of her community, she would go out to the fields to oversee laborers working there. Her behaviour towards the poor laborers was always humane.

It was paddy-harvesting time of the year, probably mid-October. I, along with other family members, was also engaged in harvesting. At noon, when other members went home for lunch, I stayed back to look after the barn in the field. Though it was October, it felt really hot and humid at noon. For a short relief from heat, I sat under the shadow of a tree. Meanwhile, coming from the other direction, perhaps from her fields, this chachi spotted me sitting there.

'Oh, it is really hot', said she, clambering up the mount under the tree, where I sat. Putting down her basket (used for carrying water) and the meal-container, she took her seat on the ground just in front of me. Holding front part of her sari with both her hands, she started fanning herself to dry her perspiring face. In the process, she exposed her twat towards me.

This was for the first time I was looking at the female genitals from such close quarters and so completely! I don't know why, but something unusual stirred me inside. Without caring for me, she remained in the same posture while talking some odd things. I showed askance at what I was seeing or what she was showing me. Despite all my efforts to turn my attention from her, I was beginning to feel hardness in my knickers. However, out of shame, I tried to conceal this from her by moving a little away to one side. Meanwhile, shaking my shoulder with her hand, she said complaining, 'Arrey, I am sitting here with you and you are looking the other side.'

At this, I turned towards her and noticed that by this time she had exposed her almost entire front towards me. Now, hardness inside my knickers had become more intense and throbbing. On my turning towards her, she noticed outward extension of my knickers, which was quite apparent. Being the experienced one, she threw a cursory glance at the protruding part and said, 'Arrey badmash (You scoundrel), what is that?'

With an amorous smile upon her face, she then put her hand on the action-ready part of my body. This was my first experience of a woman's soft touch on my crotch. It felt so sensational that I could not protest at all. I wanted the feeling to prolong. Meanwhile, she pushed herself a little closer to me and slowly began pressing my underwear, while trying at the same time to pull out my erection. Then, holding my right hand in her left, she brought it over to her clitoris and began rubbing against it as if to teach her uninitiated student. I found hers moist, very moist; and the moistness was leaking over to her thighs. Suddenly, she came even closer and speedily pulled down my underneath. Completely naked below my navel, I was now sitting in front of her. As it was rest time and the site where I was experiencing the first tinge of sexuality was in the thick of high sugarcane fields, nobody was around to see us.

Seeing my body parts standing parallel to the ground towards her, she raised her petticoat up to her navel, went down on the ground and laid herself on her back. All through, she kept an inviting smile on her face. Once there, she pulled me too with a jerk over her, and started moaning.

Her passionate moans further aroused me. Though I was not completely unaware of what was going around me, being a first-timer I still had hesitation and an obvious fear because of her upper caste background. It took me some moments to throw away the thoughts of social hierarchy and catch up with her flow.

I started melting. Then, pointing to her spread, my teacher whispered, 'Oh, what are you waiting for? Come on! Let's play the game of love.'

Player I was not, but her openness helped me ease and soon both of us were holding each other in our arms lying under the tree. My pelvic thrusts into her, shaky to begin with, soon got smoother with her doing her part vigorously from below. Her ecstatic groaning was a revelation for me. It only added fuel to fire. Then the climax reached, we both, drenched in sweat, were completely exhausted.

Lying quiet and calm on the ground, we still held closely and tightly each other. She made me realize that love was divine. That it was another name of God. That it recognized no barriers or divisions.

29

Leaders' Lip Service to Dalits

A decade after Independence, situation had changed slightly for better in favour of the weaker sections, particularly Dalits as the Congress Party had taken some steps to improve their lot. Because of protection provided by the ruling party to the under-privileged sections, attitude of the higher castes had become somewhat sympathetic towards them. Congressmen from the upper castes would always impress upon Dalits that they were their true well-wishers. Though, in reality, this never got translated into action, they were not vehemently opposed to the programs launched for the betterment of the marginalized sections of society. Introduction of scholarships for Dalit children had brought some improvement in their educational level. Despite this, there was no real improvement in their socio-economic conditions. Whatever little economic change came their way, it remained confined to the urban and sub-urban areas only.

Those days Gandhism had become a fashionable word. Anyone who followed Gandhian values in society was held in high esteem. However, Dalits' overall impression about these self-proclaimed Gandhians was not positive. In fact, these leaders would always behave contrary to what Gandhiji professed in his life.

During the General Elections, a number of local upper caste leaders would undertake tours of rural areas. During the election campaign, these white-clad leaders never forgot to visit Dalits to remind them about all what Congress Party was doing for their upliftment. A particular local leader from the trading community used to lead the Congress delegation to Dalit bastis. Dalits would feel elevated by the visits of these leaders. Leaders would address them as their *Harijan* brothers and exhort them to cast their votes en masse in favour of Congress Party, which they claimed was their real emancipator. Though in their speeches they professed to shun untouchability, they never accepted water offered by Dalits during their visit to latters' houses. General refrain was that they should not bother about such formalities. Interestingly, after visiting Dalit houses, they would head straight to the courtyard of the chieftain Thakur for refreshments. In fact, chieftain Thakur, in coordination with local schoolteachers, used to organize these visits. During electioneering, teachers appeared more like politicians and were normally busy in convassing for one party or the other.

30

A Low-caste Unacceptable as PM

Having passed my Intermediate, I wished to join some reputed university. However, given the poor resources, I had to seek admission in a local degree college. In the college, majority of students came from the farming communities belonging to Hindus, Sikhs and Muslims. Although, there was no bar as such for Dalit students to interact with upper caste students, casteism often came to the fore especially when upper caste students would make hateful and derisive caste-based remarks against Dalit students.

The period witnessed some unprecedented developments taking place in the country. Dalits in Northern India were experiencing an extreme form of hatred against them.

Political leaders of a few splinter groups had joined hands with a great zeal under the umbrella called Lok Party. They claimed that due to the policies of the then government, things had gone topsy-turvy in the country and they wanted to set them right. The Lok Party experiment failed within a short span of 18 months leading to the dissolution of Parliament and call for mid-term polls. Before dissolution of Parliament, a Dalit leader, with a long political experience, had staked claim for the top post of Prime Minister. This angered many a people in the country. Dalit students would be the constant target of their snide remarks like 'These bloody low castes that are fit only to polish our shoes, now want to rule over us! They need to be taught a lesson for their impudence for challenging us'.

Our college was reduced to a political circus. The atmosphere was bristling with all sorts of threats against Dalit students. Without caring for their sentiments, the upper caste students always made it a point to abase them openely.

Following dissolution of Parliament, mid term polls were announced. The respective Dalit Leader was again one of the claimants for the top post. He, however, was least acceptable to the people, not because he lacked administrative skills, but because of caste considerations. However, for millions of Dalits, he was an icon. They saw in him a leader who could really do something concrete for their betterment. However, all possible chances for him to reach the top were scuttled when, after the fall of Lok Party Government, the erstwhile President did not consider it appropriate to invite him to explore the possibility of forming the next government. This did not go down well with the Dalits who believed that leaders of major national political parties despite their ideological differences with each other had ganged up to prevent their leader from heading the Union Government.

Various political parties had begun canvassing to mobilize support. Senior leaders were addressing rallies after rallies throughout the country calling upon people to cast their votes in their favour. College students enthusiastically were thronging to the venues of political rallies organized for these leaders. After hearing various political leaders, students in their spare time would sit in the college canteen and teashops around the campus to plunge in discussions highlighting merits and demerits of leaders aspiring to become Prime Minister.

Barring a few, most of the students participating in the political discussions ridiculed the Dalit leader because of his not-so-good-looking face. They remarked that he was not fit to become Prime Minister as he was not only ugly but also a low caste, cobbler.

During one of such debates, a B. Sc. student from upper caste *Bishnoi* community remarked, 'Aey guys, don't you find it rather funny on the part of that ugly looking cobbler to aspire to become Prime Minister of India. Can we ever entertain the idea of a Dalit ruling over us? It was rather good on the part of President to dissolve the Parliament and call for fresh elections instead of paving the way for a cobbler to cobble up a majority to form his government. Somebody should tell that untouchable to look his face in the mirror before harbouring an ambition to become the Prime Minister. We should really be thankful to our leaders, particularly the President for not allowing that cobbler to occupy such an important position. They have really saved us from disgrace.'

His bitter words hurt me deeply. Joining the debate, I said, 'Well, Bishnoi, your remarks about our leader reek of your deep-rooted prejudice and hatred against Dalits. Otherwise, viewing Dalit leader's exemplary services to the country, no sensible person would make such snide remarks against him. In many respects, he is much better than the leader who, despite his popularity restricted to one part of a particular province, managed to become the Prime Minister. Your remarks are indicative of a mindset in which even outstanding services of Dalit leaders have no significance in nation-building.'

In response, Bishnoi first gave a bad look towards me and then said, 'So, you want us to accept that ugly cobbler as our Prime Minister? He is leader of untouchables only and not of the entire nation. We *Swarns* (golden) Hindus would never tolerate an untouchable ruling over us. He would do better if he confines his leadership to the Dalits only. He should be thankful to our big leaders who allowed him to occupy important positions like Minister of Defence and Railways. For a Dalit, there cannot be a greater honour than this! He should be absolutely contented with this. If he aspires for something higher than this, it definitely annoys us. In fact, in the new dispensation, he should be shown the door. If he continues to occupy ministerial position, he will tend to harbour bigger ambitions, something that is not in favour of the upper caste Hindus. An untouchable sitting in the chair of Prime Minister and ruling over us is unacceptable.'

Meanwhile, another student, when asked about his favourite candidate, commented 'I will prefer to drop my vote into a drain to giving it to a chamar. I would never tolerate a chamar being prime minister of the country even in my dreams.'

Then, Bishnoi looked towards other students, mostly upper castes. Almost all of them, barring one or two, spoke up in unison, 'Yes, yes, Bishnoi is quite right. How can we accept a low caste as Prime Minister of India? It seems you have begun to think big; otherwise, you could never intervene in our discussion with this kind of argument. You better focus on your studies, graduate yourself and take up some clerical job. A big ambition doesn't behove you, a Dalit.'

I guessed that had I persisted in my argument with them, situation could have turned violent. Inwardly, I really was seething with anger but without giving an air of resentment, I stood up saying, 'Well, let us leave it, we should not take it seriously.'

This was for the first time we heard a national leader talking in terms of castes. This leader who, by quirk of fate, had managed to become the prime minister, never forgot in his speeches to remind that 'Jaggu' (a diatribe for the Dalit leader) was not a suitable candidate for prime ministership because of his dark skin and ugly features. After all, as head of the government, the prime minister was also the face of the nation. Spewing venom in his speeches against the entire Dalit community, he would comment, 'The time has not yet come that we should allow our shoes to sit on our head as they are meant to be worn in the feet only.'

During dissolution of Parliament for mid-term polls, a few educated people and students would gather every evening at Panna Lal Kayastha's shop-cum-choupal in the village. Politics was a favourite subject for discussion among them. Panna Lal Kayastha, who considered himself highly knowledgeable over political affairs, would voluntarily give an expert comment on every matter discussed at these sessions.

The Kayastha was a great fan of Morarji Desai. Giving his expert opinion on the coming events, he forecast, 'Morarji Bhai would make a comeback with thundering majority; he is the most senior statesman of the country; and moreover, he is a great Gandhian; he is also a great administrator; after all, he was an ICS topper. Since Nehru's days, he has handled all portfolios assigned to him very successfully. Nehru would always consult him when the latter was Defence and External Affairs Minister.'

Many of us present there, particularly those studying in colleges and universities, were more informed than that kayastha. However, nobody tried to correct him on his facts on Morarji bhai. And the kayastha went on and on. He hardly even read a newspaper or magazine, but during such discussions, he always gave the impression as if he knew everything under the sun. He further said, 'Morarji is the only leader in the country who never lost elections; once he had even challenged Pandit Nehru to contest against him from anywhere in India. Indira Gandhi became Prime Minister by winning over some members of the Congress Party through bribery. Otherwise, Morarji would have been prime minister immediately after Nehru.'

Now that this self-proclaimed Kayastha leader was going on and on without checking his facts, I wagged eloquent. 'Lalaji', said I reverently, 'All that you have stated is factually incorrect. For your information, Morarji Desai was never Defence and External Affairs Minister. He never appeared in the Indian Civil Services examination. He was rather a PCS officer and had stood 47th in the PCS merit list. Morarji Desai was also a loser in the parliamentary elections, and he never challenged Pandit Nehru.'

'O Boy, don't try to teach me; I am thirty years older than your father. I have seen the world. My sons are more educated than you; and, by the way, how do you claim that what I said about Morarji bhai is incorrect' demanded Lalaji with a tinge of anger.

'Because, I read books, newspapers and magazines and whatever I have said about him is based on my study of various political figures including Morarji Bhai', said I with conviction.

'You are not as intelligent as our children. How come our children do not know all that you are telling me; you son of a *Chamar!* Just because you have learnt to read newspapers / books, you should not forget to respect the elders. Don't open your mouth when elders are talking; you know nothing', said the Lala, in irritating and agitated tone.

'And you know everything on earth', said I intentionally to further irritate him.

Another piece of information the Lala had about his favourite leader was that Morarji Bhai was a bania and that is why Gandhiji loved him so much. After Lala's admonishing, I tried to cool down in order to listen to all the long rubbish he was still continuing about Gandhi, Nehru, Indira, Morarji, etc. Lala further said, 'Morarji Desai was the only leader who could protect the interests of the trading class. After all, he belonged to the Bania community of Gujarat. When he was the chief minister, he protected the interests of the trading class to a large extent. Both he and Chandrabhan Gupta, the chief minister of Uttar Pradesh, had very good personal equation. Both kept Pandit Nehru under check as the entire trading community in the country rallied behind them.'

Hereupon, I wagged eloquent once again. With the intention of correcting Lala about the caste of Morarji Desai, I intervened, 'Lalaji, your facts are totally incorrect about personal details of Morarji Bhai; he was not a bania, but a Brahmin.'

'How do you know he was not a bania? In Gujarat, Desais are traders and not Brahmins' said Lala confidently flaunting his deep knowledge about Morarji Bhai, his politics and the country as a whole.

After hearing Lala, I said to myself, 'It is futile to argue with him particularly when he is not even prepared to listen to me. This is not his fault either. People like him have grown with the thought that they are born superior and what they think, do, say is always right, uneducated and ignorant though, they might be. The Lala also suffered from the same problem of self-glorification. Interestingly, the old blockhead Lala had hardly ever stepped out of his four-walled haveli. He was infamous for lending money at exorbitantly high interest rates to the poor farmers and labours, which they were never able to repay. As a result, they had to sell their land to the rapacious Lala, thereby reducing themselves to the status of landless poor. Through this business alone, the Lala had become a landlord and even richer than other landed propertied class around.

The period witnessed an unprecedented polarization among the intermediary landed classes. In the pre and post-election period, there was an unusual spike in violence against Dalits in northern India. Threatened not to go to the polling booths in a number of places they did not cast their votes. Where they tried to exercise their franchise, they had to face the combined hostilities of the dominant classes.

The Dalit leader and his Party suffered a great defeat in the elections and Indira Gandhi made a comeback with thundering majority. With this, the intermediary classes' hatred and hostilities against Dalits also subsided. Perhaps, it had dawned upon them that their ham-handed approach was a major hindrance in attracting other sections of the society to their fold.

31

Upper Castes' Participation in Community Feast

It was wedding season. Several marriages were slated to be held in different communities, including those of Dalits. According to the established customs, Dalits dined at last at the community feast organized by the respective families on occasion of their children's marriages. On the contrary, upper castes never participated in the dinner parties organized by Dalits on such occasions. Instead, Dalits had to provide raw material, such as rice, ghee, sugar, flour to the higher castes that cooked it in their own kitchens and ate. In the process, upper castes caused poor Dalits suffer doubly as the latter had to part with relatively more food material. All communities, except Dalits, were happy with this practice. Only a few Dalit families were in a position to afford this, while others could never think of inviting the entire village. Even those who could manage financially never felt comfortable with the torturous practice.

Among Dalits, there was only one family capable of matching the higher castes in terms of economic as well as educational standards. This family had somehow succeeded in arranging good education for its children. Three of them had jobs in government departments like railways, post & telegraph and district court. The family was first in the entire village to have constructed a concrete house even before many of the upper castes could do it! By virtue of their good educational and financial position, people treated them with consideration that is more respectful. Their urbane class values reflected clearly in their liberal and docile behaviour towards other residents.

This family planned to give away a party to all communities on occasion of their daughter's marriage. By becoming the first graduate in those days, the bride-to-be had done the entire village proud, especially the Dalit community. After fixing the wedding dates, the family got busy in making other preparations for the day. As the members of the family were living in different parts of India, they were familiar with the changes taking place around the country. Therefore, they wanted to solemnize the marriage with a difference. They contemplated to invite all castes over a joint community dinner where food was to be served on first-come-first-eat basis without any linear preference. The family engaged upper caste cooks to prepare food so that everyone could partake without any possible objections from the upper castes in dining together.

To translate their plan into action, the family convened a meeting of community elders to broach with them the idea of a joint community feast. On hearing about the plan, there was pin-drop silence for a few moments. Then grandfather rose to say, 'It is a good idea, but the point is whether the villagers would agree to a joint feast, especially in view of the prevailing social practice of untouchability. For this, we need first to approach the elders from other communities to know their mind, and win over them to grace the occasion with their presence. They can also be helpful in persuading the other intermediary communities who at times appear to be more rigid.'

Everyone gathered agreed with grandfather's suggestion and decided to approach the heads of upper castes - Brahmins,

Thakurs and Kayasthas etc. Dalit elders' considered opinion was that once the Brahmins agree to the community feast, other castes - Rajputs, Kayasthas, backwards and Muslims - would automatically fall in line. With this in mind, they first approached Pandit Yaggyan Dutt Sharma, head of the only two Brahmin households. All of them gathered at the raised clay platform in front of his haveli, and sent for him. The Pandit, because of his political ambitions, always pretended to be sympathetic towards Dalits. To capture the post of *sarpanch* (head of village panchayat), he needed to enlist their support. He knew that if Dalits rallied behind him, he could easily achieve his goal.

Emerging from his haveli, the Pandit smilingly welcomed Dalit elders and gestured them to have their seats on the clay platform. Sitting beside them, he asked them the reason for their visit. Charat, father of the girl to be married, stood up and said, 'Actually Panditji, I wish to render a small service to the village. I wish to invite the whole village together for a feast on my only daughter's wedding. I believe that you alone can help in making other communities agree for a common feast with Dalits. On hearing this, the Pandit's ears pricked up and he snapped, 'What did you say? Dalits? Have I heard it correctly? Do you mean Dalit and other castes - higher and backwards, Muslims - will dine together?' Then he said, 'Arrey, Charat Bhai, you know this has never been the practice in the village. You are not poor. There are several earning members in your family. After all, this is your sole daughter's marriage. You should have no problem in providing raw material for cooking.'

'No, no, Panditji! We have no problem in arranging the raw material like rice, ghee, sugar, flour, etc. for distribution, but I wish that all communities gather and eat together under the same tent. You know, my daughter is the first girl from the village to graduate. Therefore, it is her wish as well. She received her education in a prestigious university, where she came to know about the changes that are reshaping our society.

She doesn't believe in the caste system. She has proposed this idea before us and insisted upon organizing a joint dinner for the entire village on her wedding ceremony. Most qualified of all the womenfolk in the village, she wants to set an example through the proposed event for creating a socially harmonious atmosphere.'

Growing a little serious Panditji said, 'Charat Bhai, I have always sided with you people. You know, panchayat elections are round the corner. If I take initiative on your behalf in approaching other castes to convince them to dine with Dalits, they would misconstrue it, taking that I am preparing ground to contest elections with your support. Please spare me from this sensitive issue. You better convene a joint meeting of villagers to discuss the issue; I will extend my full support.'

'Panditji, you occupy the highest social position in the village and if you give your consent, nobody would oppose. Once villagers know that you had already concurred, I don't think anyone would go against it', argued Charat.

'Charat Bhai! You know it is not as simple an issue. Making all people agree to sit and eat together means breaking off from the well-established traditions of our society. This is bound to create a controversy having serious repercussions. Observation of casteism is an eternal practice enjoined upon us by scriptures. Even Mahatma Gandhi believed in jaati-vyavastha (caste system) and never advocated its abolition. How can you imagine us abandoning our eternal values in a day? No, no, please keep me away from this business.'

Panditji paused for a few seconds and resumed, 'Do you know the fate of my family if I plead on your behalf? I could be termed heretic. The Upper castes will ex-communicate us. I am not prepared to take such risk to put my entire family's survival at stake.'

'We had come to you with great hopes, particularly when you claim to be an Arya Samaji, who does not believe in the caste system. After all, we are also part of the Hindu society. If you cannot help, we don't think anyone else would do it for us', said Charat, pulling a long face.

For a few seconds, there held silence. Then, summoning more confidence, Charat said, 'My daughter is right in claiming that Panditji would never agree, because it is Brahmins who have introduced this unique concept of discrimination. Today, it became obvious that though we consider ourselves Hindus, we are not so in practice. Otherwise, what is the difference between upper castes and us that prevents us from sitting and eating together? We Dalits are also humans and practise the same religion. Therefore, it is incomprehensible to see you discriminate against us. According to Arya Samaj, only deeds, not birth decides a person's caste. If that is true, how come you don't break bread with us at our houses, nor you allow us to dine with other Hindus? When you yourself speak so highly of equality and goodwill, what prevents you from mingling with us? We now understand that your visits to our homes on festivals like Holi, Dussehra and Dipawali were just honeyfogle as you never shared food with us.'

'No, no, this is not true. I have always been with you. And why do you bother so much about eating together with higher castes? If I don't dine at your home, it does not mean that I am casteist. You are aware that whenever Dalits and upper castes clashed, I have always stood by you. And here you are accusing me of being casteist,'said Panditji in an effort to mollify Charat and his group.

'In that case, why don't you convince the villagers to participate in our community feast? I am sure if you try earnestly, they would definitely listen to you. When a Brahmin accepts, they would agree too', insisted Charat.

After a little pause, Pandit said, 'Charat, I know you are better off than many higher castes; however, your demand is something unprecedented and unimaginable. If I broach this idea with other high castes, I am not sure how they would react. Yet, as always, this time too, I accept the risk of taking up cudgels on your behalf with them. Could I then expect something in return? Hopefully, you won't disappoint me', Pandit proposed, looking at grandfather, an unrivalled Dalit leader.

'You know well that in all your feuds with Rajputs, Kayasthas etc., we have always stood by you. You can count on us in future as well. Panditji, you would recall what I did for you by risking my own life. The whole village had turned against me for protecting your son in the murder case?' reminded grandfather.

Upon this, Pandit got quiet for a while and then took out his political ace he was all this while getting on to. He said, 'Hopefully, they would listen to me. I would persuade them to agree to dine with you in the wedding ceremony; but I expect you would not ditch me when I need you. Now let me tell you, my elder son has been evincing interest in the village panchayat presidency; he is keen to do some concrete work for the development of the village, particularly for the welfare of Dalits. I know he will not be able to fulfill his desire without your backing. However, for the time being, let us keep it secret.'

Panditji undoubtedly had greater influence over most of the villagers. Although, the Kayasthas and Rajputs initially opposed him vehmently, they soon fell in line as he reasoned out with illustrations from scriptures convincing them thoroughly that it was but prudent on their part to embrace the Dalits in the changing times. What better occasion than a Dalit girl's wedding to do so, particularly when she happened to be the most educated one among all womenfolk.

In the eyes of Dalits, it was like a dream come true; for they had never thought of upper castes agreeing to their proposal easily. They felt elated at the gesture shown by the upper-castes. For them, it was a sort of Cultural Revolution as they had attained acceptability from those who had so far considered themselves born high, culturally as well as morally. Every member of the Dalit community was enthusiastic to contribute his bit to make the occasion a grand success. Overjoyed with this new sense of equality, they wanted to do everything possible to please the higher castes.

However, a few were unhappy with this development. They did not brook the idea of partaking meals with Dalits at the community feast. They were angrier to know that Dalits were going to serve them food. Some villagers raised their objections in hushed voices only but Pandit prevailed upon them finally.

Meanwhile, opposition was brewing in some unexpected quarters. With Hindus having agreed to dine with Dalits, Muslims came up with their own arguments against the proposed change. Only a day before the wedding ceremony, Muslims conveyed through the Pandit about their non-participation. Pandit made all efforts but could not persuade them. To validate their opposition, Muslims forwarded so many arguments claiming them to be postulates of Islam. Notwithstanding the lengthy arguments, even the upper caste Hindus could not convince them to join the proposed community feast. This caused Dalits a great deal of mental agony, as they had never expected this much opposition from the Muslims.

As a last ditch effort to bring Muslims on board, Dalit leaders approached them directly to talk to them. Leaders of both communities gathered at a certain place away from the public glare. Breaking the ice, Charat said, 'As you must be aware, my daughter is getting married. On this occasion, I wish to organize a joint feast for all the communities. Upper castes have accepted our proposal. However, we believe that you have reservation with this idea. Hence, this meeting. We had never imagined you would object to this new beginning in the village'.

Hearing this, Rashid Sheikh stood up to speak: 'Bhai, we are happy to know about the upper caste Hindus agreeing to eat at your daughter's wedding. You people must be feeling elated with this development. And why not? You will now be sitting and eating together as equals. This is certainly an occasion for Dalits to celebrate.

By the way, do you really believe your Hindu brothers have accepted you as equals? We still have serious reservations about their move. Maybe, there is more to it than meets the eye. Pandit, who made the villagers accept your invitation, may have had other plans to suit his personal agenda. These Rajputs, Brahmins, and Kayasthas have always treated you so inhumanly. Despite so much suffering and humiliation at their hands, you are so naive to trust them forgetting their thousand years' contempt, disdain, scorn and derision for you.

We Muslims felt let down when Pandit brought this proposal to us on your behalf. For Hindus, including you people, took us for granted. It was only appropriate to first know our opinion, but without waiting for our consent, they went ahead. We really felt hurt and humiliated as no one from you thought it fit to come to seek our support and consent.

You know, we have always stood together to ward off challenges from the upper caste Hindus. It was because of this unity that despite so many conspiracies by this clever Pandit, no one could harm us. In the past, you even contemplated en-mass conversion to Islam on several occasions. We also wanted to embrace you wholeheartedly; but these cunning upper castes always obfuscated your mind by playing tricks, whenever you planned to do that. Then, they gave you sermons from Hindu scriptures to make you feel as part of them. Special ceremonies like co-dining and *Janeyu* (sacred thread) wearing, organized by the Arya Samaj for you, were only tricks to stop you from leaving their fold. Now that they are going to dine at your place, you must certainly treat yourselves as equal to them.

For us, you will now be like other Hindus against whom we have been waging our struggle over the centuries. We expected you to come into our fold but you did not. You know we don't practise casteism in Islam, but since you have stabbed us in the back, we will also treat you the way the upper caste Hindus have treated you so far. We don't think you will be their equal by dining with them. Yes, if you convert to Islam, we are prepared to reconsider our decision and accept you as our equals.'

Dalits' understanding of Muslims' affront towards them was now quite clear. They had to either placate the Muslims by abandoning Hinduism and convert to Islam; or assert themselves as a group within the Hindu fold. Muslims obviously wanted to take advantage of Dalits' vulnerability. Earlier also, they had never dined with Dalits. They too used to accept raw foodstuff from them on occasions like marriages. However, when it came to events like elections for village sarpanch, they would always join hands with Dalits, thus making the upper caste Hindus feel threatened by this alignment. It now dawned upon Dalits that Muslims, by making them pawn, wanted to take advantage of the fluid situation prevailing in the Hindu society. Therefore, it was decided not to pursue any further the issue of their participation in the community feast.

On the day of wedding, all castes received the marriage party warmly. Indeed, a great revolution was taking place in the countryside. After guests from the groom side had dined, the villagers were served food. Majority of caste Hindus participated. However, a few who could not muster courage to accept openly the new social order made silly pretexts to avoid their participation. However, they participated in making other arrangements for the success of the wedding. Guests were surprised. They could not believe their eyes to see Dalits enjoying so good standing in the village, particularly when majority of the villagers belonged to the upper castes.

Overall, it proved to be a momentous event in the village history in that the barrier of untouchability was largely cracked, if not abolished completely. However, the attitude shown by the Muslims went beyond Dalits' comprehension. Their claims of professing equality and non-discrimination based on caste, creed and color all proved hollow. The Muslims' behaviour was rather painful for Dalits as it reminded the latter of their low social status.

32

Grass-root Politics

Six months had passed since the wedding. Elections for the *sarpanch* (village president) were now due. As usual, people began making political calculations. Thakurs, Muslims and Sainis, three large communities after Dalits, all wanted their candidate to become the *sarpanch.*

All this while, Pandit Yaggya Dutt Sharma, according to his arithmetic, was busy in the process of striking separate deals with larger communities to realise his son's political ambitions. Despite his knowledge of Dalits' aversion towards Rajputs, he made a deal with the latter assuring them to secure the former's support in favor of their candidate, if they fielded one in the elections. His game plan was quite clear. He knew well that Dalits were not going to support other candidates. He was, therefore, confident of their support for his son as per the deal negotiated by him at the wedding of Charat's daughter.

In his deal with major communities, Pandit assured them all that he would throw his weight behind their candidate, but if they fail in mobilizing the requisite support, then they would have to support his son.

The situation had taken a reverse turn once again as Muslims, the single largest community, decided to field their own candidate. They were confident of their victory, as they knew well that the fragmented Hindus would never be able to field a common candidate against them to win.

Meanwhile, Sharma was proposing to the Sainis and Rajputs to offer his support to their consensus candidate. Interestingly, he was doing this with the full knowledge that they would never agree to field a consensus candidate because of their mutual mistrust and animosity. His calculations were that with Rajputs and Sainis failing to reach an understanding for their common candidate, he would propose his son's candidature as a compromise candidate. Both the Rajputs and Sainis would then have no option but to support him, particularly when he had already cornered Dalit support for it!

However, Rajputs and Sainis too had their own agenda. According to them, Pandit was a cunning political fox and the main cause for various problems of the villagers. That was the reason why no major community came forward openly to support his son's candidature. He tried hard but failed to attract the larger communities in his son's favour. Finally, he turned to Dalits and advised them to announce publicly his son's candidature. The closer election date was drawing, the more desperate Pandit was to run after the Dalits in order to persuade them to announce their support for his son.

With no support coming his way, Pandit finally turned to grandfather, well known for his gullibility. Pandit knew that once he approached grandfather with endearment, the latter would definitely go all out to help him, easily forgetting all previous unhappy experiences.

One fine morning, Sharma descended at our chaupal. Clambering the clay-stairs of the earthen platform, he walked up to grandfather who was pulling at his *hukka* (smoking pipe) sitting cross-legged on a *charpai* (string cot). Still standing, Sharma asked, 'Kaise ho thekedar? (How are you?)' Though grandfather was nearly three decades older than Sharma, the latter considered it infra-dig to wish him because of caste consciousness. An elder Dalit too was not entitled to salutations from a relatively younger Brahmin! On the contrary, Dalits had to wish the upper castes even when the latter were visiting them to seek favors. Welcoming Sharma, grandfather offered him seat on the upper edge of his charpai, a gesture of respect in the rural India.

Taking his seat, Pandit began, 'Thekedar, you know elections are drawing near and we have not yet decided on our candidate. I have spoken to the Rajputs, Sainis and Kayasthas, but they have not yet spoken their mind. You know very well if we fail to field a consensus candidate, Muslims will easily win. We don't know how many candidates from various communities would stake claim at the last moment. If you throw your community's weight behind a particular candidate, others would also fall in line in view of large share of votes from your community. Such a candidate stands a better chance to win in the elections. Therefore, my advice is that you should announce your candidate right away. However, before that, I would like to remind you that you had promised to support my son as a consensus candidate. Now that other castes have not yet been able to announce their decision, I expect you to support my son publicly,' insisted Pandit.

'Arrey bhai (hey buddy), what is the hurry? My people have not yet arrived at a decision in this regard. There is also a growing feeling among our youngsters that if the Muslims - a little more than half of us - can stake claim, why not us? Although I am still trying to persuade them not to follow that idea, I am not sure if they would listen', said grandfather gingerly.

Hearing this, Pandit snapped, 'What! Your youngsters are thinking to field their own candidate! And who will support your candidate - Rajputs, Kayasthas, Sainis, Or Muslims?' demanded pandit.

'Well, I really do not know about the support to our candidate. However, I wish to let you know about a common feeling among Dalits. They say we would have supported you had the Muslim candidate not jumped in the fray. My men now want to compete with the Muslims, as we are larger community than they are. Therefore, we too stand a good chance to win.'

Learning this new reality, Pandit let out a sigh and with a grimace on his forehead, he said, 'You are ditching me. Uptil now I was banking upon you for support. If all that is true, I should not even think about my son's candidature. Can you imagine how much hopeful I had become after your assurance? You are well aware that I annoyed even the upper castes by pleading with them to participate in your community feast. I am disappointed to get all this in return from you. I had never imagined you would be so ungrateful. I rue the day I pleaded with the villagers to accept to participate in a Dalit girl's marriage. In fact, I went against my own conscience while doing this, as I had to deviate from the codified life based on complete abstinence from intermingling and dining with low-castes. Moreover, you tend to forget that I did all this for your sake. Any way, what is done, cannot be undone.'

'I know you must have faced stiff opposition from other upper castes in making them agree to participate in our marriage. We do recognize that and understand that without your support and personal intervention, it would not have been possible to convince them. However, please try to understand that it is premature to make an announcement of our candidate at this point of time, as it would send a wrong signal to other villagers. You must also bear in mind the fact that it is not possible for your son to win with our support only. To ensure his victory, you first need to take other major communities into confidence. What would happen if Sainis, Kayasthas and Rajputs, along with other minor backward communities, join hands against you after announcement of your son as our candidate? I, therefore, suggest that we keep quiet for the time being and see all pros and cons of the emerging political equations.

Meanwhile, you had better approach other communities as well to broach with them the idea of fielding your son. My own guess is that even if you manage to garner support from the splintered caste-groups, your son stands a chance. Please, do not lose heart early. Let us wait for a few more days for a clear picture to emerge', suggested grandfather in an attempt to mollify Pandit and keep his hopes alive.'

Notwithstanding such counsel with a tinge of hope from grandfather, a misgiving had grown in Pandit's mind. He had grown suspicious with the fears that if Dalits decided on their own candidate, there was a possibility of other lower-backward castes also joining hands with them, thus clearing the way for victory of their candidate. With this happening, there was no chance for his son to win if he decided to contest.

When Sharma rose on his feet to leave, a deep frown was clearly visibile on his face. Rising from the charpoy, he sighed and said, 'Thekedar! The only thing I can say is that my hopes are still pinned on you. If you want, you can convince your people to rally behind my son. I am sure they cannot go against your wishes. I am absolutely sure about it.'

'I am at the fag end of my life. These boys of new generation have their own minds. They hardly bother about what elders, like me, think. I can give them only an advice. I cannot guarantee whether they will act upon it. Nevertheless, I will try to explain it to them', said grandfather without any assurance about Dalits' support to his son.

Pandit was a wily politician. He had clearly read the writing on the wall. He had almost thought of his next move before he left for home.

After his departure, a group of Dalit elders arrived at the chaupal. Taking initiative, one of them asked, 'Thekedar, why had this Pandit come over here? He must have come to remind you about the assurance, which you and a handful of others gave him at the time of Charat's daughter's marriage. We are here to caution you that in no circumstances we will support this man's son. We also want to let you know that this Pandit has been hobnobbing with other groups also for his son's consensus candidature. We have come to know this through Murarilal Pal. He has informed that Pandit is also separately advising other groups, including Muslims, not to support a Dalit candidate, if they field one.'

Reacting to this, grandfather said, 'We should not jump to the conclusion so soon. We will have to wait and watch. Meanwhile, we will see Pandit's next move.'

In the meantime, he through his contacts in other caste groups ascertained what his community men had told him about Pandit Sharma. Yes, what they had informed was right.

Given Pandit's nature, grandfather had a fair idea that in case Dalits do not support his son's candidature, he would not sit idle and do something nasty to spoil the whole game. True. Frustrated over not succeeding as per his plans, and suspicious of Dalits' next move, he began to come in his true colours.

Hurt, humialiated, angry and sad, Pandit thought that grandfather had abandoned him after using as a pawn. Interestingly, he himself had played this game a number of times with grandfather, but he never realized latter's pain and suffering.

As narrated elsewhere, grandfather had saved Pandit's son from going to jail in a murder case. I too had helped his daughter by saving her from being gang-raped by some wicked boys on occasion of Ram-lila.

Sharma and his two sons were employees in a local sugar mill. Once, security men at the mill had caught his sons stealing high-cost spare-parts. My father happened to be there when security guards were accosting them. When the case came to the notice of the general manager, he almost decided to terminate their services. However, Sharma and his accused sons, in their attempt to prove themselves not guilty and place the blame rather at the door of securitymen, submitted to the general manager to interrogate father who would vouch for their innocence. Going by the case history, they were certain to lose their jobs had father spoken the truth about their involvement. Father, in fact, had informed grandfather of his intention to tell the manager truth. Pandit and his son knew this fact and were obviously apprehensive of father.

One day, Pandatayin (Pandit Sharma's wife), visited our house. Welcoming her, mother spread out a small string stool for her, and then asked, 'what brought you here, Jethaniji (elder sister-in-law)?'

'Sister, where is Devarji (younger brother-in-law)?' inquired Pandatayin.

'He has gone to the fields to collect fodder for the cattle and should be returning soon. You may please wait', said mother indulging in customary chatting with her. Soon, father was back at home. Father wished pandatayin.

'Devarji, you are aware of what is going on in my household. My husband and son are having sleepless nights after learning that you are going to testify against them. You know, if they lose their jobs, my family will be in ruins. I have three grown up daughters to marry off soon. I, therefore, have come to beg of you to save my family please. How you do that, I leave it to you. We will never forget this in our lifetime', pleaded Pandatayin, spreading out her saree's upper front part as a gesture of begging.

Father informed grandfather about Pandatayin's visit and her begging of compassion. Initially, father was not in favour of forgiving Sharma, in view of the repeated instances of his backstabbing our family in the past. Nonetheless, grandfather, in keeping with his benevolent nature, advised father to say nothing that could cost Sharma and his sons' jobs.

General Manager wanted to hear father as a witness since he had seen them stealing the spare parts. When father was going to appear before the manager, pandatayin's image in the begging form suddenly appeared in his mind. The manager was very angry when he called father for enquiry. When asked about the incident, father replied that he had overheard the security guards shouting from a distance 'Catch them! Catch them!' and that he did not see Pandit or his son anywhere near the scene. Manager wanted to ensure that father was not doing this out of fear or favour. Father repeated his statement and thus, the manager without taking any action let Sharma's sons go.

In the past also, on several occasions, grandfather and father had rescued Sharma from many difficult situations. Sharma was in the habit of using them, taking advantage of their credulity. Instead of acknowledging their gratitude, it was shocking to note that Sharma and his sons were party to several conspiracies hatched in the village to publicly debase and obliterate our family. The reason for his grudge against grandfather was the latter's popularity and influence over the village community – something Sharma was never able to achieve despite his high social status.

Political climate in the village was hot. With new equations emerging, political players were making all sorts of speculations. No community was willing to support the candidature of Pandit's son. Though there was stiff competition between the Rajputs and Kayasthas, they both were unequivocally opposed to any suggestion supporting Sharma's son.

Minor backward castes, such as Shepherds, Barbers, Telis (oil millers) etc., always depended upon Dalits (cobblers) for their meaningful survival in the village, given latter's dominant position on account of their numerical strength. Taking the intitiative, they approached Dalits with their unequivocal support in favour of their candidate. With this development, the trend was clearly favourable to Dalits, who, with the support of afore-mentioned minor backward castes, now stood a fair chance to win on the strength of their collective vote percentage.

Fear of polarization among other communities was still holding Dalits back to declare their candidate. Their apprehension was not baseless. The Pandit had begun playing his cards to prepare ground for his son by polarizing all groups minus Dalits. He instigated the upper castes not to support a Dalit candidate at any cost. He convened a meeting of high caste communities at his residence. Without mincing words, he said, 'You all know, it is I who convinced you to dine in the community feast of a dalit's wedding. However, I did that for the sake of our community's unity and strength. That you people agreed to participate in a feast organized by a Dalit, I am thankful to you all. I thought Dalits would feel grateful to us – the upper castes- for this great favour; but they appear to have mistaken us by considering themselves equal to us. Their plan to field their own candidate is a clear indication in this direction. Contrary to the traditional norm so far, instead of supporting our candidate, they also want to establish themselves politically by having their own sarpanch. I think they are in hurry. A Dalit cannot be allowed to harbour the ambition of becoming a sarpanch.'

'Then who do you think is the suitable person to become sarpanch?' asked Amba Lal, a Kayastha leader.

'Well, it is up to you to decide; but before that, we ought to take into consideration his overall support base. We have to contest the elections not for the sake of elections, but with an objective to win', quipped Pandit.

Being a shrewd player, Pandit knew well that it was not easy to arrange a consensus candidate from a complex Hindu society. He therefore, had planned first to help create a situation where no consensus candidate was able to emerge and then propose his son. Pandit was feeling the heat as the cutthroat competition for political domination had now become a reality of life in the rural areas as well.

After listening to Pandit, there was silence for a while. Then there were whispers. Heads of major communities gathered there were of the opinion that without support from the Muslims or Dalits it would not be possible for anyone to win. If major communities joined hands together and seek support of intermediary communities, then the sarpanch post was well within their reach. However, in the current situation of inter-rivalry among various groups, the possibilities were remote.

Despite long deliberations, no consensus was in sight. Pandit, who was waiting for the opportune moment, butted in offering his services to the community. Since the gathering understood his artifice well, they started shouting in unison, 'No! No!'

His face went red when several participants were vocal in protesting against him, 'How can you even think of fielding your son even when you are a minority? We strongly feel that the *sarpanch* should be from majority, including Dalits.' The last two words further dampened all his hopes. He was unable to say anything further. Frustrated, fretted and fumed, and of course, sad, he called off the meeting.

Meanwhile, Dalits resolved to assert themselves and decided to field their candidate, without succumbing to and caring for the Muslims' misplaced sentiments. They no longer wanted to remain a pawn in the hands of either Hindus or Muslims. It was increasingly becoming clear to them that they were as strong as any other group as far as elections were concerned.

Election took place. The outcome sprang a surprise! A Dalit, for the first time, had become village sarpanch! A large number of upper castes including those from the lower backward groups had supported Dalit candidate. It was the beginning of social engineering in Independent India, taking place successfully in the backwaters of countryside.

Pandit Yaggya Dutt Sharma would always credit grandfather for the victory of a Dalit candidate in the sarpanch elections. Though he never criticized or opposed grandfather openly, he would never forget this humiliating incident. Filled with enormous bitterness and animosity, he always held a grudge against grandfather.

Employment in the sugar mill was season-based only. Only a few workers were required in the off-season and father was lucky to be one of them. His continuous employment, almost around the year, had helped the family to keep its kitchen warm.

Having cleared my masters in political science with considerably good marks, my confidence level had gone up. I had joined a well-known university in the eastern part of Uttar Pradesh with the sole purpose of preparing for civil services. I was pursuing my studies with all perseverance. My efforts on higher education remained completely focused mainly due to financial support coming my way from father's income. My parents, particularly mother, would always encourage me to concentrate only on my studies and advising me not to worry about home front, especially finances.

The news about my ambitions to join civil services had spread throughout the village. While most of the people did not show any reaction, Pandit Yaggya Dutt was not comfortable with the news. Already upset and scared of grandfather's popularity and prominence, Pandit was getting apprehensive of our family gaining more power and influence over the village if I managed to realize my dream.

Dhyani's grandson as a civil servant! The idea sent shivers down his spine. He knew that my preparations for the civil services would go on undisturbed until father was in the continuous employment and financing my studies. He, therefore, wanted father's employment to go at any cost so that the source of financing my studies dried up. For this, he thought of a dirty trick. He got in touch with a local trade union leader from the communist party and assigned the responsibility to him. Father was on day-duty. As per their scheme, the trade union leader sent for father to discuss some urgent matter with regard to the union activities. On informing that during duty hours he could not leave his work place, the messenger impressed upon him that it was urgent and only a matter of a few minutes. After a lot of persuasion, father left reluctantly, completely unaware of the enemy trap. No sooner did he come out of the factory gate, than Pandit Yaggya Dutt Sharma, who himself was on duty, informed the factory manager about father's negligence of duty! The manager waited for father to return for about an hour. The leader, on the other hand, kept him engaged on one excuse or the other; despite latter's repeated pleas to let him return to his work. When father was back, he found the furious manager waiting for him. Manager enquired angrily, 'Where did you disappear?'

'Sir, our trade union leader sent for me to have some urgent brief discussion,' replied father.

'Brief discussion? I have been waiting for you for over an hour and you claim that it was brief. I am not going to tolerate this kind of callous attitude on the part of anyone,' warned the manager.

'Sir, I am a disciplined worker. And never in the past has there been any instance like this against me', father tried to explain.

'OK, let me confirm from your trade union leader if he had called you', said the manager and sent for him, through one of the co-workers. The manager then waited for the leader to arrive.

'Good morning, manager', said the union leader.

'Good morning, Mr. Chhabeel Singh,' the manager replied.

'Mr. Singh, if you have urgent work with any of your trade union members, well, you can come to the factory premises to talk to them. Please do not send for them outside the factory premises, as I do not want any worker to leave his work place unattended. This guy has been out for over an hour. He claims you had called for him. Is that true?' the manager asked.

The trade union leader feigned complete ignorance.

'Did you hear what he said? Tell me now, why and where had you gone without prior permission?' demanded the manager.

Father could not believe that the trade union leader had also conspired against him; at the same time, he was too stunned and shocked to counter him; with the result that he remained silent in standing position, unanswered. The manager mistook his silence as admission of his fault and ordered him to leave for the rest of off-season. Father had no inkling that Sharma was the director of this act. After the loss of job, a storm of frequent quarells, strifes, feuds, fights had once again gripped the family.

Pandit once called father on the pretext of disucssing another matter concerning a Thakur family. Having finished his topic, he said to father, casually, 'Arrey bhai (O brother!), I learn that your son has gone far away to prepare for collector's examination. Well, I am very glad. If he succeeds, at least we in the village shall be proud of him. Yet I am greatly concerned about you. You have five children. Your son requires a lot of money to prepare for this high-level examination. And given your condition, I doubt you are in a position to bear such expenses. It is bound to affect the well-being of your other children. If you allocate a disproportionately large part of your limited earnings to your elder son, you will be unable to pay attention to your other children. Anyway, it is up to you to decide. In my view, it is better to bring up all your off-springs in an equitable manner.'

Given his credulous nature, father, after getting home, told mother, 'Today I met Pandit Yaggya Dutt Sharma. I know he is a very clever man and has ditched us on many occasions earlier. However, sometimes he offers sensible advice. What he told me today makes absolute sense to me. It is not advisable to spend all our resources on one child only. Therefore, I have decided to bring Preet back from the city. He can continue his preparations in the village itself, if he is really serious to become somebody.'

After a brief and quiet moment, Mother said to father, 'Why do you want to recall him from the city? We are not paying for his boarding and lodging there as he is staying with his friends. Before he left, he had made his own arrangements from his scholarships and coaching others to meet his expenses. You are just sending a meager amount and that too once in two months. I think that may not be sufficient even for a week's food. Since he has been helping himself right from early age, I don't think he would agree to come back. You have hardly contributed in funding his education.'

Father did not receive mother's words kindly. Reacting sharply, he registered a couple of slaps on her face, saying, 'So, now you have become the decision-maker! I have decided to get him back. He can continue his preparations here while assisting me at the fields simultaneously.'

Within a fortnight, I received two letters. First letter was from father, who had directed me to return home immediately. Second was from mother. She wrote, 'my dear son, I know how difficult times you have witnessed from your small age. Though I have lacked in financial resources to help you develop your career, I have always stood by you in all your decisions. You would have received letter from your father asking you to come back home as he wants you to assist him in farming. His argument is that he cannot afford any longer to spend on you alone, though he has contributed hardly anything meaningful towards your education so far. I feel proud of you that you have provided for yourself enough so as not to depend upon your father. I will never advise you to return here. Continue your preparation there without distraction. For your sake, I am prepared to face your father's ire. I am confident that if you do not return, he is going to blame me. You need not be concerned about me, just be focused on your studies.'

33

A Conspirator

After civil services, preliminary exams were over; all aspiring candidates had left for home. I was still not willing to return. In the meantime, students with whom I had arranged to stay also planned to leave. Left with no option, I too finally decided to go back to the village.

I returned home in the second week of June. By that time, people in the surrounding areas had also become aware of my trial with the civil services examination. Pandit Yaggya Dutt, as narrated elsewhere, was perturbed at the prospects of my becoming an officer.

Within a few days of my arrival in the village, disturbing news started filtering to us. Someone from the backward community found out that a group of higher castes, led by Sharma, was hatching a conspiracy to nip me in the bud by implicating in some false criminal case. Their scheme was to get me caught by the police in possession of a country-made pistol. Once a police case framed and the court proceedings started, I would not be able to return to the city to realize my dream.

They had a second plan if I somehow dodged their first plan. They wanted to implicate me in a false rape case.

After hearing the rumors, initially I remained extremely disturbed. Then I said to myself, 'I should go and forewarn the Pandit against his ill designs.'

One day, after breakfast, I marched towards his haveli. On reaching his sitting room, adjacent to his haveli, I saw him lying on a wooden cot with a cushion on his side. To see me approaching, he at once sat up and said, 'Come, *beta*, come. I came to know you returned last week. Your father had told me about your preparations for magistrate's post. I am really glad to hear this.'

I was listening to the Pandit, with a faint smile. He was famous for his sugarcoated words. Responding to his sweet-talk, I said, 'Tauji (Elder uncle), thank you very much for your good wishes. I hope that in future also, you will continue to bless me so that I could realize my dream.'

'Arrey beta, my good wishes are always with you. What a great pride for the whole village to see you in the post of district magistrate. After all, it will bring name and fame to us all', said Sharma in his attempt to make me believe that he was one of my best well-wishers.

'This time, I have come to seek your advice on another matter concerning me. I have learnt that some miscreants are planning to spoil my career by having me implicated in false cases of rape and gun carrying. If this happens, it will really be unfortunate not only to me personally, but also to the entire village. I am grown enough to understand my interests and if someone tries to harm me, I am not going to sit quiet. However, I would like the village elders, like you, to intervene and prevail upon such elements to desist from indulging in such acts. I need your advice in such situation', I told him with a mixture of request and threat.

'I am shocked to hear all this. I cannot imagine that people can stoop to that extent. How can they think of even doing all this to you? Such a promising lad! I will find out and warn these miscreants against any such misadventure', said Pandit in a defensive tone.

'I know that in your wisdom, you would definitely understand the gravity of the matter. I would therefore urge you to prevail upon them, and warn that consequences of this kind of malfeasance on their part would be too costly for them', I told Pandit persisting in my veiled threat.

My last sentence brought a reflection of tension on his face. He lost no time in judging that my threat was directed against him, and that in his designs he had met his match in me. My coming-of-age fearless exchange had shaken the Pandit completely. It took him a while to readjust to the new style of mine talking to him, though it was natural from a person who found his persona and ambitions threatened. Regaining his composure, he meekly uttered, 'You are like my son. I can never think ill of you and I would never allow anyone else to think or do any harm to you. Rest assured'.

Pandit then ordered refreshments for me. After a while, his youngest daughter appeared in the verandah with a tray on her hands lined with bowls full of homemade snacks and two brimming cups of tea. She placed the tray on the table standing between the Pandit and me.

'You need not worry. There are a few jealous people in the village. Son, you are an educated person, just forget about it. Our best wishes are with you. OK, let us have tea now', Pandit said, picking up and holding out one cup to me, in an apparent attempt to buy peace.

Having finished my tea, I expressed to him my gesture of greeting and left for home. After this encounter, I was sure that the Pandit would not only himself avoid indulging in a conspiracy to spoil my career prospects, but would discourage others also from doing so.

34

A Thakurain's Frustration

It was wedding season. In the village, there was a tradition called Munh-Dikhai (first look at the bride) in which womenfolk would visit the newly wedded boy's family to meet the bride. This way, all the villagers got to know about the new bride's overall appearance. That year coincidently, almost all the newly wedded Dalit boys got beautiful wives. This remained a favourite subject during gossip sessions for several days among upper caste women.

One woman was so upset that she could not help expressing her displeasure about it. The woman in question was herself one-eyed with deep smallpox marks on her face, making her a real eyesore.

One day, we several youngsters were playing cards at the study of one of our Kayastha friends. This woman, whom we addressed *Buaji* (Paternal aunt), happened to be part of a kitty party in another room in the Kayasth haveli. Unaware of my presence, Buaji was expressing her lamentation. Her pains, sadness and despair were loud and clear.

'Alas! It is virtually bad time! You see, low caste boys have found beautiful brides! I don't understand how these low caste girls could be so fair colored, tall and beautiful. Where is this crop of such beautiful girls growing in Dalit families? I think the sacred Ganges has begun flowing upwards to the Himalayas; perhaps God also has turned against us and begun bestowing His blessings upon the low castes. Otherwise, these beautiful girls would not have born in them. If it goes on like this, you cannot make a clear differentiation between them and us after a few years', Buaji said heaving a long sigh.

The Kayastha women simply kept listening to her with intermittent nods. None of the boys, except me, seemed to be paying any attention to her. Her so manifest grudge against Dalits obviously was agitating me. I felt like gorging out her other eye also, but somehow I controlled my anger and anguish. My negative thoughts soon disappeared when the young and beautiful girls of the family arrived to serve us tea and homemade snacks.

35

First Experience at a Metropolitan City

Having finished my civil services examination, I returned home in early December. Within a few days of my arrival, I received a telegram from a Central Government organization in Mumbai to join them as an officer. As I was the first boy in the entire Dalit community to have made it, the news of my oppointment sent my family into rapture. After two days of rejoicing, I began my preparations to proceed to Mumbai city. Before my departure, grandfather called me and said, 'I feel proud of you. I can see a bright future for the whole family. Since you are going far away and would be living alone over there, I would like to offer a piece of advice for you to be borne in mind. There is an age-old adage *'Zubaan, Haath aur Langot; Inko Rakho Vash Mein; Kabhi na Khaoge Chot'* (If you want to achieve success in a distant land, you ought to keep away from three vices—bitter tongue, pilfering hands and restless crotch). If you follow these principles in life, nobody will harm you and success will be yours.

'OK, I will keep your advice in mind', I nodded in agreement. Having said this, I took leave of him and other family members, to drive to the nearby town to catch train. Several relations and friends saw me off at the station. After a long journey of nearly 28 hours, I reached Mumbai for my training.

After getting off the train into the milling crowd at Victoria Terminus, Mumbai, I felt a little insecure. Holding my suitcase and bedding, I somehow, exited the station to look for a cab. Soon, I got one and hurriedly, keeping my belongings in the trunk, I asked the driver to take me to Kurla, location of my training.

Next day was Sunday. By morning, all thirty-four trainees, including twelve females had arrived. Truly, our batch represented the whole of India, as the trainees hailed from all parts of the country. After breakfast, all trainees planned to visit Juhu beach. From Kurla bus stop, we boarded a bus towards Juhu. After alternating bus at two places in between, we reached the beach. This was for the first time I was seeing the blue sea. It really felt pleasant to be on the seaside. The city was an entirely different world.

After coming back from the site scene, I wrote a detailed letter to one of my friends in the village, giving a detailed description of Mumbai city:

'The city is in constant motion. Everybody is busy. There is life 24 hours. All kinds of people - rich and poor, businessmen, industrialists, trade-unionists, actors, actresses, professionals, educationalists, politicians, bureaucrats, hawkers, laborers, beggars, criminals, pimps, prostitutes et al, -live in this unique, multi-faceted city of India. I am surprised to see large families and that too from upper-middle and middle-classes living in two or one-and-a-half room flats. People are always prepared to make adjustments with everything—corruption, evils, crimes, flesh-trade, business, trade, mafia, burgling, gang war, and of course entertainment by bollywood. Actors and actresses, the outward role models for the society, also are not immune to these characteristics of city life.

On the one hand, I see high-rise buildings, housing business establishments and luxury hotels catering to the rich and influentials; on the other hand, in between the tall structures, there are embedded slums, full of beggars - both male and female – some of them without limbs.

The city presents a true picture of socio-religious confluence. Almost all cultures, sub-cultures and religions are visibile in this magnificent metropolis. Interestingly, there is no business - legal or illegal- not running in this fascinating city. Everything - *Matka, Jhatka, Satta* and *Tapka*, go side by side. Workers are always vociferous in pressing for their demands at various firms and establishments in and around the city. Sadly, it is different that their own trade union leaders silence them to compromise on their demands. Toiling workers, even after having lived in the city for decades, have largely remained confined to slums. Corrupt and murky businesspersons, politicians, bureaucrats, cunning intermediaries, smugglers, gangsters, mafia dons and other dreaded criminals, all hand in glove, have thrived manifold during the same period or even earlier. The *Kuber Nagari* (city of wealth), as it is called, appears to have been more benevolent to the law-breakers!'

The ambience in the hostel, where we resided, was truly of a composite and multi-hued culture. Everyone had something to offer to other colleagues.

On Monday, our classes began. The first day went by in introduction only. Each trainee gave a brief description about his background, including family, education, and experience. The day was full of fun and the session was over earlier than expected. In the training hall, eyes met with eyes. Several trainees had, through their eye contact only, established intimate relationship with each other. How intimate their relationship had become within a short time after meeting each other could be gauged from the spectacle at the dining hall. Newly formed couples had occupied seats of their choice on the dining tables. Then everyday something or the other began coming to light. Principal was, of course, not oblivious to the attractions developing between pairs. Though these were permanent appointments for the posts, management would keep all the trainees under observation during the first three months to assess their character, integrity and personality.

Within two-three months of training, things became quite clear about each trainee's personal traits. Several boys and girls had paired off. They had started courting each other frequently and within no time, stories of their blooming love affairs surfaced. Although, there was no evidence available about their physical involvement with each other, their conduct on the dining tables, tennis courts, badminton courts and inside the gym was a clear indication that something serious was transpiring among them.

On a few occasions, the institution director summoned some couples to explain about their relationship. Swearing off anything objectionable in their relationship, they avoided punitive action. Yet, director remained apprehensive of their scruples as their activities gave ample reasons to be distrustful despite their claims of innocence. At times, some of these love couples were found behaving with each other in questionable manner. Interestingly, whenever accosted, they would rather put the authorities in the dock by asking them to produce evidence. Thus, authorities could not initiate any action against them without evidence. Taking advantage of this situation, they continued mating clandestinely.

Hard regimen was in place to discipline the trainees. Authorities looked at even casual talks with suspicion. Therefore, as a reaction, several couples were seeing each other secretly. The harder the rule, the more frustrated and disappointed they felt. A few trainees, just to keep their affairs under cover, began pretending non-objectionable relationship of kinship.

One such pair was of Saleena Begum and Somesh Chandra. Saleena belonged to an orthodox family from northeast and Somesh from a holy city in eastern Uttar Pradesh. They eluded everyone in the institute by giving their relationship a pious name of brother and sister. Both of them would visit together religious places like Laxmi temple and Hajimalang. Saleena would invariably say her namaaz five times a day. Somesh also displayed religious orientation by his regular visits to the famous city temples. Everywhere - entertainment club, tennis lawn, badminton court - in the institute where trainees would gather in the evening for sports and other recreational activities, Saleena and Somesh were always butt of jokes. Somesh was always vociferous in protesting against such leg pulling. Initially, trainees used to indulge in teasing just for fun. However, subsequently, it was for all to see an emotional upswing in their interaction. And gradually, it raised a suspicion bar in everybody's mind.

Excursion program was one important component of the training in which trainees would visit the various industrial establishments in and around the city to familiarize themselves with the running and functioning of these plants. Once, all the trainees were taken to the industrial compound of a private limited concern, where the company welfare officer warmly received us. He took us around the premises informing us on the security measures put in place for the welfare of the employees. Afterwards, we had an interactive session with the management to learn about security, wages, compensation, accidental claims, protection for dependents of the workers and other welfare measures to safeguard workers interests. After that, many of us returned to the plant to see the functioning of various units there. For most of us, this was for the first time we had the opportunity of looking from a close range at the giant machines running automatically.

As per the instructions, we were supposed to return to the institute by the evening. After the tour was over, we had some personal time at our disposal. Trainees were scattered in different rendezvous places. Those of us who stayed behind had to gather at the designated place from where a bus arranged by the management had to pick us to drive back home. A few of us including me stayed behind in the premises of the company. Scattered here and there, trainees were watching giant machines with keen interest.

As I was watching a huge machine in operation, I happened to notice Somesh and Saleena at a little distance moving together in a corner. Their movement together, and that too in a dark corner of the factory, where nothing was visible, raised suspicion in my mind. I therefore decided to follow them up. Oblivious of my pursuing them, they walked into the corner, stopped and looked around. I immediately hid myself behind the huge machines and tall pillars. Once certain that nobody was around to see them, they hurriedly walked into the darkness.

What I saw next was astonishing. Dragging Saleena into his arms, Somesh started hugging her passionately. For a few moments, they stood still holding each other tightly. Somesh now slid his right hand into her blouse with his left hand still around her back. Taking out one of her twin assets, he began fondling it. Then pulling out the other one, and holding both in his hands, he put his mouth on them and started kissing and sucking them wildly. In response, voluptuous Saleena was also planting kisses after kisses upon Somesh's well-rounded cherubic cheeks. The next spectacle between them was unbelievable and, of course, unbearable to see given their public protestations. With Somesh unbuttoning and pulling down his trousers, and Saleena raising her saree up, he started moving his hands up her thighs. I was just a few steps away from them behind a steel post. Then, I heard Saleena whispering, 'Somesh! Let us go behind that heap of scrap. It is darker over there.' Soon, they walked into that corner, unaware of my tiptoeing them. Having walked a few steps towards the heap, I stopped short to hide myself behind it. Somesh, who was still holding his unbuttoned trousers in one hand, helped Saleena with other arm to lie on the ground. Somesh now pulled his trousers down to his knees. 'Please hurry up, come in', said Saleena, holding out her arms towards Somesh, still standing in between her spread out legs. It looked really funny to see them in the act. At the same time, I had some sense of guilt, but overall, I was also enjoying their passionate act.

She now pulled her sari further up. Holding her both legs up, Somesh quickly dealt a push forward. With Saleena moaning and groaning something undecipherable, Somesh was now fast pulsating back and forth. Saleena, in the meantime, had wrapped her legs around his waist. I thought it was wiser to leave the place immediately as I had also begun feeling hot and hard. I therefore rushed to the factory exit. A few steps further, a bus was waiting for the trainees to return. A few others, including Saleena- Somesh and Malini Khobragade-Pyush Ratan Joshi were yet to come back. Perhaps, like Saleena and Somesh, they too were having fun in another desolate and dark corner of the factory!

Soon, all the trainees were back and aboard the bus. Somesh and Saleena took their seats in the row next to me. I noticed that normally talkative, they were unusually calm and quiet. It was very common on Somesh's part to crack spicy jokes, particularly on these occasions. However, this afternoon, he was rather quiet. 'Somesh, you are not sharing any jokes today', said I, taking initiative. 'No, yaar, I am feeling a little headache', replied Somesh, perhaps evading a reply. I did not persist further. Saleena and Somesh got off at a stop well before the hostel. It was already dusk. After taking quick shower, all the trainees collected at the dining hall around 0900 hrs. I looked around and found that Somesh and Saleena were conspicuous by their absence. All of us were there at the dining table except for them.

Looking through the windowpane, I noticed both Saleena and Somesh climbing up the stairs to the residential block, holding big plastic bags in their hands. That night they did not appear in the dining hall. Instead, they spent their time in the recreation hall untill late night. I passed by the recreation room without a glance at them and straightway returned to my room in the boys' residential block. I then relapsed into my bed immediately. While looking up at the ceiling, I was pondering over the clandestine manner in which the two were carrying on, even without letting out a hint to anyone. Interestingly, it was baffling to note that both were pretending to be extremely pious in their relationship. Hypocrisy, thy name was Saleena and Somesh!

Our cook Pujari always served the same food over lunch.Immediately after looking at the food, all the trainees at the table would knit their eyebrows, sniffing their nose. Trainees from across the country had varied food habits but Pujari's menu for breakfast was idli-sambhar; and one small bowl of rice, a bowl of lentil and four chapattis for lunch and dinner each. Despite repeated pleas and complaints, he never bothered to change his menu during our six months training. Rumor was that he was doing this with the tacit understanding of some officials of the institute, who received a cut from the big money he was making by providing sub-standard food in the mess.

One day, in order to observe their behaviour closely, I deliberately occupied a chair around the same dining table where Somesh and Saleena sat. Surprisingly, their outward conduct had no sign of intimacy that they were sharing privately. I left immediately after a quick lunch.

I was getting impulsive to share all that I had seen at the plant but somehow restrained to keep the secret to myself. Had I gone ahead, there was a possibility of this all, boomeranging on me. My apprehension was not baseless viewing the support and backing both of them had from the upper caste trainees in their conceitedness. I thought it was wiser to keep my mouth shut and avoid any trouble.

However, I was naïve to think that only I knew about this relationship. The news had traveled to senior faculty members as well as they had their own mechanism to keep tab on the activities of the trainees. Within a month, an interesting but stunning incident took place in the hostel.

One night, around 1:10 am, there was a sudden hubbub in the girls' residential block. I quickly woke up when I heard someone tapping on my door. I immediately got off the bed, switched on the lights, and walked up to the door. I put my ears to the door and asked, 'Who is there?'

'Sir, I am Sangale', a voice came from the other side.

Sangale was a residential caretaker in the institute. He had also been assigned the job of round-the-clock watch over the activities of trainees. Unlatching the door from inside, I pulled it a little in and said, 'Yes, Sangale, what is the problem?'

'Sir, I am sorry to trouble you at this late hour. Please come out, Sir. I am going to wake up others also. Today, I have caught somebody red-handed from a female trainee's room', whispered Sangale into my ear.

Within minutes, almost everybody gathered in front of the entry gate to the female block. Then we noticed that Dr. Sethu, a senior faculty member, was also there. In the presence of all the trainees there, he instructed Sangale to unlock the gate. At once, all the boys along with Dr. Sethu entered the block to awaken all the female trainees. Most of them, after sensing commotion, had already woken up.

Dr. Sethu came forward to knock at Saleena Begum's door himself. Strangly, there was no response from inside despite repeated beatings and calls. By that time, the female trainees had come out of their rooms. Finding so many male members in their block along with Dr. Sethu, they began whispering among themselves. However, none of them had yet any idea about the reality on the ground. Then, they began enquiring from Dr. Sethu. A few of them were guessing about some untoward incident in the hostel.

Dr. Sethu instructed Sangale to inform the female members about the reason of their visit. Upon this, Sangale said, 'I have seen Somesh entering Saleena's room. I am certain he is still inside.'

Hearing this, Sarvati, one of the female trainees, who also hailed from a northeastern state, started screaming at Sangale saying, 'What non-sense are you talking? What is Somesh doing here at this late hour? How can you be so sure about his identity?' she demanded sternly.

Encouraged by Sarvati's fulmination, more female trainees came forward to complain that all this was a conspiracy by male trainees to defame them. For a few moments, Sangale stood stunned to see the angry and united front presented by the female trainees. Trying to regain his composure, he maintained that he had seen Saleena ushering Somesh in. Reacting to this, Sarvati shouted at Sangale saying, 'Buzz off. Do not try to outrage a female's modesty by vilifying her. You are a liar'.

At this, Dr. Sethu, who normally maintained his cool, flared up, 'Madam, don't call us liars. Do you know what is going on here? I am aware that many of you have grossly violated the rules of the institute, vitiating the whole atmosphere. Sadly, you are one of them. If you want me to let other trainees know more about your affair with Patnaik, I will produce a detailed report on your activities to the board members.'

Hearing these plain words from a senior faculty member, Sarvati fell silent. Realizing the gravity of the situation, in an attempt to divert attention, she said, 'Sir, I am sorry if I have annoyed you; but are you sure, Sir that somebody has entered Saleena's room?' Thereupon, Dr. Sethu offered, 'If you don't trust us, you may check for yourself her room.' Now Sarvati gingerly walked up to Saleena's room and began tapping on it wildly. When there was no response from inside, everybody got scared. They suspected that Saleena and Somesh might have caused some harm to themselves out of fear or shame.

Sarvati then volunteered to cross over to Saleena's balcony through her room. After Dr. Sethu nodded, she came to her balcony to scale up the wall into Saleena's balcony. The balcony door in Saleena's room was open. After entry, Sarvati tried violently to shake Saleena up, who pretended to be fast asleep. Finding no one inside, Sarvati herself opened the main door from inside to let Dr. Sethu and others come in. She informed Dr. Sethu that there was no one inside. Hearing this, he grew a little mortified.

He turned to Saleena and asked, 'Saleena, be honest and truthful. Tell us who came to your room.' Saleena said nothing. Dr. Sethu reiterated his question, but Saleena remained silent. His persisted attempts to make Saleena confess and tell the truth to everyone around failed repeatedly. Saleena disclosed nothing about her late-night visitor.

During the questioning process, my eyes kept roving around the room to look for a good proof suggesting a visitor's arrival into her room. Suddenly, I spotted two water jugs resting on the side table. Elbowing Dr. Sethu, I pointed towards them, who immediately picked up both the jugs in his hands. While one jug had little water in it, the other was full and appeared to have been filled just an hour ago, as there were still drops of water all over. While Dr. Sethu was still holding the jugs, I continued to look for more evidence. I noticed a bigger size pair of chappals lying on the ground. Bending on my knees, I peeped under her cot and could see another pair of chappals. I pulled it out with the help of my foot and drew Dr. Sethu's attention to have a look at them.

Dr. Sethu then asked Saleena if she was still maintaining that there was no visitor to her room. If that was the case, then why was there a pair of chappals, which did not fit her apart from a jug that was also not hers? Dr. Sethu recalled that in his knowledge both the items belonged to Somesh.

At this point, Saleena broke down. She said crying, 'Please forgive me, Sir. At this moment, I am more concerned about Somesh safety.'

'Why? What happened? Where is he?' demanded Dr. Sethu.

'Sir, we heard someone latching our iron gate. Scared that someone had noticed him entering the complex and that he would get caught now, Somesh jumped off from the balcony door', informed Saleena.

As Saleena's room was on the third floor, all of us including Dr. Sethu rushed to the backyard that had a banana orchard and thick bushes in it. We saw no one there, but a banana grove was found crushed to the ground, an indication of the fact that Somesh had jumped down over there and escaped undetected.

Immediately, Dr. Sethu informed police to trace out him. They asked for his photo identity, which was made available from his personal file in the record room to enable them to undertake search operation. Throughout the night, police team continued to search for him in various parts of the city without any success.

In the morning around 7:00 am, a police inspector arrived at the institute to inform that police had taken Somesh custody from Dadar railway station. Finally, police brought him to the institute, where he tendered his apologies to the management.

Atmosphere at the institute had hotted up. All around, there were whispers. Lovebirds, among us, had reason to be concerned, as the next day, management expelled Saleena and Somesh from the institute on the grounds of moral turpitude.

Somesh Pandey was a staunch advocate for the preservation of the institution of caste system. He would often quote the scriptures and Mahatma Gandhi to buttress his arguments. He would say, 'great seers of India have established social classification for the stability and progress of the society and all enlightened people should work in this direction.'

In his pursuit, he was so arrogant and insensitive that he would not hesitate in using condescending words for Dalits, without realising that it might hurt them. Obviously, on occasions, Dalit trainees, including me, felt humiliated at his snide remarks.

As Saleena and Somesh were taking leave, I walked up to the exit gate where a taxi was awaiting to take them to the station. When both of them, along with a few others, reached close to the taxi, I walked upto them. With Saleena having got into the car and Somesh still climbing in, I greeted him with the advice that he should take good care of his *dear sister*!' This was my way of letting out my pent up emotions. For a moment, he looked threateningly at me. Shame-faced, he quickly got into the taxi and drove away without making eye contact with anyone over there.

This was not the only couple indulged in such an activity. There were others too who were doing the same thing in a clandestine manner.

In the institute, there was groupism among the trainees, reflecting separate identities of their caste, religion and region. Initially, I associated myself with a group from Northern India. In this group also, members prided themselves more on their caste identity as most of them belonged to upper castes such as Aggarwal, Gupta, Saxena, Mathur, Maheshwari, etc. Personally, I never felt comfortable talking in terms of caste, religion and region. Since members, irrespective of their groups, insisted on revealing caste identity, I gradually disassociated myself with any of the groups. I was aware of 2-3 more Dalit trainees at the institute but none of them was prepared to reveal his identity.

These groups would organize and celebrate their cultural events and festivals with gusto. On a few occasions, I too participated in their festivities. However, subsequently I stopped as I noticed that, even on such joyous occasions, they would rake up in their discussions, irrelevant and unnecessary issues concerning Dalits.

Another interesting aspect that my interaction with them brought to light was that though their job was to educate the workers about their rights, none of them appeared to be sympathetic towards them. Issues like eradication of untouchability and caste system, abolition of exploitation and other forms of discrimination against workers formed part of the syllabus for training. These issues also figured prominently in the discussions and debates on labour problems. After attending the programs on these issues, many trainees would express their disapproval of such an approach, saying, 'Who bothers about these issues? They have been part and parcel of our society. We are not here to abolish them. Our aim is to earn our livelihood and lead a good life'.

On one occasion, a Muslim faculty member happened to ask me in front of several trainees, 'Which caste do you belong to?' I was stupefied at his question. It felt awkward that a senior officer, and that too when he himself practiced a religion that does not recognize caste system, was talking in terms of such a social hierarchy. When I told him that I was a human being, he audaciously said, 'All belong to humankind; but I just wanted to know the sub-caste you belong to. I know you are a Rajput.'

'No, no, Sir, I am not. By the way, what made you to think that I am Rajput? Being a Muslim, do you still believe in the caste system, Sir?' I asked in mock disbelief.

'Well, in Islam, there is no such division. Since I am a Rajput Muslim, I can easily read a person's lineage. I firmly believe that blue blood recognizes blue blood; your appearance suggests you are a Rajput,' he asserted confidently, giving a biological tinge to his explanation. I just let it pass with a smile.

Outside the training hall, parallel to the passage to the kitchen, sat several benches for probationers to lounge. One day, sitting there, I was glancing through a newspaper when a female probationer, namely, Neena Dwivedi waved at me from the entrance of their residential block. When I returned the courtesy, she utilized the opportunity to come down and sit with me. I gestured to her to take a seat on the bench to my left. Picking out a leaf from my newspaper, she sat down. Posing as if she too was reading it, she began, 'Preet, do you know Tapat Mishra? The boy from Lucknow, connected to a political family, always keeps talking against you in abusive language. I think he hates both of us. He has been repeatedly warning me not to interact with you at all.

'Then, why don't you stop that? Do you have any idea about why he is opposed to our meeting? I have had no dealing with him so far. So, I wonder what grudge he is holding against me.'

'You don't know his mindset. He is from an orthodox and obscurantist Brahmin family who believes in the caste system and untouchability as part of their religion. Last night after the dinner when I was sitting along with my female friends, he walked up to me in the lawn outside. Calling me aside, he asked if I knew which caste you belonged. When I informed him that I knew everything about you, including the caste, he told that despite knowing everything why I am friendly to you! He added that I should be ashamed of myself for being interested in a Dalit boy. When I rejected his discourse, he flared up and left fuming and commenting "go to hell".

'So, what have you decided? Would you like our friendship to continue or follow his diktats?' asked I.

'Don't be crazy. I don't care what he and others think about our friendship. We have done nothing disgraceful in our relationship that we should feel ashamed of. Moreover, you know well that I don't believe in bloody caste system or untouchability, even though I am a Brahmin myself. Let Tapat Mishra and others of his ilk hang themselves if they are not comfortable with our meeting each other. I think Tapat is jealous of you. On several occasions, he made advances towards me. However, I sternly warned him not to get close to me. That could be the cause for heartburn in him.'

I was delighted to hear such comforting and encouraging words, shorn of any bias or prejudice, spoken with honesty and truthfulness. Looking at each other, we remained seated there for some time and then left for our respective blocks.

My room in the hostel had become a chatting *adda* where we would gather very often to indulge in all sorts of bizarre gossipings. One day, three colleagues—a Jat from Haryana, a Dogra from Kashmir and third a Sayyed Muslim from UP—had descended in my room to spend the afternoon. We were regaling each other with various anecdotes on people from rural as well as urban areas. Then suddenly, Tapat barged into my room without any prior notice. It was totally unexpected as he had never visited me earlier. Since he was already in, I gestured him to take the chair standing nearby. Pulling up the chair, he sat on it. For a few minutes, he remained quiet. He appeared to be oblivious to what was going on around him.

Suddenly, to everyone's bewilderment, he began, '*Arrey yaar*, what are you talking? I find nothing interesting. *Aajkal desh ki dasha badal rahi hai. Saale, neech jaat, achoot bhi afsar banane lage hain. Khaskar chamaron ka bada dimaag kharab ho gaya hai.*' (Our country is witnessing great changes. Bloody, low caste, untouchables have also joined to become officers. Particularly, cobbler community in my province has gone crazy.)

Stunned, enraged and humiliated, I felt deeply anguished but I somehow managed to restrain myself from retorting back. I spared him by giving a slightly angry look only. He, however, continued with his vituperative tirade. '*Yeh saale, kam jaat wale bhi bari bari rajniti karne lage hain. Kal tak yeh hamare pairo ki jooti the aur aaj hamare sir pe char baithne ki koshish kar rahe hain*'. (These bloody low caste people have also started participating in big party politics. Those who until yesterday were not worthy of being our shoes, are now trying to sit on our heads.)

He used many more highly provocative and abusive epithets. No one with any self-esteem could put up with such offensive. However, since he was my (uninvited) guest at the time, I somehow controlled myself in responding to his casteist onslaught.

Soon, the situation got out of control. Despite no contribution from my side, it took a nasty turn when he attacked me directly, '*Is saale ko dekho, yeh bhi to chamaar hai aur kitni bari bari batein karta hai. Apne ko Brahmin aur Rajput se bada samajhta hai. Saala baat karte samay yeh bhool jata hai ki iski jaati kitni neech hai.*' (Look at this bloody cobbler, himself a low caste, but talks big. He thinks himself no less than a Brahmin or a Rajput. While talking, he forgets his low-caste origins.)

Stung and hurt, it felt that my body from head to toe had numbed. Moreover, I was unable to understand the reason for his insulting me at my own place. I simply asked him, 'Yaar Mishra! Why are you trying to drag me into these things? And why do you call me names?'

What he said next was again unbelievable and inexplicable. Firing his salvo, he added, 'Abe saale, chamatte (even more derogatory term), you dare argue with a Brahmin! You, a low caste, do not deserve to be here. You are fit only to polish our shoes.'

That was enough to put an end to the tether of my restraint. His acid remarks had thrown me into an uncontrollable rage. In electrifying manner, I rose swiftly from my chair, lifted my sandals from the floor and began thrashing him. I did not stop until I was out of breath. While doing this, I chased him out of my room, kicking on his back from behind.

The incident reminded me what grandfather would say about such people, 'By reminding you repeatedly of your low caste status in the society, these people want to make you believe that you are naturally born low. With such derogatory words used frequently, at some stage, we also begin to believe in such notions and consequently resign to a status thrust upon us. This generates inferiority complex and one tends to accept meekly what others say, think and do about one. On the contrary, if you retort back in belligerent manner, it does have impact on the other side.'

After thrashing, Mishra never crossed my way. Grandfather's observation was quite honest. I could clearly see its impact on Mishra.

36

Interesting Revelations in the New Job

Six-month training period in Mumbai was over. Successful trainees had received their deployment orders. I had to report for duty in an eastern state, then notorious for the practice of extreme form of casteism and untouchability.

Before proceeding to the place of posting, I visited my family, as grandfather had taken seriously ill. After treatment for over a month, he breathed his last. His departure undoubtedly created a void in the family, his community and the village. Known for his fearless, plain, bold approach and well-grounded wisdom, he had won laurels from all sections of people in the whole region. Despite being rude, cruel and spiteful at home, especially towards mother, he commanded great respect in society. He always showed his affection towards me, especially after I started performing well in the studies. His dream was to see me become a *Bada Sahab* (senior officer). Apart from his love and attachment for me, this would obviously enhance his social standing within and outside the village community. Sadly, the dream could not be realised in his lifetime. After his demise, the role of head of the family passed on to father.

Not comfortable with the people or places where one had to first reveal one's caste identity, I landed in the city with a bag of mixed feelings - happy about my first job but a little tight over the possibility of being blatantly identified based on my caste affiliations.

I got accommodation in the residential colony meant for management and employees. The colony housed over 30000 officials and employees and perhaps the only such corporate residential block. After dumping my bag and baggage in my bungalow, I straight away proceeded to the office to report for duty.

The first day went by, in introduction only. One week into my job, I was still in the process of settling down. Then, one day my boss, Shri A.K. Lal Prasad, the regional director, summoned me in the office and asked, 'How do you find the new place?'

'Well Sir, the place appears to be good', I replied.

Proceeding ahead, he enquired, 'Are you aware that our zonal director (ZD) is visiting next week for inspection? All officers need to go to the airport to receive him. In addition, we are required to present him some good gift at the time of his departure. We have to make his stay comfortable. Boss is Bengali; he loves Basmati rice and fish. I need to arrange at least one quintal of good quality Basmati rice to dispatch along with him. To arrange a suit-length for boss and a good silk sari for ma'am, all the officers need to contribute. Now that you have joined, you will also make your contribution.'

'I have just arrived, sir. I do not have money for such contribution. In fact, I need advance from the office as I am still in the process of settling down. So, please exempt me this time at least' I said naively to him, without realizing that it would offend him

To my utter shock, boss retorted angrily, 'You appear to be from a very low background. I wonder how you have reached this far. Surely, you must be the first educated person in your family, who has moved out in the real world. That is why you have no idea of how the system functions. You need to understand the system to survive here. I see no point in taking you to the airport for reception of the visiting dignitary.'

His curt remark about my background hurt me deeply. Though entirely unexpected, it was an eyeopener. Apologising to him, I again expressed my inability to contribute.' At this, he said dismissively, 'It's OK'.

There was a lot of hurly-burly going on in the office on the day of the visit. Officers as well as staff were busy in preparations for a rousing reception. A senior staff walked into my room enquiring: 'Sir, are you coming to the airport to receive ZD?'

'No' I replied.

'Why? Didn't regional director inform you? You are a senior officer you must come. May be, RD did not invite you to come because you have just arrived and are still in settling stage', he said.

In the afternoon, all officers left office earlier than usual. Only I was sitting until 5:30pm. In the evening, officers and staff, led by RD received the Zonal Director at the airport. From there, they escorted him to the hotel in a cavalcade. RD hosted a lavish dinner in honor of the ZD at the hotel restaurant itself. All officials and staff, except me, participated in it.

Next day ZD, accompanied by boss, set out for sightseeing. All officials and staff remained absent from office most of the day. At 1:30pm, the corporate management hosted a lunch for ZD. Every one, barring me, (as the RD had not informed the corporate management about my joining the office), attended it. After lunch, RD escorted the guest back to the hotel.

Again in the evening boss hosted dinner at the hotel. All officers and staff attended the dinner. After attending the dinner, on way back home, a colleague from office dropped in my residence. It was 11:00 pm when he knocked at my door. As

I was quite new to the place, I was a bit hesitant to open the door. A visit by someone at this late hour was quite unexpected. Rising from my chair, I walked to the door and putting my ear to it, I asked, 'Who is there?'

'Its me, Sinha, your colleague from office', was the reply from outside.

'Who Sinha?' I asked to reassure myself about the identity of the visitor.

'It is M.K.Sinha', said he.

I opened the door to let him in. I noticed a lady standing behind him. Introducing her, Sinha said, 'Meet my wife, Chandra'. Then turning towards her, he said, 'This is Preet who joined office last week only', he added introducing me to her.

Chandra was really a buxom beauty. 'Namaste Bhabhiji' I wished her.

'Namasteji', she returned my wishes with a sweet voice and a mystifying smile.

Offering them chairs to sit down, I, as a matter of courtesy, asked them, 'What would you like to drink'.

'I won't mind a cup of tea, and what about you Chandra?' said Mr. Sinha looking towards his wife.

Mrs. Chandra appeared to be a more understanding woman. Realizing that I may not have settled yet, she said, 'Arrey, why do you bother Preet especially when he is not settled yet. We will come some other day to have tea with him.'

'Arrey Bhabhiji, please don't worry about my settling down. At least, I can offer you tea. That should not be a problem', I insisted.

Having said this, I walked into my small kitchen. When I was boiling water in the kettle, Mrs. Chandra entered the kitchen and offered to help. 'No bhabhiji, why you take the trouble. Please sit with Mr. Sinha' I said politely, with a sweet smile.

'No, no, I will assist you', she persisted.

After preparing tea, Mrs. Chandra took out three teacups from the cupboard overhead. Meanwhile, I drew a small plate and a box containing snacks from the cupboard, lined the plate with some homemade snacks and placed them on the tray. Mrs. Chandra followed me to the drawing room holding tray in her hands. She first handed out teacups to us. Then picking up hers, she started the conversation, 'Bhai Sahib, you must be hassled that we disturbed you at this late hour.'

'Oh, this is not a big deal', said I.

We had just begun sipping when Mr. Sinha said, 'Yaar, we really feel bad and find it rather strange that RD did not invite you to the dinner.'

'Well, it is his prerogative. I have nothing to say on this', said I.

'It's nice of you that you think like this, but everybody at the dinner was talking of you. And you know, ZD himself enquired of you', added Mr. Sinha.

'You will be surprised to know that ZD in the presence of everyone asked RD the reason for your absence, but he was shaky and uncomfortable in giving a convincing reply. He only kept quiet. I have a feeling that tomorrow ZD is certainly going to check this directly from you', informed Sinha. I listened to him attentively and then in an attempt to change the topic, I casually asked, 'How was the dinner and who all were present there?'

Having mentioned the names of the participants in dinner, Sinha said, 'You won't believe, yaar, throughout the party RD appeared to be completely forlorn and disturbed. Though he himself was the host, he did not appear to be enjoying. In an apparent effort to placate the boss, he simply kept asking, 'anything else Sir? Please try this one, Sir', 'Please try that one, Sir' pointing to different cuisines laid out at the dining table. 'You should have brought madam along Sir. Weather here is pleasant; she would have definitely enjoyed this place. RD spared nothing to flatter ZD. While RD was busy appeasing ZD, we all were enjoying the dinner.'

He continued, 'There were around 25 invitees. Boss' daughter-in-law was in-charge of the arrangements. She had decided upon the list of invitees as well as menu.'

'Daughter-in-law!' I exclaimed and asked Mr. Sinha, 'Why daughter-in-law? Doesn't boss have wife?

'Don't you know that boss is a widower for over a decade? His son, who migrated to the USA a few years ago, left his doctor wife behind to take care of his father. He visits his father and family every two years. Boss' daughter-in-law is very social and broad-minded woman. Stunningly beautiful, her charms are extremely captivating, her social networking is really admirable. In the absence of her husband, she is looking after her father-in-law quite well. Boss is also rumoured to be taking really good care of this heady cocktail of brain and beauty.' Sinha updated me with a mischievous smile.

The titillating and spicy way in which Sinha gave me these interesting details about boss' family background got the better of me, making me probe even further.

'Yaar, Sinha, you appear to be rejoicing in sharing these details. I can sense a kind of wicked pleasure in your narration. I can also sense that today you are here to brief me more on boss. Please feel at home, cast away the shyness. Tell us something more.' I said prodding him in an attempt to dig his mind further on the matter.

'Arrey yaar, this is a long story. It is already late. We will talk about it some other time', said Sinha, and rose to leave.

It was past mid-night and I was feeling terribly sleepy. Therefore, I did not insist upon him further. However, my curiosity about RD's personal life grew further, when Mrs. Chandra commented, 'Bhai Sahib, your boss is a colorful man. We will talk about this great story when we have some leisure.' Saying this, Mr. & Mrs. Sinha left my residence. I saw them off to the gate and walking back bolted my room from inside. Soon I reclined into my charpoy and fell asleep. I got up a bit early next morning. Having done some yogic exercises, I hurriedly prepared myself for the office with the intention of stopping by a restaurant to have my breakfast.

I had just stepped out of my house when Pandit Radha Shankar Tiwari, a local priest called me out. Approaching me from the opposite end of the street, he asked, 'Preet*ji*, you are leaving quite early today. Do you have a meeting? Or, are you going somewhere else?'

'Tiwari*ji*, I could not prepare breakfast at home. So, I plan to eat at the restaurant near that auto-rickshaw stand', I replied.

Within a fortnight of my arrival in the locality, people had become quite familiar with my name. I also knew almost all of them personally.

'Preetji, yesterday, I performed Satyanarayan katha at one of my jajmans' (host) house. A lot of foodstuff, like sweets, fruit, purees, came as offerings. We have a plenty of it still left at our place. If you don't mind, let's have breakfast together', offered Tiwari inviting me to his house. I could neither accept nor decline. Taking a subtle stance, I informed him that because of sensitive stomach I could eat only freshly cooked food. Upon this, Tiwari remarked, 'Arrey Preetji, we pandits are used to such food even if it is two-three days old. For you, I will arrange fresh paranthas or purees. Please don't say no to have breakfast with me.'

We both walked along the street in the direction of my way to the office. At the far end of the street, he stopped by his house, a few yards away from the market where I would take a cab to office.

'Preet*ji*, don't be hesitant; feel at home; after all, we are neighbours. Moreover, you are the seniormost officer in the locality. I am very happy to have you here,' Tiwari welcomed me holding my hand and conducting me to the gate of his house.

I could not say no and followed him.

'Arrey, Listen! See who's come!' Tiwari called out.

A middle-aged woman with wide eyes and well-shaped oval face appeared in the room, where I was seated on a bamboo chair. Tiwari himself sat with his back to the door.

I rose to my feet to say my regards to the lady in the room who, by now, I knew was none other than Mrs. Radha Shankar Tiwari.

'Namastey' I wished her with folded hands.

'Please be seated', returned Mrs. Tiwari before leaving the room.

Tiwari this time called his daughter, 'Pinki, come and say Namastey to uncle'.

Soon a young beautiful girl, hardly 16-17 years of age, appeared from the adjoining room.

'Namastey uncle!' she said with hands lifted jointly.

'Lay out the breakfast, my child; uncle has to go to office. In fact, he was reluctant, but he relented only on my insistence; he is in hurry, there is an urgent meeting for him to attend', Tiwari told his daughter, conveying to her that I was an important person! Pinki soon left the room to help her mother in the kitchen.

Pinki appeared with two plates in her both hands full of purees, kheer, burfis and bowels of vegetables, nicely arranged on the trays. Bending on the table sitting between us, she deposited the two plates on it and went out to bring water. Signaling towards the food on the table, Tiwari gestured, 'Lets start, Preetji, you are getting late.'

During the breakfast, Tiwari was talking so many bizarre things, mostly weird and meaningless. I was somehow bearing with him. Most of the stuff was passing over my head. However, I kept pretending as if I was attentively listening to what he was uttering throughout. Meanwhile, a particular comment by Tiwari truly caught my attention. He said, 'You know Preetji, I know all your colleagues, their families and their backgrounds. I also know your boss, Prasadji very well. I am certain that you would be interested to know anything flavorsome about him'.

By now, I had finished my breakfast. I savoured a freshly cooked stuffed parantha with a small bowl of curd. On hearing the word 'flavorsome' from him, my ears pricked up. Pretending that I was not much enthusiastic in any story about my boss, I just made some nocturnal noise. Then, interrupting Tiwari, I said, 'Tiwari Sahib, you know I am already late; can we reserve this discussion for some other day'.

'Oh yes, why not. We shall keep meeting. I am sure you would love to hear more about your boss', Tiwari said.

After thanking Tiwari for the sumptuous breakfast, I left for the office. Standing up at his place, Tiwari requested me to hold on for a few moments. This said, he hurriedly went inside and soon emerged in an elegant dress. Then walking together, he conducted me to the door. Turning towards him, when I wanted to say Good Bye to his family, Tiwari immediately spoke up, 'Preetji, for the last several months, I have not been to that part of the city. Therefore, I will also accompany you'.

I did not understand the reason behind his sudden decision to go with me. We took a cab and drove away. I thought Tiwari would get down somewhere midway but he did not. Having reached the designated place, we left the cab. I paid the driver and hurried up to the stairs to the second floor of the building where the office was located. Immediately after entering the chamber, I got busy in work. All this while, Tiwari was meeting individually with official staff members in their rooms. Sitting in my room, I could overhear him addressing everyone –from RD to peon – by first name. After spending a few hours in office, Tiwari went away only to return in the evening.

Nanhe, our peon, was an old hand. For the largest period of his service in the department, he had worked with A.K. Lal Prasad, the RD. Wherever, the latter transferred, Nanhe always went with him to that place. This was Prasad's third stint in here and so was of Nanhe.

Presuming that Nanhe, by way of his long stint in the office, should be the most suitable person to know about Tiwari,

I called him in my room. I asked him, 'for how long he had been working in this office.'

'Sir, it's nearly eighteen years since I have been with Bada sahib, he said referring to Prasad.'

'Nanhe, then, you must be personally known to all visitors who frequent to this office', I asked him.

'Of course, Sir. No one can escape my keen eyes. I know all the trade union leaders, mediators, arbitrators, managers and officers, who visit us frequently' confirmed Nanhe, with a tinge of justified pride in his voice.

'Yes, I do appreciate your knowledge about people in the city. By the way, could you enlighten me on Tiwari? What sort of person is he?' I asked Nanhe innocently and directly.

'Tiwari Sahib has been associated with this office for many years. He has interacted with most of the officers and regional directors. He facilitates in organizing workers' camps in different parts of the region. He is very close to Prasad Sahib, whom he knows from latters early days in service. Tiwariji once happened to be a trade union leader and was very powerful and influential. He was instrumental in brokering peace between the striking trade unions and managements of several industrial concerns of the region.' Nanhe revealed.

It was about 5:15 PM. Nanhe was still around in my room when Tiwari walked in. 'Sorry, Preetji, I had gone to see someone in the Heavy Engineering Corporation (HEC), where I got stuck. Hence, this delay', he tried to explain away laughingly.

'It's OK. You have a long life! We were just talking about you. I suppose, you and Nanhe are quite familiar with each other', I said.

'Yes, I know him since he was a young boy. And if I am not mistaken, for most of the time in course of his service, he has been with RD A.K. Prasad', informed Tiwari. Nanhe supported him with an expression of pride.

'It is time to go home, Preetji', said Tiwari. I looked into my watch; it was quarter to six. I checked from Nanhe if other officers had left. 'Yes, sir, everybody has gone', he informed.

I collected my personal papers and putting them in my briefcase I rushed out down the the stairs with Tiwari leading the way.

It was pitch dark all around. No one was visible on the streets. A little far away from our premises, on the main road, a few streetlights were dimly blinking. 'Tiwariji, I hope we get a cab at this late hour to reach home', I said.

'Arrey Preetji, do you really need a taxi to get home? Why do you worry about it?' said Tiwari looking towards me.

Then pointing to an Ambassador car in the parking lot, reserved for para-military forces, he speedily stepped towards it, waving at me to walk behind him and taking out at the same time a car key from the right pocket of his thick woollen coat. Soon, we stood near the car. Tiwari quickly opened the front door and asked me to get in.

On way back home, Tiwari said, 'Preetji, you appear to be a simple, honest and plain-speaking person, far away from all those essential qualities that make a person resourceful, influential and successful. In the past, many officers like you came and went. You would soon learn from people that I gave several of them necessary tips to be in real profession. Today, they are the most successful officers in their career. I may prove wrong, but I still hold that honesty, simplicity and plainness are the qualities that people mostly appreciate in abstraction only. However, these values are of no good use in leading a decent and comfortable life. If you try to live with your natural traits, you are only going to invite more trouble for yourself than appreciation'.

Tiwari's philosophical monologue continued, 'Look at me. I have never bowed before anyone. People respect when you put on the veneer of honesty and idealism. We all have many facades and adjust ourselves in accordance with the situation in view of our self-interest. You cannot change a single person, let alone the world. When you advise someone to live with ideals and principles, they might admire you in the face. However, the truth is that they laugh at you behind your back. The moment they find you interfering with their stakes, they will not hesitate to wipe you out, even if it means physical removal. It is not advisable for a gentleman like you to mess up with goons, who are always well connected. Therefore, to pursue your interests and survive in this world, you need to be clever, highly connected, well informed, resourceful and sometimes even forceful and farcical. The reason for my telling you all this will be clear to you from what I am going to tell you now.'

Before Tiwari could go ahead, I interjected, 'Tiwariji, how can I change my intrinsic qualities suddenly? Though born in an under-privileged family, I was brought up with certain values. I can hardly abandon them now'.

'When you face the reality, you will find that your so-called values are rather a hindrance than a facilitating means in your upliftment. You see, after graduation I decided to take up cudgels on behalf of the poor labour class and soon emerged as a popular trade union leader to reckon with. I began mobilizing workers of both organized as well as unorganized sectors to push for their demands. Within no time, my hard work and sincerity paid off; and I gained a great deal of popularity among the working classes. On the other hand, all that I had earned in public life was lost on family front. Being away from home for long stretches of period due to my continuous engagement in intensive labour activities, my family began suffering on all counts. Managements of several industrial concerns, where I had done tremendous amount of work for the welfare of working class, created dummy trade union leaders, paid them hefty sums to spread rumours involving me in several cases of tribal women's molestation and rape. They falsely implicated me in other cases of bribery and blackmail. All this caused me a great deal of humiliation and insult, apart from creating a general feeling of mistrust in my mind. Faced with a social boycott from all sides, I had to distance myself from public life. However, I was now like a wounded tiger. I, therefore, pledged to teach my detractors a lesson of their life.

I would collect all sort of information about the murky activities of the dummy trade union leaders, like their involvement in sale-purchase deals, down the table payments received from managements, their indulgence, along with several management personnel, in sexual exploitation of tribal girls. Once the clinching evidence was in my possession, I would then contact them sounding out on their activities.'

Interrupting him in recounting of his long personal history, I asked Tiwari straightly, 'Tiwariji, could you please be brief and tell me what you exactly achieved by indulging in these sorts of bickerings and wranglings.'

'Of course, I achieved a lot. Within no time, my income graph soared up. No management personnel or trade union leader could afford to say no to me. Would you like to know how this happened,' asked Tiwari.

'Yes, go ahead please,' said I.

'That is because I know all the secrets of these people's murky dealings. Your own boss cannot afford to ignore me for anything I put up to him', said Tiwari with a whiff of arrogance, aimed at frightening me as well.

With rapt attention, I continued listening to him, without allowing myself to miss real implication of his avowals.

'I am like your father. My advice should help you learn things faster to achieve your objectives in life. You are new in this place. I am sure you will gradually know everything about your colleagues as well as boss. If you need any help, please do not hesitate to contact me. Otherwise, I myself will remain in touch with you. I can see a trustworthy person in you as a friend. Therefore, I wish to have a solid, reliable and steadfast relationship with you. Don't worry at all. Nobody here can dare harm you in any way', declared Tiwari, trying further to overawe me with his reach and connections.

'By the way, how do you know so much about the cloudy activities of high-ranking management personnel and trade union leaders, particularly when you are no longer actively involved in trade union politics or social work?' I enquired.

'Being a pujari (priest) in the colony's temple has proved highly advantageous for me. People of all ranks—management personnel, babus, government officials, trade union leaders, workers—visit me there. Though religious in nature, I try to utilise their visits as an opportuny to glean indiscernibly all the valuable information about simmering scandals. You know people respect me as a priest and as such they reveal voluntarily everything I ask them.' said Tiwari, stopping the car and telling me 'You are home, now.'

There was no light on the streets. It was dark all around. Stepping out of the car, I noticed that the car had halted in front of Tiwari's house. Thanking him for the lift and stretching my hand for a parting shake, I said, 'It was really interesting talking to you. See you later, Tiwariji.'

I had just started walking towards my residence when Tiwari suddenly called, 'Arrey Preetji, don't be so formal. Where will you go in this dreadful dark? I had informed my family to prepare dinner for both of us. Let us have dinner and then I will escort you to your place.'

'Tiwariji, don't pamper me so much that later it becomes difficult for you to get me off your back', I said in a lighter vein.

'Arrey, why do you say so? It will always be a pleasure to have you home. It will be a good company when you visit me', said Tiwari, insisting further to have dinner with him.

From the road down below, we climbed up the flights of stairs to the entrance of his house. Standing on the last step, he knocked at the door calling out his daughter, 'Pinki bitiya, please open the door. It is papa here.'

Soon, Pinki opened the door and after letting us in, she slammed it again. She then straight walked into the living room to announce, 'Babuji, dinner is ready. If you want to freshen up, we will wait to lay the table'.

'Would you like to wash?' asked Tiwari.

'Yes, I will.' I replied.

Tiwari conducted me to the toilet, handing out at the same time a freshly rinsed white towel. I hurriedly splashed cold water on my face and hands as I was feeling the hunger pangs. Just when I was coming out of the bathroom, Tiwari entered, saying 'Just wait, Preetji. Let me also freshen up'.

While Mrs. Tiwari was still busy in the kitchen in her pre-dinner preparations, Pinki walked into the living room and took her seat on a bamboo chair opposite me. She was really a well-reared child. While seated, her body language and manners were clear indications that she was keen on talking to me.

Slowly bringing her lips to motion, she murmured, 'Uncle, you know, daddy always admires you so much.'

Stopping short of calling me uncle confidently, she said, 'Do you mind if I address you uncle? If you do, I will not address you so. I simply don't know what I should call you.'

We were still chatting when Tiwari emerged from the washroom. Presumably, he was already out, but we could not notice him. He seemed to have heard our talks. I was right. Tiwari, while walking into the room, said, 'Pinki bitiya (my daughter, Pinki), if Preetji does not like it, you may call him Bhai Sahib.'

'Yes, it is ok with me' said Pinki, looking smilingly towards me. Her beautiful face, with a sweet and captivating smile, really made me a little restless.

'Pinki, my child, please lay out the table now. Mice are hopping in my stomach,' said Tiwari jokingly.

Pinki soon walked out; only to return with two thalis (plates) arranged nicely with four medium-sized bowls of curries, pickle, chokha, rice, puree, et cetera. Placing thalis on the table, sitting between Tiwari and me, Pinki said, 'Please begin,' and at once returned to the kitchen to assist her mother. While dining, my gaze was intermittently traveling to her. I noticed that she too was looking towards me unblinkingly. When I reciprocated her constant stare, she smilingly waved at me.

Now, I was eating less and looking more towards kitchen. We kept exchanging affectionate looks. Although it was premature to seek meanings from her manner of uninhibited looks, it somehow gave me a feeling that she had developed an affectionate attitude towards me.

I returned home after the dinner; but I continued to think about Pinki until late in the night. Next day, when I woke up I felt her images floating and drifting before my eyes. Somehow, I managed to distract my attention and prepared to leave for office. Sitting alone in the office, her images again began appearing before me. I felt something unusual was going on in my mind. Despite all my efforts, it was flying back to the previous night when Pinki had emerged as a focus of my all thought processes and attention. Then, I somehow succeeded in putting my mind back to work with the result that in the evening when I was returning home, I did not even look into the direction of Tiwari's house.

After mulling over the whole affair, I decided not to visit Tiwari frequently. And I did not go near his house for over a month.

Tiwari seemed to have developed a liking for me. One day, he descended at my office quite unannounced. 'Arrey Preetji, you have forgotten us completely; nowadays I rarely see you. Are you too busy to see us?' asked he with a tinge of mock-annoyance.

'It's not that, Tiwariji. I did think of visiting you a few times. However, I could not do so as the last few days have been extremely hectic in the office. The whole month, I remained rather busy in clearing pending cases, apart from undertaking two trips to the neighbouring town in connection with labour disputes. Therefore, despite my keenness to visit you I could not do that.' I told Tiwari giving an easy and believable pretext.

'Humn. I thought so. Anyway, forget it. In fact, I also could not visit you as I myself was pre-occupied with several household matters this whole month. I wished to visit you last evening but again could not make it as I was quite late in returning home.' said Tiwari.

'How is your family?' I enquired.

'They are fine. Mrs. Tiwari and daughter Pinki remember you a lot, and have asked me to bring you home.' responded Tiwari.

'Oh, it is so nice of them. Kindly convey my regards to your family,' I returned.

'Preetji, I have come to inform you that due to some urgent work I have to go out of town for over a month. Therefore, we will have dinner together tonight. I need to tell you something more about your boss. You would recall our talks about him were incomplete that day. So please do not make any excuse to come with me,' insisted Tiwari.

I nodded in confirmation to his invitation. I hurriedly finished my office work as I too was longing to see Tiwari's family, especially his young daughter, whom I had not met for over a month now. In fact, I was looking for some pretext to visit them. So, without much of apparent excitement, I accepted his invitation.

At around 5:00 PM, Tiwari drove me straight from my office to his residence. There he parked his car under a sheesham tree on an empty municipality plot just opposite to the street.

We got out of the car and moved up the flights of stairs to his house. Tiwari, while tapping on the door, called out, 'Pinki, my child, its papa. Open the door, sweety.'

'Just coming, Papa' came a voice from inside. Obviously, it was Pinki. Meanwhile, I deliberately stepped aside into a corner so as not to be visible to her when she opens the door. My guess was that she would be a little sad not to find me at the door. And this is what exactly happened when she opened the door. Not finding me there, her usual liveliness disappeared and she asked in a spiritless tone, 'Papa, where is bhai sahib? Has he not come?'

'No, he was not in office today,' said Tiwari smilingly.

'Look here my child. There he is', added Tiwari, while swiftly pulling me out of my hiding place from behind the door. Craning her neck a little out of the hinges of the gate, and roving her eyes from one side to the other, when she spotted me standing on the left side of the gate behind Tiwari, she just uttered, 'Papa, you are impossible!' The usual exuberance, as if magically, immediately returned on her beautiful face, and the voice and gait regained their natural liveliness.

Then, slamming the door shut behind, she guided us to the living room. After seating me, Tiwari walked out, enquiring, 'Where is your mummy, dear baby?'

'Mummy was waiting for you to come home till five. When you did not return, she went alone to market to buy vegetables. She left a message for you. You have to go to the vegetable shop near the city center to assist her come home with the stuff,' Pinki told her father.

'It is ok my child. I am going right now', said Tiwari. He then turned towards me and said, 'Excuse me, Preetji. I have to dash to the market. I should be back in an hour or so. Pinki daughter is there to give you company, and here are the magazines and newspapers you may like to read.' Before leaving, he asked Pinki, 'Baby, please close the door from inside and take good care of Bhai Sahib.'

Pinki at once closed the door. She then walked up to me and asked, 'What would you like to drink - tea, coffee or cold drink?'

'Cold drink' replied I at once.

Pinki immediately vanished into the kitchen and in a few moments returned with a tray in her hands with two tumblers on it, filled nearly up to neck, with Limca. Placing the drink on the center table, she said, 'Here is your cold drink'. Picking up my drink, and pointing to the other placed on the table, I said, 'You too, please take yours'. When we were sipping our drinks, Pinki, with a mesmerizing smile, said in a soft and sweet voice, almost in whispers, 'Bhai sahib, you have been staying here for almost two years now. Don't you feel homesick? I always see you busy in your office work. Don't you like to chill out sometimes?'

'Of course, I do. But I don't get time for such things,' I replied.

To my great surprise, Pinki asked, 'By the way, what is your impression of my father? I believe you will be honest in giving your true opinion about him.' As I did not expect this coming from her, I was unable to gauge as to why she was asking me this question. To me, Tiwari was apparently a loving father and a caring husband. When I asked Pinki about this, she said, 'Bhai Sahib, we should not go by the face value of a person, as it is generally deceptive. As for my father, let me tell you, his true character is seated behind the facade of his genial disposition and decent behaviour.'

'So, you are trying to tell me that your father is not what he appears to be?' I plainly asked her.

'I think you got my point' said she.

Though I was absolutely stunned, I cajoled her to be more forthcoming with the caution, 'you should not cast aspersions against someone until you are sure about the veracity of such allegations. Else, it might reflect on you. And here you are casting doubts on your own father. So, better tell me all that is on your mind, that you claim is contrary to his public image.'

For a few moments, I noticed Pinki was cagey. Then regaining her composure, she said, 'It is a long story. I think he has not told you yet that I have one elder brother and a sister. Sister has since got married and comfortably settled with her husband. My brother has gone overseas. He never visits us. Do you know the reason behind his not visiting us?'

'I don't know. It is only you who can tell me', I replied.

'You know, my brother was only a few months into his marriage when he got a lucrative overseas job offer. Grabbing the opportunity, he proceeded abroad leaving his young wife in our custody. Father acted as a very caring father-in-law to ensure that we look after all her needs.

Within a couple of months, my parents fell out. Mother, sitting in a remote corner of the house, used to cry quietly but never confided into us the reason for her sorrows. However, we got to know soon the reason for the strained relationship between them' said Pinki and then paused.

'Could you be a little more candid on this sudden fall out?'

For a few moments, Pinki remained quiet and then said, 'I am prepared to share this secret with you, Please ensure that you never cross check with my father.'

Once I promised her, she began, 'After our brother's departure, everything seemed to be going quite well for the first few months. Then the unusual started happening. My sister-in-law, who otherwise is very affectionate and good by nature, began showing tantrums by putting up unreasonable demands on mother. She would often ask for costly costumes and cosmetics. She stopped coming to the kitchen to help mother. Instead, everything had to be delivered to her in her private room. When it was getting difficult for mother to bear her petulance any more, she tried to resolve the matter in consultation with father, in our presence. Though fully aware of what was going on in the house, father would silence us by saying 'You know, she is living here away from her husband. In this emotional crisis, let us take good care of her even if she is a little unreasonable'.

Pinki continued, 'Mother was not happy with father's defence. Since he always sided with sister-in-law in the altercation between mother and her, she had reasons to get suspicious. She began probing into his indulgences to clear her doubts. Soon, mother's apprehension turned into reality when one day around 3 a.m. she noticed father tip-toeing quietly out of sister-in-law's room. Although mother did not confront father, she increased her vigilance level. Then one night she discovered something unbelievable between a father-in-law and a daughter-in-law!'

At this point, Pinki paused and seemed hesitant to carry on. After a little encouragement, she resumed, 'Mother lay on her bed in their room opposite to father's bed. He had no inkling that mother was still awake. Suddenly, father was stepping out of his charpoy. Noticing him leave his place, she was now alert to see what he would do next. However, she pretended to be asleep. Father, in his misplaced complacency that mother was asleep, easily walked into sister-in-law's room, which was adjacent to mother's. With this, mother's suspicion about the relationship between her husband and daughter-in-law resurfaced. She was still unable to summon courage to follow him, but thought it wise to sit up and wait for him to come out. After 10-12 minutes, when father came out, she mocked coughing while sitting. Father did throw a glance at her while walking towards his place. It was difficult for him to miss that mother was not only awake, but also aware of his dalliance. He could no longer keep this liaison with his daughter-in-law shrouded.'

In order to know more about Tiwari's other hues, I asked Pinki as to why her mother did not accost her husband. 'Of course, she did, but was shut up by him. Thereafter, they would very often quarrel with each other on trifle matters. Mother always looked for a pretext to pick fight with him.'

'Did you and your sister ever talk to your father on this?'

'No, we never did.'

'But, did your mother share with you all that she had seen?'

'Yes, she did share with both of us - my elder sister and me with the advice that we should not talk about this outside.'

'Did your father demonstrate repentance by morphing himself into a refined person after your mother's frequent quarrels with him?'

'Of course not. In fact, he was even bolder as he unhaltingly continued to fool around with sister-in-law.'

'How did your sister-in-law look at this episode?'

'You know, it was not possible without her consent and willingness.'

'Did you, along with your sister and mother, ever try to reason out with her that what she was doing was the most outrageous and thoroughly reprehensible act?'

'Yes, all of us – mother, sister and me - tried to explain to her. Her reaction was amazing.'

'What was that?'

'Instead, she, without any sign of shame, frankly said, 'Like any young, beautiful and lively married woman, I also have my physical needs. Being suitably employed I can look after myself well without sacrificing my joys and pleasures. There is no life after my husband is gone away. If not the son, let it be the father. If you are not comfortable with this arrangement, then allow me to rent out a house elsewhere in the city.' Having heard her plain words, we all fell silent. Thereafter, we never broached the issue again.'

'Then what is your objection? After all, it has her consent. She is a fairly highly educated person; she ought to understand what is good and bad for her.'

'You seem to be taking the issue very lightly. It is not as simple a matter to let go. It had disturbed our household's peace.'

'But now I can see everything normal here. Your mother also seems to have accepted this. Your father is showing all his affection and love towards your mother and you. He is so concerned about his wife that he left immediately to help her there in the market. It shows his deep concern for the whole family.' I said.

'Peace has returned to our household after a long time. All this became possible only when sister-in-law left to join my brother abroad. Thereafter, she never returned. However, she left behind an unbearable sense of guilt, shamelessness and disgrace for the entire family'

'I think it is better for all of you to bury the past.' said I, offering a piece of conventional wisdom.

'It is easier said than done. I still find something seriously objectionable in his conduct,' said Pinki.

'Is there still something detestable on his part?' I casually asked.

'I told you, his character has many shades. However, it is impossible for me to reveal all the colors. '

'If you have trusted me and confided so serious secrets, I think, everything else is insignificant to be revealed.'

'It is too much on my part. Let it go, Bhai saheb.' Pinki said, turning her head to the other side.

'Come on! Please tell me what's on your mind. I can see you want to share more.' I prodded her.

'This is not something very serious, but it does show his shameless behaviour. It concerns him only,' she said with a visible mark of blush on her cheeks.

Looking at her face, I got further curious to know more about Tiwari's misdemeanour. I said to her, 'I think, you have more but find it embarrassing to explain. You better relax by emptying your mind out.'

'In fact, this is about father's explicit sexual behaviour. When he is in mood, he doesn't care for anyone else including me. Now that my brother, sister-in-law and elder sister have gone, only I am left in the house. Earlier, my elder sister, who had seen father on several occasions dragging mother into his room and force himself upon her, was sick of him. And I too feel the same way now. I myself saw him forcibly dragging mother from her cot, which I share with her, to his room and force him upon her even when I am awake.' said Pinki smiling and looking at me with a meaningfully wicked glimmer in her eyes. Before she could complete, we heard someone patting on the door. Tiwaris had returned from the market.

Pinki opened the door. Tiwari and his wife, laden with two bags full of vegetables entered. Walking towards the kitchen and unloading themselves of the bags, they said, 'Arrey Preetji, you must be feeling bored. Sorry to keep you waiting for so long. We hope Pinki looked after you.'

'Its fine with me, Tiwariji' said I.

Mrs. Tiwari called out Pinki to the kitchen to help her arrange vegetables. Pinki immediately walked into the kitchen and got busy in cooking. Tiwari rushed into the washroom and within minutes came out with beads of water still visible over his face, hands and feet. Pulling down a hand towel from the rope tied at both ends across the outer wall of the washroom, Tiwari cleaned his face and walked into the living room. Pulling up a chair, he sat next to me. He said, 'Sorry, Preetji, dinner will be a little late. I have brought fresh vegetables, I am sure you would relish the food. You would recall I had promised to tell you about your boss' colorful life.'

'Tiwariji, I do not know why everyone, including you, is so keen on telling me about boss.' I casually remarked.

'You mean there is somebody else who is also privy to your RD's private life?' Tiwari asked of me.

'Of course, a number of officers and staff have offered their services to read to me boss' story.' I returned.

'Do you mind to give me their names?' asked Tiwari.

'In fact, everybody in the office appears to be overtly interested in dishing out one secret or the other of his life. Mr. Sinha and his wife Chandra seemed to be particularly eager to brief me on various pieces of boss' life.' said I.

'Oh, how come Sinha and his wife claim to be in the know of RD's life? By the way, when did you meet them? Sinha, I can understand, you meet him everyday in office. What about his wife? Did they invite you over dinner or the meeting took place elsewhere?'

'On their way back home from the dinner reception that boss threw when ZD was here last time, they dropped by my place. In course of our informal chat, Sinha took the initiative to discuss RD's life. He appeared to be quite excited. I was surprised when Chandra, Sinha's wife, in her parting shot remarked that boss was very 'romantic'.

'Humm. How can Sinha point his finger at others? He should sweep clean his own house before making comments at others. It is interesting that Mrs. Chandra calls RD 'romantic'. What about her?'

'You can enlighten me.'

'Would you like to hear her story too?'

'Of course, I would be delighted to hear all that you have about her. The more, the merrier.'

'You know, this lady Chandra had wormed her way into RD's heart so much so that he, could hardly ignore anything demanded by her. She held absolute sway over him for years. Her husband, Sinha, got his promotion superceding several of his colleagues because of RD. It is an open secret that she warmed RD's bed for several years. These are not rumors. Any of your colleagues can corroborate these facts. Perhaps, over a period of time RD got tired of her, with the result that Sinha fell out of favour. But the Sinhas know very little of his past.'

'I know in your office there is no one who is in the know of complete story of RD' life. From your vast experience, I guess you know more than anybody else, about not only RD but also others in the office. So, you are the best person around to get true and clear picture of boss.'

'Tonight, I will restrict myself to a few revealing things that should be of interest to you. Otherwise, it needs months to talk on him.'

'You are right. I am interested only in his present family life. I have no interest in knowing about his past escapades with other women.'

Meanwhile, Pinki called out from the kitchen informing that dinner was ready. 'Yes, my child. Please lay the table. I feel terribly hungry. And so must be Preetji.'

'OK Papa'.

Soon, Pinki and her mom laid the table. Several nicely cooked spicy and delicious curries like spinach, mushrooms, okra, eggplant and cauliflower were served, along with chokha. As we were nearly starving, our appetite went up after looking at the delicacies laid for us. Both Tiwari and I, without losing a moment, began to devour the food.

After having popped a few morsels in his mouth, as expected, Tiwari came back to his favourite subject, 'So, I was going to tell you in a short-cut manner some of the fascinating portions of RD's life.' I nodded in agreement and gestured him to move on.

'By now, you are aware that your boss' son has been staying abroad. During the last five years, he visited his father only once. He is rumored to have married another woman there and fathered two children from that lady. Your boss is fully aware of this. His daughter-in-law was very enthusiastic to go and settle with her husband abroad. However, when she came to know about his affair and marriage, she changed her mind and decided to stay back. Since then, she has never thought of this again. Being away from her hubby for a long period and living under the same roof with her widower father-in-law, the enevitable happened between the two. RD on his part has been looking her after quite well. However, you know a young woman has natural physical desires also. She, therefore, needed someone to fulfill those needs and this came to her easily within the four walls of her own house. To cut short the story, RD and his daughter-in-law are virtually living as sex-partners. The child is, in fact, not his grandchild but his biological daughter! After RD's advancing age, the daughter-in-law has now started courting influential people in the city and most of us are aware of this fact. This is your boss life - interested, conceited.'

I just smiled while humming soft sounds in affirmation.

37

Dalit Women Sheer Objects of Pleasure

I landed in a village around 150 kms away from the headquarters with the assignment and responsibility of organizing labour camps to educate unorganized sector workers. It was a five-day camp where, apart from educating them, the workers were to be provided with free food and cash. I was required to stay in the village for four nights. Being peak winter, the biting cold welcomed me there. The village sarpanch, who was coordinating the organization of the camp, arranged my lodging in the community hall, which had no intact windows or doors left in their places. However, I was provided with a good string cot and an earthen pot full of coal ambers in one corner of the room to act as room heater to protect myself from the freezing cold.

The Sarpanch, at night, mindful of my importance for his village, served me well. He himself brought dinner for me. Before dinner, he offered me whisky, which I politely declined. Then, we had dinner together. He kept me absolutely engrossed through out the dinner in giving demographic details of the village. After the dinner, the Sarpanch collected dishes and began to leave saying: 'I know it is not comfortable here in this terrible cold. I feel bad that you did not stay with us. However, I deeply appreciate that you are observing the official propriety by not accepting hospitality when on duty. Bearing this in mind, I did not press you hard to stay with us. Anyway, I will try to make your stay as comfortable as I can.'

'This is workers' camp. One must live their way while with them. By doing so, one can understand their problems better. I have no problem here.' I told the sarpanch.

'Arrey Preet Sahib, I know it is not going be easy to spend these four nights in this open-like room. You need some hot stuff to keep you warm through the night. Don't worry, I will be back soon after dumping this stuff at home.' Said sarpanch with a smile and mischievous glean in his eyes, and walked out before I could read between the lines, especially his 'hot stuff' offer.

After sarpanch departed, I immediately pulled over the puffy blanket I had brought along, as the cold had begun its effect on me. Having slipped into the blanket, I soon fell asleep. I had hardly had half an hour's sleep when the hot stuff guy knocked at the door. On hearing patting on the door, I suddenly got up calling out who was that. 'It's me the sarpanch, Sir' responded he. As the door was almost broken and hard to latch from inside, he had already pushed it open to walk in before I could react. By now, I had sat up on my cot. A lantern was still flickering in a corner. Although the lantern was generating dim illumination, even in that, objects were easily visible. I could see someone walking behind the sarpanch. The sarpanch slammed the door shut and whispered to me, 'Preet Sahib, I have arranged a good stuff to keep you warm through this knifely cold night.' He then pulled forth the girl from behind in my full view and said, 'Here she is at your service tonight'.

Taken aback, my immediate reaction to his shocking gesture was that I got highly enraged, and felt like breaking his cheekbones. Aware that people in this part of India were feudal and extremely caste-conscious, I had sensed that the girl brought there was from a weaker section of the society. My suspicion further crystallized when, after my polite refusal, the sarpanch revealed, 'Arrey sahib, I have been preparing her for the occasion over the last so many days. She has got a good soap bath, apart from being massaged with *itr* (fragrant oil) only for this day. Please enjoy your night with her.'

'Sarpanchji, Thank you very much. However, I am not used to this kind of treatment. Moreover, I am a responsible government official. I am on duty here in connection with welfare of poor workers. It is unbecoming of us to exploit the people whose welfare we are supposed to ensure. Perhaps, you are not aware of the consequences I will be facing in case my involvement in such a case comes to notice. How did you decide this on your own without checking with me first? Anyway, you should not have taken it for granted.'

'Arrey sahib, I am very sorry. But it is my duty to serve you' said he.

'I appreciate that you made good arrangements for my stay here; but this is not the way to serve. In case, I needed something, I would have told you. I am really feeling anguished.'

'OK Sahib, I admit my mistake. I should have checked with you before. Now that she is here, could you allow her to stay for the night? Otherwise, I will have to shell out from my pocket.'

'Oh, she has been arranged on payment-basis? My God! For Heaven's sake, you may go now' said I handing out a 50-rupee note to him trying to get rid of them quickly.

'Arrey Sahib, so much money! You need not worry. I will give her five rupees, which is more than sufficient for these people. After all, she is from that poor Dukhi Ram Chamar's family and the amount you have given is equivalent to what they get after working for three days in our farmlands. These Chamars and Dushads deserve not more than this', advised he while asking the girl to leave. Hearing him say all this, I was about to fulminate but somehow I restrained from creating a spectacle of that poor girl and myself. I was feeling like dragging his tongue out of his mouth and smashing his head with hammer.

I could not sleep that night. Thakur sarpanch's disdainful remarks about poor Dalits had shocked and hurt me deeply. Next day, the camp started with sizeable participation of workers from unorganized sectors. The participants were happy to get both food as well as cash for just their simple attendance.

For the remaining three days, the sarpanch did not show up anywhere near the site of event. However, on the fifth day, he arrived after lunch when workers were about to leave after receiving their payment for attending the program. He was perhaps scared to see me due to the episode of the first night of my stay. I could now sense that he was there to meet me. Realising this, I called out, 'Arrey sarpanch ji, I did not see you for last four days; where were all this time?'

'Sahib, I am really ashamed of what happened that night. Without checking from you, I should not have done that. Though I wanted to come and see personally if you were comfortable here, I could not do so. Instead, I ensured through others that you were looked after well. Finally, I am happy to note that you had no problem during your stay in my village.'

'Arrey, you should have come to attend the program to see for yourself how the poor and illiterate workers can benefit from my teachings about their rights. After all you are sarpanch and it was necessary for you to show up at least once or twice.'

'Believe me, Sahib. I wanted to come, but I was feeling terribly guilty. I also wanted to tell you that it was not my idea. In fact, I became a pawn in someone else's game.'

After hearing his regretful explanation, I was now inquisitive to know the key player behind this game.

'Whose idea was this to serve me that way?' I enquired of the sarpanch.

'Sahib, before your visit, I got a call from Radha Shankar Tiwari in your city to look after you well. He sent a clear message to arrange a young girl for you. I thought he was familiar with your personality. That is why, without your approval, I proceeded as instructed by Tiwari. When I proposed to recheck with you, he advised there was no need for this. So please forgive me for my impudence.'

I was shocked to hear this, particularly when I never did or displayed anything in my conduct vis-a-vis Tiwari to create this kind of impression. For the moment, I thought it appropriate not to prolong the issue any further and decided to let it go.

'Sarpanch ji, if you have realized your mistake, I no longer hold you accountable' I told him.

After my assurance, I could sense that the fear writ large on his face had vanished. Regaining his lost confidence, the sarpanch said,

'Sahib, I would like to say something. Before you, several sahibs have visited us and I have entertained them all. The demand to arrange girls for their comfort during the nights used to be put up by the visitors themselves. In almost all such cases, their preferences have been for the well-built, tanned-skinned, volumptuous girls from the communities of Chamars and Dushads. Sir, the girl that night was a virgin. On Tiwari's instructions, with great allurement, I had made her agree to sleep with you. Any way, sir, you are different.'

'Sarpanchji, what do you think is so special about the girls that you prefer them to supply for your visiting sahibs and that your guests prefer these girls only?' I asked him casually without making manifest any fellow feelings for poor Dalit girls.

'Kahe, Sir. We have been fucking women from these communities from times immemorial. They are really hot. And the more they resist our advances, the more pleasurable becomes the act of outraging their modesty. They are nothing but sheer objects of our pleasure', bragged the sarpanch with great audacity.

Such extreme claims of sexual birthrights over low caste females by the sarpanch set my blood on fire. However, I was not yet prepared to reveal my identity to him. The Rajput sarpanch was under the impression that I was also a fellow Rajput and therefore I was sharing his glee over self-chest-thumping.

'Don't you think that being the sarpanch, it is your duty to protect the dignity of womenfolk of your area irrespective of their castes and religion?' asked I.

'Preet Sahib, I do protect all of them, but in so far as the low-castes are concerned, the responsibility towards protection of their women is not ours as we consider them outside our fold. There is nothing new in it. This has been going on for thousands of years. We just consider them as objects of our comfort. You may say it is as if we kill chicken for pleasure whenever we wish. Just because we eat chicken that does not mean that chicken has become a part of us.' argued the sarpanch audaciously, equating the low-caste status with animals.

Enraged and shocked though I was, I let it pass, as I did not find it appropriate to engage in any further discussion with such a xenophobic, intolerant and bigoted person as this sarpanch was making himself out to be.

As common elsewhere, here too, poor, helpless and oppressed people were just tools meant to serve the privileged upper castes. The wretched souls had no control over their own being! While Dalit men lived, only to work, mostly as bonded labour, for the upper caste landlords, their women were to provide comforts to their feudal lords.

38

Quitting the Job

Flooded with millions of negative thoughts about the sarpanch, I returned to headquarters. After reporting for duty, I sat quiet in my office throughout the day. Deeply perturbed, I did not feel like eating or doing anything. In the evening, I left for home a little earlier than normal. Realizing that I had been under constant pressure to fall in line and accept things in the prevailing system, I had begun to lose interest in my job. Initially, I put up resistance to it, however I was soon able to sense that behind the curtain, there was a conspiracy to either co-opt or force me out, by all means, including bullying and use of physical harm.

In a few weeks, things became quite clear to me. My continuation in the service had become almost difficult. No one in office was happy with my style of functioning. My colleagues were never comfortable with my probing nature, as I possessed substantial information about their involvement in a number of cases of graft and embezzlement of government funds. Though they never dared uttering anything on my face, they had been harbouring grudge against me. It was easy for anyone to smell a rat in the situation from the fermenting atmosphere in the office. I decided to help myself get out of this rut. After weighing all pros and cons, I finally decided to put in my papers.

Next morning, I visited all the colleagues in their chambers. After having brief chats with them, I returned to my office. I had not revealed my plan to any one. Back in my chamber, I prepared my resignation letter and put it up to RD, the boss, to forward it to the competent authority for acceptance.

Taken aback by this sudden move, RD called me in his office and asked mollifyingly, 'What provoked you to take this decision. You know people nowadays get jobs with great difficulty, and here you are who is resigning from such a good job without any valid reason. By the way, where would you go from here? Have you got any better job?'

'No, Sir. But I am not willing to continue here.'

'Well, this is purely your decision and even if I wish I cannot change your mind. I have found you are quite resolute in your decisions,' said RD.

I left his office without further discussion. There was only a day left for the month to end and my resignation was with effect from the first of the coming month. Therefore, I was waiting for my salary to finally pack and leave.

As I had great dream to join the civil services, I boarded next train to Allahabad, considered then as the nursery for civil servants, to prepare for this examination. I had already tied up with one of my old acquaintances to provide me place to stay there.

39

Mother's Demise

Exams were round the corner. Just when I was in the middle of my hectic preparations, I received heart broken news of mother's sudden demise. It was hard to accept that she was no longer around and that how it happened so abruptly, especially in view of her excellent health. Initially, I thought the news should be a pretext on the part of father to get me back home. This suspicion arose because the flow of funds to him had dried up since quitting my job. Yet the negative thoughts concerning mother gripped me to the extent that I had the instinct that not all was well. I tried to overcome this negativity and concentrate on my studies but to no avail.

One evening, I boarded train to visit my native place. An unusual silence in the household welcomed me. The sense of fear had now begun intensifying as all the family members, except mother, were there. When I would visit home, she was the first one to come and greet me. Surprisingly, she was conspicuous by her absence. Immediately, I made an enquiry of her. All my siblings were silent. Father was at the chaupal. I went there straightaway to confirm if the news sent to me about mother was true. He was mum. This was painfully disturbing for me. My suspicion crystalized when one of the villagers standing there, gestured towards me with his head, to come aside. He then left. I got up from my seat after a few moments and then went into the backyard of a thatched house where he was waiting for me. He gave me a detailed description of the circumstances in which mother had ended her life.

On the ill-fated day when mother took the extreme step of taking her life, the woman, with whom father had an affair, visited our house. She wanted father to go to a distant place to see a prospective groom for her daughter. Mother, who was suffering from malaria that time, saw the woman whispering something to father, who was simply nodding. Once the woman left, father started getting ready to leave. Seeing him dressing up, mother reacted by complaining that he never had time to take her to the doctor, whereas even a small dictat from that wicked woman had a swift effect on him. Showing rare boldness, mother threatened of serious consequences if he still went away for her work. Ignoring her, when father was stepping out, mother jumped out of her cot and waylaid him. She again warned him that he was free to do that but only over her dead body. He rushed angrily towards her and began slapping her furiously. She was soon on the ground but he was still kicking her all over. He then went off leaving her there, unconscious.

When she returned to her senses, she was struggling to sit up. Somehow, she managed to get up. Sitting there, she kept weeping unconsolably before falling silent. For a while, she continued to brood over all the humiliation, pain, distresses, abuses, insults etc. she had been enduring over the years. With great difficulty, she stood off the ground and dragged herself to go in.

Her mind was now flying into the past. Bitter memories of her consistent persecution by her husband were now tormenting her immensely. Her enormous patience finally gave in. Haunted by her dreadful past, in a moment of reckoning, she decided that her life was not worth it anymore. In the heat, she decided to finish herself by consuming pesticide.

My mother – my source of support, strength and encouragement – had gone forever. With a heavy heart, I returned to Allahabad to resume my preparations for the civil services.

40

Joining the Civil Service

After exhausting preparations for a year and a half, I finally made it to the Foreign Service, to serve mainly in Indian missions abroad.

Since my school days, I had a very high view of Civil Services. Therefore, I always aspired to join it. However, my this perception changed, immediately after joining training in the Administrative Academy, Mussourie. A few probationers and faculty members had no qualms to reveal their real objectives for joining the civil services. Once, a probationer from administrative service, very candidly admitted that his sole purpose for joining the civil service was to make five hundred crores rupees within a span of ten years. He would then establish an industry to provide employment to the people in his respective province. On one occasion, a senior faculty member went to the extent of telling that members of Indian Foreign Service remained below poverty line. Implication of his telling this was obvious.

Village visit was one of the components of probationers training program, under which, our group of probationers landed in Uttar Kashi District to cover a part of rural area, to get first-hand knowledge about its socio-economic conditions and related problems. While camping in a village there, we had an opportunity to visit a local school. The headmaster, C.M. Joshi, received us well and briefed us on various educational activities in his school and the accompanying problems they were facing in implementation. As we were discussing day-to-day problems, including those of the students from far-flung hill areas, the headmaster suddenly, brushing aside crucial matters, spoke up.

'Sahibs, in your career ahead, you will be holding important positions in government departments formulating policies and programs for the welfare of people. That way, you will be controlling our lifeline. You see the situation is changing fast. Old paradigms seem to be breaking down. We, the upper castes, have always had upper hand. However, now these low caste people are trying to grab our place. God knows what has happened to our children. They appear to be very complacent; do not pay adequate attention to their studies. Contrary to this, low caste children are taking keen interest in learning. This new development and the resultant declining gap between their and our children is becoming a matter of concern.'

'Masterji, you should be glad to see this happen. You know, as per our constitution and government policies, it is the responsibility of the state to lift the backward and the underprivileged sections of the society. Therefore, you teachers have a crucial role to play in bringing about that transformation. I wonder as to why you are worried if the lower caste children are coming themselves forth to get uplifted' I asked quietly while my colleagues looked on.

'Sahib, it is easier said. You know the very thought of low caste people taking our place makes our hair stand and we start getting goose bumps', admitted the headmaster with a long sigh.

Then pointing to a dark–skinned and half-clad boy, he said, 'Look at that boy there, in the corner. He comes from a

Dalit family. His father is not able to provide them even two square meals. Yet the boy is so focused on his studies that he has outshone almost every student in the school. He has never missed classes even in severe winter when he is half-clad. You know, he is thrashed for even the trifle mistakes in order to get him demoralized and force him to drop out of the school. Despite the odds, he is doing amazingly well,' said the headmaster Joshi in whispers bringing his mouth near my ears.

For a moment, headmaster's words worked to send me back to my school days.

Reacting to his audacity, I said to myself 'Oh God! Save our country from these criminals.'

41

An Encounter with Harlots in Mumbai

After the completion of the six-month long foundation course at the Administrative Academy, Mussourie, Probationers proceeded on Bharat Darshan to various parts of the country. During our tours to the coastal states, our group landed in Mumbai.

A few of us planned to go for an evening out in the city. Having walked for an hour or so in the busy lanes of central Mumbai, we entered a restaurant for dinner. Here, we met three young and beautiful waitresses attending to the clientele. Two of our colleagues engaged in intimate talks with them. After they were served their wine and liquor, one of them whispered something to one of the waitresses. She, in return, just nodded and walked away. A little later, the other waitress came to our table. Putting a tumbler full of beer in front of one of our colleagues, she, in a hushed voice, uttered something to him. Our colleague at once took out a fifty-rupee note and handing it out to her, said, 'Thank you very much.' I could hear these only four words clearly.

After dinner, we came out on to the lane leading towards our place of stay. We were just walking along when one of the colleagues shook me from behind by tapping my shoulder. I turned back and asked, 'What is the matter?'

'Lets go there', said he pointing to a lane leading to the other direction.

'Why should we go there? It's time to go to bed as we have to get up early in the morning to catch train for our next destination.' I demanded.

'Don't bother about your train. We will all go together. It will not take much time. That waitress in the restaurant told me about a place in that lane. I just want to see there something for my entertainment,' insisted he to accompany him.

Having walked a few yards along the lane, we spotted several middle-aged women surrounding and whispering to men in the dark alleys. Seeing the women, our two colleagues walked straight up to them. Perhaps, based on their previous experience they had identified them. I walked with them without any knowledge of what was to follow.

Approaching the women, they stopped; and then they waved at them. Soon, I saw a group of 4-5 women walking towards us. Meanwhile, one of my colleagues turned around and said to me, 'Look here. All these are hookers.'

'How do you know they are streetwalkers?' I demanded.

Without any response, they slowly walked towards the women. Seeing them approaching, immediately two women rushed towards them. They began whispering with them. I still looked on. Then, my two colleagues, while waving at a woman, walked up to me. Meanwhile, I overheard one of them saying to the other, 'My friend, I am not interested as I don't have sufficient money to spare to do this. You can go ahead if you want'.

Then the other colleague, approaching me, said, 'Friend, could you lend me three hundred bucks? I want to go with that woman to entertain myself.'

Meanwhile, the other colleague withdrew himself and joined me, saying, 'lend him some money, yaar. He seems to be completely turned on and taken over by fleshly passion'.

I lent him three hundred rupees without any fuss and we two walked away.

Putting the money into his pocket, he walked along with that full-bosomed woman towards the stairs of a neighbouring multi-storey building. Holding each other's hands, they climbed the flights of the stairs and we soon lost sight of them. We stood on the pavements when two good-looking women in their early thirties approached us, perhaps looking for their prey for the night.

'Hi Gabru (Hunk)! How do you do today?' asked one of them.

'Come, I will give you real pleasure, come, don't waste time', said the other.

As this was for the first time, at least for me, to chance upon such women, I was stunned to hear such open invitations from them.

Things did not stop here. Within a few seconds, we both found ourselves surrounded by several women who were jeering at us making obscene gestures and comments. Faced with their over frank, obscene and lewd talks, we also became a little bolder, and sought amusement in making fake negotiations for the price to have sex with them. In truth, neither of we two was serious enough for that kind of thing. However, we both were certainly enjoying talking with the female strangers who were behaving as if we were known to them for years.

During one of the lighter moments in our talks, I somehow happened to ask one of the women, 'How much would you charge?'

'Not less than one hundred', she said.

'I don't have that much money in my pocket' said I.

For a few moments, she remained quiet. Then she walked away. After a while, she returned to us and said, 'OK, it's getting late now. If you agree, I would entertain both of you for 100 bucks.'

'No, we cannot offer you that much.' I returned.

'How much are you going to give me? Tell me quickly.' said she desperately.

As we were not serious about it, and our engagement in talks was only for pleasure, we found ourselves in a confused state of mind, not able to give a straight reply.

Again, she walked away. We still were at the same place, waiting for our friend to return. Perhaps, guessing that we were not in a position to spare the money asked for, she returned one more time and proposed in sugary voice, 'I believe you don't have enough of money. This is my last offer to you. Please give me 50 rupees to entertain you.'

We remained silent. Finding no reply from us, she, in her last ditch effort, offered us sex for 10 rupees each. She perhaps got no client that day and was desperately looking for any amount come her way. There was no response from us. Sensing that we had no interest in her at all, she walked away and did not appear at the spot after that.

Meanwhile, to our great amazement, another middle-aged woman, well built, tall and very good-looking, emerged there from nowhere. She walked straight up to us, asking, 'I notice you standing here for last half an hour. Are you interested here?' she asked, pointing her finger to the meat between her thighs. The way she uttered these words and crudely gestured to her private parts, we got red in the face.

Not finding any reply from us, the woman went on, 'If you don't have that much money, you can still do it. But please give me some money at least so that I could buy today's meal for my children.'

It was an apt demonstration of the fact that hunger can make anyone stoop to any level, not just prostitutes. The woman had displayed her utter desperation in offering her body for money for a simple meal. However, without thinking over what she had just said and why, I carried on in my same old un-serious and zestful negotiating way and offered, 'Will you accept one rupee? This is the best I can offer you'.

'Go away, bastards! Go and buy your sister for that money. I don't need your khairaat (charity)', shot back the hurt woman, who until a few moments back was pleading us to sleep with her for any money. She continued, 'I must tell you, I am not a regular lower caste prostitute. I belong to a higher caste Maharashtrian Brahmin family. I hold a higher social status. You must accord me a certain respect that I am entitled to by virtue of my birth. Instead, you here dared offer me one rupee for offering my body to you'.

The woman was still in a belligerent mood when my other colleague, to enrage her further, commented, 'How would you expect us to know without being told that you were a Maharashtrian Brahmin? Only a few moments back, you were ready to offer yourself for any amount, and this is what we can afford to pay. Never mind. We respect your higher caste status. We are ready to pay double this amount if we can be assured that a Brahmin female would provide double the heat!'

It blew the lid off woman's patience. She furiously knelt, took out her slippers, and brandishing them, rushed towards us. Before any harm could come to us, we scooted for safety, leaving our other friend behind.

42

Boss's Frustration

My first assignment as a Diplomat was in a west Asian country. During preparations before departure, many sweet thoughts were floating on my mind. I thought that, serving abroad in Indian mission I would not experience any of the problems that were so common within the country. The reason for this enthusiasm flowed from the fact that my service had the reputation of being above the petty considerations.

My father, brothers and in-laws saw us (my wife, a forty-day-old son who had yet to open his eyes completely and myself), off at the airport. The scene was really emotional – heavy hearts, tearful eyes but no words. With a scheduled halt at Dubai, we landed at the place of our first posting.

As a language trainee, apart from attending Arabic classes at the institute, I was assigned responsibilities in the office as well. That time, we were two language trainees in the Embassy. The other trainee was senior to me in the sense that he had joined the Mission nearly ten months before me. Otherwise, he was from the same batch.

We were among several hundred foreign students learning Arabic in the institute where my other Indian colleague had already completed a full-term session of Arabic classes and was now in preparations for appearing his language test. He took his language test with full preparation and appeared quite confident and optimistic about his success. Sadly, the results were quite contrary to his expectations.

Meanwhile, time for my language test was fast approaching and my preparations were in full swing. This time, both of us were scheduled to take our exams together in the next language test to be conducted by the Ministry of Defence. I was in a hurry to clear the mandatory language test as soon as possible to qualify for my next promotion.

One day, Ambassador called me in his office and said, 'You know, Preet, your colleague did not clear his language test. I feel sorry for him. He has spent a considerable time on learning the language. Now it is high time for him to clear it. I am doubtful if he can clear the language exam along with his office responsibilities. Therefore, I want him to be divested of all his other duties to enable him to concentrate only on his language skills. Since you are familiar with his area of responsibilities by sharing the same office room, you take over all his work. I promise when it is your turn, you will be given equal opportunity to prepare for the test. Now you may go and relieve him,' instructed the Ambassador.

I took charge of the office desk handled by my trainee colleague to free him to focus on his language. Frankly, I was finding it quite difficult to cope up with both the office work as well as evening language classes in the institute. Somehow, I managed to keep attending the classes to prepare for the test. Exams were round the corner. I called on Ambassador to request him to give me the same treatment for the language test. Ambassador retorted, 'You are not supposed to remind me. I have given a rethought to it. I feel there is no need for you to show hurry to take your language test. Who will handle two desks – yours and that of him - if I free you as well from the office responsibilities?'

'Sir, you had promised to give me equal opportunity. That is why I am here.'

Upon this, the Ambassador flared, 'Do you want me to close down the office? If you are so desperate, discover your own ways and means; but I am not going to release you from the official work. Okay? Now, no further discussion; language is your problem; you need to sort it out. Do you want me to take over your responsibilities?'

Disappointed and stunned, I left Ambassador's office. Back on my desk, I mulled over his ham-handed approach towards me. My colleague, who had already spent over a year on the language, was completely free from office for his second attempt, whereas I had to deal with both - mine as well as his – desks in office and simultaneously putting several hours in preparing myself for the language test. I had cordial relations with my trainee colleague. Even after Ambassador's decree in his favour, I held no grudge against him. However, no positive feelings for the Ambassador were left in my heart. My emotional instinct was impelling me to prove that Ambassador was neither fair nor impartial in my case.

The language test took place in the Embassy in Ambassador's direct supervision. We both appeared together in the test. Coincidently, the weekly meeting, taken by the Ambassador, felt on that day. After the test was over, we both colleagues attended the meeting. Before starting the proceedings, Ambassador inquired about our performance in the language test. Looking smilingly and confidently towards my colleague, Ambassador asked, 'So, how did you do in the test, Samreet?'

'It was excellent, Sir,' replied he.

'You must clear with flying colours this time. I am confident.'

'Sir, I guess so.'

'Good. You have been under very stressful situation. Now go and relax for a couple of days before your resume your duties,' instructed Ambassador shaking his head up and down, his face filled with happiness.

He then turned to me and asked, 'Yes, what about you, Preet? I hope you attempted all questions. In any case, it doesn't matter as it is only your first attempt. I don't expect you to be doing well.'

'Sir, I have attempted all questions and feel that I have done well. I don't know what my score will be but I am sure I will not fail,' I replied softly.

'Oh! I see. Let's hope so', Ambassador replied with a cynical smile on his face.

During the period between the test and announcement of results, Ambassador was more anxious than we to know about our result. Results of our language test sprang a surprise, particularly for the Ambassador. I cleared my language test with good grades. Unfortunately, my colleague had plucked once again. Because of his carefree nature, Samreet did not take his failure to his heart. Instead, he came and congratulated me on my success.

I straight went to Ambassador to inform him about my results.

'Sir, there is a good news,' I said.

'What is this all about?' he asked.

'Sir, I have cleared my language test,' I replied.

'Humn! Its' really good news! Anyway, congratulations! I knew you deserved it. What about Samreet, by the way?'

'Unfortunately, he could not clear his test this time as well.'

'Oh! No. He had prepared so well. What was wrong with him?'

Reflections of sadness, embarrassment and frustration were clearly visible upon Ambassador's face. When he said nothing further, I left his room.

Ambassodor then called Samreet to his office. When Samreet returned after meeting the Ambassador, he lit a cigarette and began taking deep and long puffs rather quickly. He then lit another cigarette and pulled deeper and heavier puffs. I could guess he was doing this only in desperation. I kept looking but said nothing. All this while, Samreet remained unusually quiet. Then breaking his silence, he said,

'Preet, I had very high image about this Service. I thought officers were above the petty considerations of caste, creed, region and religion upholding secular values. But I am disappointed today.'

'Why do you think so?' I asked.

'By the way, what was Ambassador's reaction when you informed him about your successful attempt in the language test?' He enquired.

'Well, he congratulated me saying it was well deserved', I replied.

'Do you believe he is truly happy with your success?' he asked.

'Well, I have no reason to disbelieve him'

'Preet, your hard work has paid you handsomely. Honestly speaking, I don't have the knack to learn this language. Therefore, I don't mind my failure. However, I am happy that you have cleared. Interestingly, would you like to know Ambassador's reaction?' asked Samreet.

'Yes, I would like to hear it,' I replied.

'Let me tell you honestly, Ambassador did not feel happy with your success,' said Samreet.

'How can you say so?' I enquired.

Ambassador felt highly embarrassed at your success. Giving me a dressing down, he said, 'How are you feeling, Samreet? You have failed twice despite the fact that you were totally free from office responsibilities.'

'Sir, I am very sorry.'

'You are sorry! You should be ashamed of your upper class background. Do you understand how much embarrassment you have caused us all? Is it comfortable to see a Dalit boy from the backwaters of Uttar Pradesh excelling himself, despite so many unfavourable conditions created in his way? On the other hand, you come from a distinguished family; you are son of a Secretary to the Government of India. It is shocking indeed.'

I could not believe that Ambassador would react to my success this way simply because of my humble social background. However, without any apparent expression, I thanked Samreet.

Index

C

D

N

O

P

T